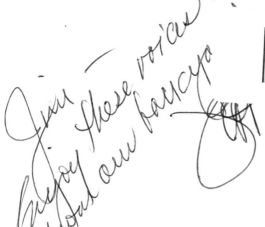

Ma, Wee Got Nuthin Here But Mud & Muskeeters

The 1862 Peninsula Campaign – Yorktown to Seven Pines

A composite diary as recorded by soldiers, sailors, marines, engineers, farmers, citizens, newspapermen, surgeons, naval constructors, river-boatmen, clerks, signalmen and nurses' assistants in their diaries, letters and journals.

Jeff Toalson – Editor

Pale Horse Books
Williamsburg

1

Ma, Wee Got Nuthin Here But Mud & Muskeeters

The 1862 Peninsula Campaign:
Yorktown to Seven Pines

ISBN: 978-1-939917-42-3

www.palehorsebooks.com

Available through PaleHorseBooks.com; Amazon; and Barnes & Noble

Cover Design: "Why the Army of the Potomac Does Not Move" Sketch by A.R. Waud (courtesy of the Library of Congress), portrait of Seaman Richard Curtis (courtesy of descendants Curtis Watkins and Cathy Watkins Thomas), and the letter is from the author's personal collection.

Cover Layout: Sally Stiles

"If on the battlefield bones should be left,
and this diary of mine is found, let not
the finder keep it as a theft, but send
it home safe and sound."

A note on his inside journal cover
Private Luther Calvin Furst
Co. D – 10th Pennsylvania Infantry

Dedicated to the common soldier, who is often forgotten in stories of the glory of battle and in praise of generals. They are the ones who suffered, lived in terrible conditions, endured the bad food, the rain, mud, mosquitoes, disease and death. Many of those men lie in unmarked graves on battlefields near Yorktown, Williamsburg and Seven Pines.

Books by Jeff Toalson

Butternut Series

No Soap, No Pay, Diarrhea, Dysentery & Desertion

A Composite Diary of the Last 16 Months of
the Confederacy from 1864-1865

Send Me a Pair of Old Boots and Kiss My Little Girls

The Civil War Letters of Richard & Mary Watkins, 1861-1865

Mama, I Am Yet Still Alive

A Composite Diary of 1863 in the Confederacy

I Got Nuthin Strange to Rite

A Selection of Forgotten Southern Letters, 1861-1865

Ma, Wee Got Nuthin Here But Mud & Muskeeters

The 1862 Peninsula Campaign – Yorktown to Seven Pines

Transcriptions

The 1863 Diary and Letters of Lt. George Buswell – Co. H, 33rd Virginia Infantry

(Transcription, with annotations, from the documents provided
by his daughter, Jean Buswell Sutton, of Mulberry, Indiana)

Contents

Cast of Characters

Southern:

Private Milton Barrett	18th Georgia Infantry
Sergeant Hamilton Branch	8th Georgia Infantry
Flag Officer Franklin Buchanan	C.S. Ironclad *Virginia*
Miss. Delia Bucktrout	Nurse's Assistant – Bruton Parish Hospital
[Private] [S.] A. Bumgarner	unit undetermined
Private Beaufort Buzhardt	3rd South Carolina Infantry
Private Newton Camper	11th Virginia Infantry
Mrs. Harriette Cary	Williamsburg resident
Marine Private William Cline	C.S. Ironclad *Virginia*
Mrs. Cynthia Coleman	Williamsburg resident
Brig. Gen. R. E. Colston	Department of Norfolk
Private William Corson	3rd Virginia Cavalry
Seaman Richard Curtis	C.S. Ironclad *Virginia*
Lt. John Eggleston	C.S. Ironclad *Virginia*
Private John J. Flournoy	3rd Virginia Cavalry
Dr. John Minson Galt II	Superintendent – Eastern Lunatic Asylum
Miss. Sally Galt	Williamsburg resident
Private Thomas J. Head	6th Georgia Infantry
Private William P. Holland	11th Virginia Infantry
Asst. Engineer E. A. Jack	C.S. Ironclad *Virginia*
Lt. Catesby Jones	C.S. Ironclad *Virginia*

Mr. John B. Jones	Clerk, CSA War Department
Private Eli P. Landers	Cobb's Legion
Mr. John T. Martin	Farmer & School Teacher
Maj. Gen. Lafayette McLaws	McLaws Division
Captain William Norris	C.S. Army Signal Corps
Private James T. Petty	17th Virginia Infantry
Surgeon Dinwiddie Phillips	C.S. Ironclad *Virginia*
Sergeant Benjamin Porter	11th Alabama Infantry
Mr. John L. Porter	Naval Constructor– Gosport Naval Yard
Chief Engineer H. Ramsay	C.S. Ironclad *Virginia*
Private J. W. Reid	4th South Carolina Infantry
Private Tally Simpson	3rd South Carolina Infantry
Pvt. Randolph A. Shotwell	8th Virginia Infantry
Sergeant William Smith	17th Virginia Infantry
Private Nathaniel V. Watkins	King and Queen Heavy Artillery
Private Richard H. Watkins	3rd Virginia Cavalry
Lieutenant E. V. White	C.S. Ironclad *Virginia*
Private James P. Williams	Richmond Howitzers
Lieutenant John Taylor Wood	C.S. Ironclad *Virginia*
Mr. George Randolph Wood	Schooner *James Buchanan*
Mr. Thomas G. Wynne	Farmer

Northern:

QM Aldis Brainerd	5th Vermont Infantry
Gun Captain Frederick Curtis	U.S.S. *Congress*

Colonel W. W. H. Davis	104th Pennsylvania Infantry
Pvt. Lyman A. Dickey	2nd New Hampshire Infantry
Corporal Henry E. Dunbar	3rd Vermont Infantry
Private George M. Englis	89th New York Infantry
Private Wilbur Fisk	2nd Vermont Infantry
Corporal George French	3rd Vermont Infantry
Corporal Luther Calvin Furst	10th PA Infantry / Signal Corps
Lt. Dana Greene	U.S. Ironclad *Monitor*
Lt. Charles Haydon	2nd Michigan Infantry
Private Charles Johnson	Hawkins Zouaves
Sergeant Robert W. Johnson	8th New Jersey Infantry
Corporal Joseph B. Laughton	38th New York Infantry
Corporal Patrick Lyons	2nd Rhode Island Infantry
Fireman Joseph McDonald	U.S.S. *Dragon*
Lieutenant E. P. McKinney	6th New York Cavalry
Lt. Austin Pendergast	U.S.S. *Congress*
Captain George Quinby	4th Vermont Infantry
Sgt. Major Elisha H. Rhodes	2nd Rhode Island Infantry
Private Edgar Steele	85th New York Infantry
Chief Engineer Alban Stimers	U.S. Ironclad *Monitor*
Corporal Marshall H. Twitchell	4th Vermont Infantry
[Private] George [ ]	[3rd] Vermont Infantry
Captain John L. Worden	U.S. Ironclad *Monitor*

Introduction

Inspiration arrives unannounced. In this case I was reading the booklets of Richard Curtis and E. V. White recounting their service on the C.S. Ironclad *Virginia*. Seaman Richard Curtis was the bow gunner on the *Virginia* and was involved in all action directly in front while attacking the U.S.S. *Cumberland, Congress, Minnesota* and *Monitor*. Junior Engineering Officer E. V. White was the only engineering officer on the main deck and relayed all engine orders, via speaking tube, from the Captain of the *Virginia* to the engine room. They, and many other common sailors and soldiers, are too often neglected in the telling of history.

It was time to start collecting voices, not just about the naval actions in Hampton Roads, but a book that covered the Peninsula Campaign from Yorktown, through Williamsburg, to Seven Pines on the doorsteps of Richmond.

I already had the marvelous letters of Private/Lieutenant Richard Watkins from my publication of his wartime letters in *Send Me a Pair of Old Boots & Kiss My Little Girls – The Civil War Letters of Richard and Mary Watkins, 1861-1865*. I knew that the archives at the Swem Library at the College of William and Mary held the letters of his brother, Private Nathaniel Watkins, of the King & Queen Heavy Artillery, who served at Gloucester Point and then at Seven Pines. This was a starting point.

Fred Boelt, a local James City County historian, brought my attention to the farm journals of Mr. John Martin, who farmed on the western end of the county toward Richmond, and Mr. Thomas Wynne, who farmed on the eastern end of the county about two miles from Lee's Mill and Lebanon Church. These journals offered a perspective from two farmers and the impact of soldiers, from both armies, on their farms. Mr. Wynne is Fred's great, great, uncle.

The Swem Archives also holds a great many individual letters, both Southern and Northern, which add marvelous personal insight that is lacking if we just study military movements and battle tactics. A sister in New Jersey writes Sgt. Robert Johnson, of the 8th New Jersey Infantry, asking if their dead friends, from the battle of Williamsburg, can be brought home for burial. Robert explains on May 21, 1862, that it would be *"utterly impossible to precu those bodies . . . they are decayed a great deal by this time and then they where not buryed in coffins . . ."*

You will see, listed in my "Cast of Characters" that I have used 42 Southern voices and 25 Northern voices to tell the story. Over the twelve-month span some of the voices will speak 20 to 30 times and become your good friends and guides. Other voices may only speak once or twice but will add great texture and understanding. These are the voices of the common citizens and soldiers. Generals, politicians, and people at the top of society are intentionally avoided. Quite frankly, their commentary is usually self-promoting and offers no insight into the plight of the common soldiers and civilians. General Lafayette McLaws is an exception to this rule and is one of the major voices in this book.

I chose Private Luther Furst, of the 10th Pennsylvania Infantry, because he was in the Union Signal Corps and would offer some insights not seen from the usual soldier serving in the infantry, cavalry or artillery. His journal rests quietly in the archives at Slippery Rock University in Pennsylvania. When Dr. Judith Silva, the University Archivist, forwarded me the link to his journal his opening line on the inside cover became the opening line of the dedication for this book. It will be the first quote you will read. It just might hide in a corner of your mind forever.

Through it all there is rain, mud, mosquitoes, disease, death and a growing realization that this is not a lark and that this war will not soon be over. For a large percentage of these men this will be their initial exposure to campaigns and battles. In their letters, diaries and journals, they will share their thoughts, feelings and fears. You will be moved by the power, humanty and magic of their words.

Editor's Notes

It is my belief that documents lose their historical flavor and magical feeling if the spelling, punctuation or wording is modified. In many cases, because of scarcity of paper, our writers did not use paragraphs and even wrote in the margins around the edges of their paper. I will not be creating paragraphs, correcting spelling or changing punctuation.

Those readers who are familiar with my editing style know that I use [. . .] to indicate that I have left out text before or after other text: *". . . the sun was very hot . . . it was a most sickening offensive place . . . we helped bury a good many of our dead . . ."*

Many writers had unusual habits for using both periods and capital letters. This type of sentence structure is normal: *"Mr Baker was planting corn . . . I inquired about the shoats we got from Mr Redd . . . we are going to plant cabbage on saturday."* Periods are typically used at the end of sentences and seem optional in other situations.

Some of the writers whom you meet, Private Edgar Steele, of the 85th New York Infantry, in particular, leave gaps after each thought rather than using a period: *" . . . the monortor [Monitor] is here in the harbor   I have also catch a glimpse of the rebel merimac [Merrimac] much oblige for that paper . . ."* Quite often a writer will spell a name or place incorrectly. As above, I will put the correct spelling in brackets. I will normally only do this the first time since the writer will no doubt continue to spell the item incorrectly.

Certain abbreviations are used on a regular basis. YrAff [Your Affectionate], Gen or Genl [General], &c [etc} and CH & CoHo [Courthouse] are the most common. You will see consistent misspellings of recognizable words and phrases and these will not be changed: Troope, comlads [comrades], rashuns [rations], provishun [provisions], git, tolrable, enuf, sevrel, prey for us, close [clothes], and ber footid [bare footed] are some key examples. You will be amazed at all the different ways to spell diarrhea and mosquito.

There are terms such as a quire of paper, redbugs, and graybacks which will be explained in the editor's notes at the end of the letter in which the phrase or word first appears. Redbugs are chiggers and graybacks are lice. Along with wood-ticks and mosquitoes these pests drove the soldiers to distraction. Their letters are full of their frustrations and complaints. It should be no mystery how muskeeters became part of the title of this book.

I have tried to stay true to the style of the writers and have sometimes wished that my computer would quit trying to correct what I was typing. It will automatically turn befel to befell and saturday to Saturday. It would not let me type tolrable, it just had to add an "e." It is necessary to go back and correct the computer.

There is something magical about the way Sgt. Benjamin Franklin Porter, of the 11th Alabama Infantry, closes his letters to his mother: *"Ma . . . I want you to prey for me all the time for preyers are of great youse to us."*

In the chapter introductions and in the paragraph above, I have quoted two individuals, but have provided no footnote. The quote will appear, and be footnoted, in the chapter where it is part of the story. In the case of Pvt. Steele and Sgt. Porter, you will find their quotes in April and June, 1862, respectively.

It is my pleasure to offer you these remarkable voices.

April, May and June, 1861

On April 13, 1861, Fort Sumter surrenders and on April 15, President Abraham Lincoln calls for 75,000 ninety-day volunteers to put down the insurrection. Calling on states to invade other states violates the United States Constitution and in short order Virginia, Tennessee, North Carolina and Arkansas secede from the Union. These four states had all voted against secession, some of them had voted against secession more than once. President Lincoln made an error in judgement that would cost hundreds of thousands of lives. Without the troops and the manufacturing capacity of North Carolina, Virginia and Tennessee, the seven Cotton States would have been a much easier group to persuade to come back into the Union. Calling for troops to invade the Southern states was the tipping point.

George R. Wood, writes from Hampton, Virginia, *"The Federals set fire to Portsmouth Navy Yard on Saturday night* [April 20]. *The old battleship Pennsylvania and the Merrimack and several other vessels were burnt."*

On May 3 President Lincoln calls for 42,000 more volunteers for 3 years or the duration of the war. On May 6 the Confederate Congress declares that a state of war exists with the United States. President Lincoln cannot admit that a southern government and country exists as he plays word games for various political reasons.

The United States Navy is small and has to grow rapidly to support troop movements and to begin to enforce a blockade of the southern ports. There is no Confederate Navy and the only solution is to create one, and they do.

On June 11, 1861, the loyal counties of Western Virginia secede from the rest of Virginia in a convention in Wheeling. The Union recognizes this secession but not the other secessions. It should be noted that when the various states ratified the original United States Constitution several of them, including New York, Pennsylvania and

Virginia, reserved the right to secede from "these United States" if they felt their rights were being abused.

On the Virginia Peninsula, there is a small Union force at Fort Monroe, a large grouping of Union naval ships and a small force of Confederate troops under the command of Col. John B. Magruder. Work has begun building some Confederate fortifications at Gloucester Point, Yorktown, Mulberry Island, Jamestown, Fort Huger and other select points to deter Union navigation on the York and James Rivers. The peninsula area is currently of minor importance as the focus is in the northern Virginia areas near Washington, D.C., and out in the Shenandoah Valley near Harper's Ferry.

In Yorktown, Private James Williams, of the Richmond Howitzers, writing to his Aunt Mary notes, *"This is the hottest place I ever saw . . . not a shade tree on the place . . . We have fine salt water for bathing every morning and evening . . ."* Bathing twice a day seems to be worth writing about. In a few months if James gets to bathe twice a month he will be very happy.

The first issue of Confederate currency is authorized on March 9, 1861, by the Confederate government in Montgomery, Alabama. The initial issue of $50 to $1,000 notes is dated from Montgomery, Alabama. The Confederate capital will not move to Richmond until May 24, 1861. The National Bank Note Company of New York, New York, prints most of the issue. A total circulation of $1,000,000 is authorized. The Southern Bank Note Company of New Orleans, Louisiana, is contracted to produce $50 and $100 notes to help with supply and demand for these denominations. These notes bear various hand-written 1861 dates in May and June.

(*The Civil War – Vol. II, The Picture Chronicle,* Ralph Newman & E. R. Long, 1956, New York [Hereafter cited as Chronicle by date.]; *Confederate States Paper Money,* Arlie Slabaugh, Iola, 2000, p. 22-26 [Hereafter cited as Slabaugh])

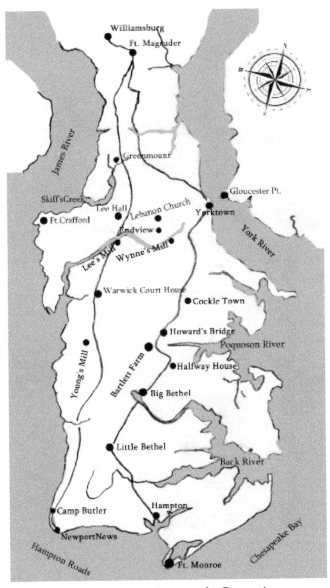

1862 Virginia Peninsula Campaign
Ft. Monroe to Williamsburg

April, May and June, 1861

April 20, 1861 – Hampton, Virginia
George Randolph Wood – 14-year-old resident

The Federals set fire to the Portsmouth [Gosport] Navy Yard on Saturday night [April 20]. The old battleship *Pennsylvania* drawing 28 feet of water and used as a receiving [vessel] for years, *Merrimack,* and other vessels were burnt. The frigate *Cumberland* and the steamer *Pawnee* came down to Sewell's Point and anchored to blockade the river.

(A Young Virginia Boatman Navigates the Civil War – The Journals of George Randoph Wood, edited by Will Molineux, Charlottesville, 2010, pp. 13-14. [Hereafter cited as Boatman].

- - - - -

April 21, 1861 – Portsmouth, Virginia
Lt. E. V. White, City Light Guard, Georgia Infantry

My command, the City Light Guard, of Columbus, Ga., arrived in Portsmouth, Va., Monday morning, April 21st, 1861. The Navy Yard was burned and destroyed on April 19th, two days before our arrival. We were quartered at the Naval Hospital, and on the day of arrival I visited the Navy Yard and there looked upon the smoking, smouldering remains of the *Merrimac,* upon whose hull was subsequently erected the great naval wonder of the world, the Iron-Clad *Virginia.*

(The First Ironclad Naval Engagement in the World between the Merrimac-Virginia C.S.N. & the Ericsson-Monitor U.S.N. in Hampton Roads, March 8 & 9, 1862 – E. V. White, New York, 1906, p. 5 [Hereafter cited as White].)

- - - - -

April 21-23, 1861 – Hampton, Virginia
George R. Wood, 14-year- old resident

The pilots, being state warrant officers, had been ordered not to pilot U. S. vessels and offered their service to Gov. John Letcher, although they were nearly all Union men. They took their property (boats) from Hampton to Norfolk or [up] the James River.

The pilot boat *Plume* [owned by George's father Robert C. Wood] was loaded with moveable furniture such as beds, carpets, chairs, crockery, stoves, cooking utensils, bedsteads, safes, etc. The families of Robert C. Wood, Richard Bully and Joseph Wingfield were on board [April 22] waiting for next morning to start up the James River. The war talk was strong on all sides of the water. Steamboats had stopped running. Two Massachusetts regiments had arrived at Old Point. . . . We slept on the boat that night, some aft and some in the forward bunks. I remember two cockroaches falling in my face waking me up with a start.

We got underway next morning [April 23] . . . beat out of the creek, never to be entered again by several of the people [on board]. . . . We reached Jamestown that afternoon and fastened to the wharf while a thunderstorm passed over. [Enroute] we passed the Warwick River, Pagan or Smithfield Creek, Mulberry Island, where the Confederates afterward had a battery [Fort Crafford]. Just across the river a little higher up was Harden's Bluff where they had another battery [Fort Huger]. . . . Next was Kingsmill, College Creek and Spratley's until we reached Jamestown . . .

(Boatman, pp. 14-16.)

- - - - -

April 22, 1861 – Greenmount Farm, near Lee's Mill
Mr. Thomas George Wynne, Farmer

The navy yard of Portsmouth, as we learn, was fired and then deserted by Federal troops . . . It is now in the possession of southerners who succeeded in extinguishing the fire and saving a good many cannon.

(ed: Thomas farms 400 acres adjacent to his father's farm at Poplar Hall. The parents of Tom's wife, Fannie Curtis Wynne, own farmland at Lands End on Mulberry Island and Dr. H. H. Curtis of Endview is a brother-in-law. Tom's full blood bother, William Baker Wynne lives at Locust Grove. All of the families attend Lebanon Church which is on land in front of Endview. Thomas serves in the local militia but his poor health, from childhood, keeps him from active service.)

**(*James City Cavalry Picket Lines*, Williamsburg, Virginia, monthly, 2008. Articles entitled *Greenmount Farm Journal* edited by Fred Boelt and appearing April p.3; May p.2; June p.2-3; July p. 2-3; August p. 3; September p. 4-5; November p. 4; December p. 3-4. [Hereafter cited as Greenmount Journal by month])

- - - - -

April 26, 1861 – Greenmount Farm, James City Country
Mr. Thomas Wynne, Farmer

. . . Yesterday the ordinance of secession passed the Convention [in Richmond].

(Greenmount Journal by month.)

- - - - -

May 8, 1861 – Gloucester Point, Virginia
Pvt. James P. Williams, Richmond Howitzers

Dear Sister [Nannie]

. . . We reached West Point, the terminus of the road [railroad], yesterday morning just as the sun was fully up, and the river and everything together was the prettiest sight I ever beheld. . . . the Mattaponi comes down on your left, and on the right Pamunkey, and just at the end of the rail road they both unite and form York River . . . after breakfast we all marched down to the wharf, put our guns on board the steamer *Logan,* then jumped aboard

19

ourselves and struck out for this place. . . . we got here about 11 o'clock and found an engineer and about 60 negroes and carts throwing up breastworks, and they had already accomplished a good deal. The Point here is on the north side of the river and Yorktown is right across on the opposite side. . . . The Point here is a low sandy piece of land running right down into the river, and further out from the point and behind it is a high steep bluff. This is the narrowest, and deepest place in the river and the only place where we can well stop vessels from passing with our small guns. The river here is about a mile wide . . . we sent a dispatch to Richmond yesterday . . . we are on the lookout for the rest of our company. . . All we lack is large guns. We couldn't possibly defend ourselves against a regular man-of-war with the guns [field artillery] we have. . . . There are two big 9-inch columbiad at West Point which we are expecting down today, and if the rest of the company come down today I reckon they will bring some large guns with them too. . . .We have oysters fried, for breakfast, dinner & supper and . . . we take them right out of the river. Some of the boys are out now fishing for crabs. . .

(ed: James is from Halifax County, Virginia, and was 17 years and 3 months old when he enlisted in the Second Company of the Richmond Howitzers on April, 21, 1861.)

(Papers of James Peter Williams 1854-1899, Alderman Library, University of Virginia, Accession #490, Charlottesville, Virginia [Hereafter cited as Williams, by date.])

- - - - -

May 11 & 16, 1861 – Yorktown, Virginia
Mr. Thomas Wynne, Farmer

Went down to Yorktown with father [Richard Cary Wynne] to see the fortifications which are being erected there. There will be a line of fortification guarding the entrance of the road from Hampton, also a fort on the back to guard the river. Went over to the Gloucester side. There are 400 men, 4 Columbiads, 4 six pounders and 4 rifle barreled cannon.

Thursday, May 16th - Went to Yorktown this afternoon. Two Columbiads were landed there from Richmond, also a company of
soldiers. Several companies are expected tomorrow.

(Greenmount Journal by month.)

- - - - -

May 23, 1861 – Greenmount Farm
Mr. Thomas Wynne, Farmer

Thursday – This day will be ever memorable in the history of Virginia and should be celebrated as the anniversary of Virginia's escape from Northern rule and the despot's thraildom. Mr. Wood
[Wynne's overseer for Greenmount] and myself went up to Williamsburg and cast our votes for the Ratification of the Ordinance
of Secession. Left Fannie and Bet with Nora and Mat making
clothes for the soldiers.

(Greenmount Journal by month.)

- - - - -

June 10-11, 1861 – Greenmount Farm
Mr. Thomas Wynne, Farmer

Monday, June 10th . . . A fight took place today between our men
and the Yankees near Bethel Church in which the latter were repulsed . . .

Tuesday, June 11th . . . Sent a communication to the [Richmond]
Dispatch giving our account of the battle near Bethel Church.
Today's account make the killed and wounded over 400 men.
Thanks be to the God of Heaven for his goodness in destroying
those who would destroy us. . . . Sent down to Capt. Cosnahan's
company 42 lbs of shoulder meat and 1 bushel of meal.

(Greenmount Journal by month.)

- - - - -

June 11, 1861– battle at Big Bethel
Pvt. Charles Johnson, Hawkins Zouaves

Our Regiment did not participate in the action, though three Companies (A, B and G) engaged in bringing up supplies . . . the fact can not be concealed that our forces were entirely defeated, that our first battle is a decided repulse of the Union arms.

. . . another fact . . . is that the troops . . . are certainly lacking in discipline . . . for on our return march if the enemy had pursued us . . . the Vermonters, Massachusetts men and Germans presented nothing but . . . a horde of stragglers. . . .

(ed: The 9th New York Infantry was known as Hawkins Zouaves.)

(The Long Roll – One of the Hawkins Zouaves 1861-1863, Charles F. Johnson, Shepherdstown, 1986, p.23. [Hereafter cites as Long Roll.]

- - - - -

No date – Portsmouth, Virginia
Asst. Engineer E. V. White, C.S. Ironclad *Virginia*

The *Virginia* [constructed on the hull of the U. S. S. *Merrimac*] was covered amidships with a roof 170 feet long, built with an angle of 45 degrees, constructed of 20-inch heart of pine, and covered with 4-inch oak. Upon this wood backing there were two iron plates two inches thick and seven inches wide, one laid horizontally and the other vertically, making the armament 4 inches thick. These plates were bolted through the wood and clinched on the inside. Her bow was armed below water with a cast-iron prow about 6 feet long, to be used as a ram. Her weakest element was her motive power, her old engines and boilers having already been condemned. Her ordnance consisted of ten guns: two 7-inch steel-banded Brooke rifles, mounted as pivot guns at the bow and stern; two 6-inch rifles of the same pattern and six 9 inch Dahlgren smooth-bore broadside guns. Her commander was Franklin Buchanan . . . Second in command was Lt. Catesby Jones. Her crew numbered 350, most of whom had volunteered from the army . . .

(White, pp. 6-7.)

- - - - -

June 12, 1861–Greenmount Farm
Mr. Thomas Wynne– Farmer

Wednesday – Between 5 and 6 hundred Zouaves from Louisiana reached the Grove Wharf this morning directly from Fort Pickens [Florida]. They went down to York. They are a brave, desperate looking set of men, the sight of them will frighten the Yankees. Their commands are given in French.

(Greenmount Journal by month.)

- - - - -

June 15, 1861 – Yorktown, Virginia
Private Thomas J. Head, Co. B – 6th Georgia Infantry

My dearest Sallie

I now seat myself to write you a few lines acknowledging the receipt of your most lovely letter dated June the eighth, and I assure you it was with the greatest pleasure that I received it. I have been moved as you will see from the heading of this letter to the great place York Town. This place is a very old and dilapidated town there has not been a house erected since Cornwallis delivered the sword to General Washington.

The old fortifications of Cornwallis are very visible in some places I visited his cave the other day, it is situated right on the river banks and it has a hole just large enough for a man to crawl through it is hewn out of solid rock and is about ten feet square inside. We are making great preparations for a fight here. The soldiers are throwing up breast works for a mile out of town.

I have been sick ever since I came to this place but am getting nearly well and who could help from getting well when they get such consoling and loving letters as the one I received from you last night it is almost enough to revive the dead.

We are expecting a fight every day we have been sleeping under arms for two or three nights and we don't know what moment the enemy will attack us. We received orders the other day to march immediately to the other side of town that the enemy was in two miles of this place but it was all a farce. I think it was done to see how the men would stand it. There was about two hundred in the regiment that was excused from duty that day but when the orders came I don't think there was excusing a dozen men who stayed in camp. It seems that they all anxious for a fight. The Virginia and North Carolina regiments had a fight the other day with the abolitionists and our men killed about two hundred of the enemy and they only got one man killed and five or six wounded. You asked me to write you a long letter I would do it with great pleasure but I have so much to tell you and about so many important things that I hardly know which to write first. And another thing we must not expect a soldier to write much at a time because we are not fixed for writing as we would be if we were seated in our quiet country homes where we have nothing to disturb us. I am now sitting on the ground in my tent beside my trunk writing and my chum laying sick with fever and some of the boys in the tents near mine are playing the violin and some of the companies are out on drill with drums beating and amidst all of this confusion I am trying to write to the only being on earth that is nearer to me than a Father & mother.

And as you say I hope that the day will not be far off when we will spend a great many pleasant hours together. If I am not with you now my thoughts are ever with thee there is not a day that passes over my head but what I think of thee.

And if I am called out on the battle fields I will remember thee and the more I think of thee the more I will strive to conquer my enemies. I will know that there is one being that cares for me and one I care for Dearest Sallie you must not think I am a flatterer when I say that you are the most lovely being I ever saw.

You must write to me immediately when you receive this letter for we may be removed from this place in the course of two or three weeks. Write soon, and may god bless you I remain forever you true lover

T. J. Head

PS

Address T J Head

6th regt of Ga Vol

York Town

Va

(ed: T. J. is a private. He enlisted on May 20, 1861, in Dade County, Georgia. The swampy environment of the lower peninsula and contact with soldiers with a wide variety of diseases results in Thomas receiving a disability discharge on September 20, 1861, while still stationed in the Yorktown area. He will serve in Co. H of the 6th Georgia Militia beginning on April 15, 1864, and will be discharged from service in Augusta, Georgia, on April 9, 1865.)

(ed: In the middle part of the letter when he writes of the "fight the other day" and "killed about two hundred of the enemy" he is making reference to the battle of Big Bethel which was fought on June 10, 1861.)

(Private Thomas J. Head Letter, SC00117, Special Collections Research Center, Swem Library, College of William & Mary, Williamsburg, Virginia)

- - - - -

June 18, 1861 – Greenmount Farm
Mr. Thomas Wynne, Farmer

Tuesday – One of our picket Guards stationed at the mill [Blow's Mill on Skiff's Creek], Mr. Garland Hanes, called on me today to supply them with some buttermilk and bread, which we were glad to do. A soldier's life is one of hardship and privation.

(Greenmount Journal by month.)

- - - - -

June 18, 1861 – Camp Butler, Newport News Point
Pvt. Charles Johnson, Hawkins Zouaves

Am not doing duty to-day. Am both bilious and feverish, feel cold and hot by turns, with other strange sensations, the result of not having our food properly cooked and from sleeping on the damp ground.

(ed: The 1858 edition of 'Mackenzie's 5,000 Receipts' notes that bilious fever is caused by peculiar poisonous vapours from ponds, marshes and decaying vegetable matter. The recommended treatment is to cleanse the bowels with an emetic and use calomel. From 10 to 20 grains of calomel [mercury chloride] combined with molasses and repeated until copious evacuations are produced.)

(Long Roll, p.24. and Mackenzies 5000 Receipts of the Useful and Domestic Arts, Pittsburg, 1858, p. 199 [Hereafter cited as Mackenzie].)

- - - - -

June 22, 1861 – Camp Butler, Newport News Point
Pvt. Charles Johnson, Hawkins Zouaves

I have reported myself well to-day, although I do not feel strong enough to do much. I have had chills and fever, or the ague, and have actually eaten nothing for the last three or four days, and I do not remember much that has transpired during that time, except that Beith [tent mate] would occasionally put blankets over me when I was shaking.

(Long Roll, p. 24.)

- - - - -

June 24, 1861 – Yorktown, Virginia
Pvt. James P. Williams, Richmond Howitzers

Aunt Mary

. . . All the fortifications are about finished . . . this is the hottest place though I ever saw we are right down in the sand, and there is not a shade tree on the place, the water also is very mean, but there is plenty of it and we are getting use to it. . . . We have fine salt water bathing and go in the river every morning and evening. . . . We have no such thing as lard for Biscuits, but generally use the grease from fried bacon. The other morning one of our mess saw some barrels of lard lying out on the wharf, and went down and stole some out of a barrel to make biscuits . . . The biscuits were baked and nearly all ate up when a fellow from another mess . . . came up and told us that what we had supposed to be lard was Tallow used for making candles. . . . I think I had managed to get down three biscuits before I found out, and really thought they were very good. . . .

(ed: The Richmond Howitzers have been moved from Gloucester Point to Yorktown where they will become more involved in scouting, support of infantry probes, and foraging operations.)

(Williams, by date.)

- - - - -

June 26, 1861 – near Newport News, Virginia
Pvt. Charles Johnson, Hawkins Zouaves

. . . for the first time I have witnessed the pure wantonness of destruction . . . a carpenter-shop . . . was set on fire and everything that could not be appropriated was destroyed. . . . Who can blame Southern citizens for not staying here to witness the destruction of their property and the desecration of their homes? Their cause as men and freemen is just. We are the invaders, and it were right for them to drive us from their soil. . . . I often said to myself, "God help this poor, distracted country."

(Long Roll, pp. 25-26.)

- - - - -

June 28, 1861 – Greenmount Farm
Mr. Thomas Wynne, Farmer

Friday – Supplied breakfast and supper to the picket guards stationed at Lebanon Church.

(Greenmount Journal by month.)

July, August and September, 1861

On July 21, at Manassas, Virginia, the Union army under General Irvin McDowell met the Confederate army under Generals Pierre G. T. Beauregard and Joseph Johnston. The Confederates win and rout the Union army which clogs the roads to Washington with fleeing troops, wagons and carriages of politicians and ladies who came out to watch the victory. General George B. McClellan is given command of the broken army. He views himself as the one who will save the Union.

Private Charles Johnson, of the 9th New York Infantry, watches a comet and muses, *"wondering if that little visitor was tired . . . or disgusted with the appearance of things on . . . our planet."* Confederate Colonel Lafayette McLaws, in Williamsburg, advises his wife that *"measles and mumps are prevalent . . . I was in town, and visited the General Hospital where there were . . . a hundred patients with measles, mumps, and all kinds of diseases . . . it is a sickly country."* Things are quiet on the Peninsula with both armies scouting, foraging and the Southerners in particular building a primary line of fortifications across the Peninsula between Yorktown and Mulberry Island. A secondary defensive line is being constructed at Williamsburg between the York and James Rivers.

The second issue of Confederate currency is authorized by the Act of July 24, 1861. $20,000,000 is authorized and printed by Hoyer & Ludwig of Richmond. These notes are all printed in black ink and the backside of the notes are blank. Hoyer & Ludwig is the producer of Confederate postage stamps and had been a printer of cards and poster lithographs pre-war. The issue is printed in denominations of $5, $10, $20, $50 and $100.

General Sterling Price and his Confederate troops win battles at Wilson's Creek, Missouri, on August 10 and Lexington, Missouri, on

September 20.   There is great consternation in St. Louis as the Confederate forces seem to move at will. On the Peninsula, in Virginia, Private William Corson, of the 3rd Virginia Cavalry, writes Jenny about foraging, camping on a bluff over the river, spending leisure hours bathing and fishing. He then notes, *"There is a great deal of sickness . . . particularly in Yorktown where three or four die every day."* Life in the swampy, marshy environs with the summer heat takes a heavy toll on soldiers in both armies. Life in both armies is drilling, picket duty, scouting, foraging and dealing with disease.

On September 2, 1861, a third issue of currency is authorized in the amount of $100,000,000. Hoyer & Ludwig share the contract with J. T. Paterson of Columbia, South Carolina and Augusta, Georgia; B. Duncan of Columbia, South Carolina; Keatinge & Ball of Richmond and later of Columbia, South Carolina; and prior to the seizure of their plates by Federal authorities, the Southern Bank Note Company of New Orleans, Louisiana, is able to provide a limited amount of $5, $10, $20 and $50 bills. In September the Confederate dollar is worth 95 cents versus the United States dollar. Inflation has not yet become a problem.

In Virginia, Private Richard Watkins, of the 3rd Virginia Cavalry, in a letter to his wife Mary pens, *"The Yankees do not venture more than three miles from Fort Monroe . . . Since coming here I have commenced drinking coffee and find no inconvenience from it."* Private William Corson is on picket duty when he is attacked by *"muskeeters"* who swarm him and *"have bitten my face and hands till they are perfectly spotted . . . I feel out of sorts this morning."* The Yankees do not bother the 3rd Virginia Cavalry but the muskeeters attack all day long. A few days later he writes that *"musquitoes are on the increase."* William is not alone is his struggle to spell mosquito.

Out west a new general named Ulysses S. Grant is in charge of Union forces at Cairo, Illinois. Confederate forces have occupied Columbus, Kentucky, overlooking the Mississippi River, just to the south of Cairo. Grant moves some forces across the Ohio River and occupies Paducah, Kentucky, at the mouth of the Tennessee River.

The recent Confederate victories, both in the east and west, has boosted the volunteering of troops for the Confederate armies. In the Union, they have to institute the draft to fill the ranks. Once the fighting begins in earnest, and the dead and wounded fill the cemeteries and the hospitals, it becomes necessary to have drafts in both the North and the South. Currently the soldiers on the Peninsula are bored with drilling, building fortifications, foraging and scouting. Both sides need to enjoy the quiet times while they last. Being a soldier will not be a lark much longer.

(Chronicle by date; Slabaugh, pp. 26-46.)

July, August & September, 1861

Early July, 1861 – Yorktown, Virginia
Pvt. William C. Corson, Co. G – 3rd Virginia Cavalry

My dear Jennie

. . . I had a hard chill the day we started from Williamsburg and had to ride all the way to Yorktown in the baggage wagon. I am now suffering with rheumatism contracted from sleeping on the cold ground. We reached York a little after sunset Friday and pitched our tents on the very ground where Corn Wallace delivered up his sword . . .

(ed: Company G is from Cumberland County, Virginia, and their official name is the Cumberland Light Dragoons.)

(My Dear Jennie – Letters from a Confederate Soldier to his fiancée by William Clark Corson, edited by Blake Corson, Richmond, 1992, p. 22. [Hereafter cited as Corson].)

- - - - -

July 2, 1861 (Tuesday) – camp near Williamsburg
Col. Lafayette McLaws, 10th Georgia Infantry

My dearly beloved Wife

. . . I am in command of forces in and around Williamsburg, including an area of country about 10 miles long and three or four broad. The camp of the 10th Regiment is my head quarters and is immediately in the rear of an immense redoubt [Redoubt #6] now in the course of erection under my control.

. . . Parties of the enemy are constantly making inroads in the country around Newport News and stealing negroes and all kinds of property and committing so many degradations that the inhabitants have fled leaving their homes, fields and worldly goods behind. . . .

(ed: Lafayette will begin almost all of his letters to Emily with either 'My dear wife' or 'My dearly beloved wife.')

(A Soldier's General – The Civil War Letters of Maj. General Lafayette McLaw;, John C. Oeffinger, editor, Chapel Hill, 2014, {Hereafter cited as McLaws by date.]).

- - - - -

Early July, 1861 – Yorktown, Virginia
Pvt. William C. Corson, Co. G – 3rd Virginia Cavalry

My dear Jennie -

. . . Nearly all of our men went down to the river and bathed in the salt water. Some rode their horses out in the water and sat on them fishing for crabs. There are plenty of fish down this way and we buy them for a mere trifle. After the tide commenced falling we caught oysters and gathered shells. . . .

(ed: The 3rd Virginia Cavalry has companies from Halifax (2), Cumberland, Prince Edward, Mecklenburg, Nottoway, Dinwiddie, Charles City, New Kent, James City and Hampton/Newport News Counties. That is 11 companies and a regiment normally has 10. In April, 1862, the James City Cavalry will be transferred to the 5th Virginia Cavalry.)

(Corson, p. 22.)

- - - - -

July 11-17, 1861 – Greenmount Farm
Mr. Thomas Wynne, Farmer

Thursday, July 11th . . . Have to send a man [Jake] and cart down to [Grove] wharf tomorrow morning to assist in throwing up entrenchments.

Saturday, July 13th . . . A skirmish occurred between a plundering party of Yankees and Chas. City Cavalry [3rd Virginia Cavalry] near Capt. Smith's in Warwick, in which 15 or 20 of the former were killed and thirteen were taken prisoners. My man and cart are still employed at the wharf.

Monday, July 15th . . . Sent Jake to the wharf again this morning . . .

Tuesday, July 16th . . . Again Jake, with cart had to be employed at the wharf. Two deserters from the Yankees came to Yorktown this afternoon.

Wednesday, July 17th . . . Sent Jake to the wharf again this morning . . .

(ed: The government requests workers from surrounding farms to assist with the building of fortifications. Mr. Wynne will be paid for the days of work provided and will get some type of rental fee for the cart. Confederate soldiers will also be employed in work details building the fortifications, clearing fields of fire and stacking limbs and tree trash in ravines and fields to impede the advance of an attacking enemy.)

(Greenmount Journal by month.)

- - - - -

July 17, 1861 – near Newpot News Point
Pvt. Charles Johnson, Hawkins Zouaves

Have just gotten two letters with more than ordinary pleasure: one from my Father in Minnesota and the other from my Sister in Hudson City, the first news I have had from either of these homes since I left New York. All well so far.

. . . a most beautiful night. . . I watched the comet, wondering if that mysterious little visitor was . . . now tired of his visit to these regions of space, or disgusted it may be with the appearance of things on this side of our planet, for he is now leaving in seemingly greater haste than he came, with his tail between his legs, for the unknown regions out yonder. . . .

(Long Roll, pp. 30-31.)

- - - - -

July 18, 1861 (Thursday) – Williamsburg, Virginia
Col. Lafayette McLaws, 10th Georgia Infantry

My dear Wife

. . . The measles and mumps are prevalent to be sure . . . The enemy have been extraordinarily quiet .. . I do not think he will march in this direction. . . . I will subscribe to a newspaper for you – either the *Richmond Dispatch* or the *Whig,* the latter is said to be the most reliable. . . .

Good bye my darling –

(ed: In an August letter he informs Emily that he has taken out a 6 month subscription to the 'Richmond Whig' to be mailed to her in Georgia.)

(McLaws, by date.)

- - - - -

July 19, 1861 – Greenmount Farm
Mr. Thomas Wynne, Farmer

Friday, . . . Heard that a battle has been fought near Manassas Gap in which we were victorious.

(Greenmount Journal by month.)

- - - - -

July 21, 1861 Tuesday – near Williamsburgs, Virginia
Col. Lafayette McLaws, 10th Georgia Infantry

My dear children

. . . To day I was in town, and visited the General Hospital where there are about a hundred patients, with measles, mumps, and all kinds of diseases such as soldiers have . . . it is a sickly country. . . . Everything there is out of order, because of the neglect of the Department in Richmond in not furnishing supplies and because the doctors do not know how to conduct a hospital.

(McLaws, by date.)

- - - - -

July 22, 1861 – Greenmount Farm
Mr. Thomas Wynne, Farmer

Monday . . . Fannie sent a market cart up to the Louisiana camp at Littleton and found a ready market for everything.

(Greenmount Journal by month.)

- - - - -

July 24, 1861 – Williamsburg, Virginia
Col. Lafayette McLaws, 10th Georgia Infantry

. . . Went to town [on the 23rd] and found the hospital improving, put guards under more strict orders . . . The weather dried to day the 24th but the country filled with pools of water. The works were considerably damaged by washing but will soon be in good repair again. . . .

(ed: In heavy rains the freshly dug redoubts and fortifications have a certain amount of their dirt washed down their sides and back into the moat. Repair work will be needed. Eventually weeds and vines will grow on the outer dirt walls of the battlements to help hold them in place. Being new they are very vulnerable to heavy rains.)

(McLaws by date.)

- - - - -

37

July 24, 1861 – Geeenmount Farm
Mr. Thomas Wynne, Farmer

The soldiers are still among us very much, visiting homes in quest
for something to eat. Many of them are the merest rowdies, des-
titute of self respect. If the regiments from Louisiana be sample
of the people of that state I must confess that they are very low
bred and uncivil. There are some gentlemen among them but
very few. . . . July 25th . . . The Yankees continue to steal Negroes
from the farms near Newport News.

(Greenmount Journal by month.)

- - - - -

July 25, 1861 – Williamsburg, Virginia
Col. Lafayette McLaws, Camp of the 10th Georgia

. . . Intended finishing this letter to be sent off this morning but . .
. obliged to leave and go off about a mile to put a working party
with axes to cutting down a grove of trees that obstructed the
field of fire of one of the batteries and to entangle the ravine that
led up to within a few hundred yards of one . . . redoubt. By entangling I mean cutting down trees and making them fall across
each other in the direction the enemy is expected to come . . . it
makes it very difficult for them to get over [the obstructions and
charge a redoubt]. . . .

I put twenty men to cutting and went off to examine . . . another
fortification [Redoubt #1] which commands another mill dam at
. . . Tutter's Neck. . . .I [also] have some 400 negroes at work . . .

(McLaws, by date.)

- - - - -

July 26, 1861 – camp near Newport News Point
Pvt. Charles Johnson, Hawkins Zouaves

I saw a paper of the Twenty-third last night, and it corroborates the worst. Our forces were defeated [at Manassas] and made a shameful stampede . . . without the least attempt at order. . . . the people at home must feel worse about it than we do. . . . One of our Buglers is dead, and as I write, Col. Allen's band is escorting the body to its last resting-place.

(Long Roll, pp. 33-34.)

- - - - -

July 29, 1861 – Camp Cockle, Virginia
Pvt. William C. Corson, Co. G – 3rd Virginia Cavalry

My Dear Jennie

. . . The Yankees are leaving Hampton and concentrating at New-port News. Nearly all the forces from Williamsburg and all from this place have been below here near Bethel church for five or six days and passed here today on way back to camp. . . . Our fare is quite scanty sometimes and our scouts frequently are 18 hours without any thing to eat. Sometimes we can get a plenty of fish and Salt-Water clams for which we readily discard mess-pork and camp-made bread. We rarely ever get any thing to eat from home now as there is such difficulty in getting boxes here. Watermelons are plentiful a few miles from camp but they sell very high. . . . Dear Jennie I am so anxious to see my darling. One sweet kiss from my love would entirely cure me . . .

(ed: Camp Cockle and Cockle Town are near present day Grafton.)

(Corson, pp. 25-26 and xxi.)

- - - - -

July 30, 1861 (Tuesday) – Fort Magruder, Virginia
Col. Lafayette McLaws, Camp of the 10th Georgia

My Dear Wife

. . . The main work here called Fort Magruder [Redoubt #6] is fast approaching completion, and on the right and left redoubts of formidable strength . . . will be [finished] within a week. . . .

. . . I have several friends who are . . . endeavoring to have me appointed Brig Gen and they say with a good prospect of success, but we shall see . . .

The weather is excessively warm and the mosquitoes very active all the day long, but I have on tar & when in bed am independent. This morning I received a tin bucket of tomatoes from a lady in WmBurg who at the same time sent a basket of biscuits for 'The Georgians" and about two & a half gallons of buttermilk . . . the ladies are exceedingly kind to the sick, giving all kinds of delicacies, supply quantities of bedding of all kinds, clothing of every description, and above all giving them constant personal attention. The attending surgeon . . . informed me that fifteen ladies . . . were from time to time attending in person to the wants of the sick in one hospital alone . . .

(ed: In this letter, and his letter of July 21, when he speaks of visiting the General Hospital he is referring to the major hospital in Williamsburg which is the Female Academy Hospital. It is located on the grounds where the Colonial Capitol was located prior to it being destroyed by fire. The Williamsburg Female Academy closed with the outbreak of the war and it provides space for the only large hospital in Williamsburg. Prior to the battle, the other three significant hospitals are the College Hospital (in the Wren Building), the Episcopal Hospital (in Bruton Parish Episcopal Church) and the African Church Hospital (in the African Baptist Church). Many other buildings will be pressed into service following the fighting of May 4 - 6, 1862.)

(McLaws, by date.)

- - - - -

July 31, 1861 – Yorktown, Virginia

Pvt. James P. Williams, Richmond Howitzers

Dear Sister [Nannie]

. . . I received Aunt Mary's letter while I was down the country and the Box also came . . . the boys knew I would be absent for several days, and were afraid the contents would spoil: they therefore opened it, but ate only a few cakes and didn't touch either of the jars. The cakes were first rate & the pickle & jam were the best things I ever tasted. . . . I should like very much to have had some fried chicken. . . . obliged to Aunt Mary for the socks and will need them after a while . . . tell her I can make out very well for a month or six weeks longer. If I want them sooner . . . I will write for them.

Our company has been split up and very much divided within the last two weeks. They have taken about ¼ of the men & Capt. Brown over to Williamsburg . . . to drill raw artillery companies stationed there. . . .

(Williams, by date.)

- - - - -

August 8, 1861 – Greenmount Farm
Mr. Thomas Wynne, Farmer

Thursday . . . Heard that Hampton was burned last night.

(Greenmount Journal by month.)

- - - - -

August 9, 1861 – Bethel Church, Virginia
Pvt. James P. Williams, Richmond Howitzers

Dear Aunt Mary

. . . I left Yorktown a week ago today and in the week have been tramping all over the whole Peninsula, arriving at this place yesterday morning. I received Pa's letter Monday, while at a place called Young's Mill, over on the James River . . . Old McGruder [Magruder] is down here in a large force scouting, and trying to get up a fight, but I believe in vain. . . . we drew up the line upon the very outskirts of Hampton, but the cowards had actually left the place although strongly fortified and retired to Fortress [Monroe]. . . . That night McGruder determined to burn the town and . . . deprive the rascals of its many advantages and accommodations . . . All the citizens had left long ago and . . . the Yankees had already destroyed everything . . . and were using the houses for quarters and hospitals . . . the cavalry with one Virginia regiment of infantry [applied] the torch about 12 o'clock . . . We looked on until three o'clock in the morning when we took up the line of march for Bethel . . .

(Williams, by date.)

- - - - -

August 10, 1861 – Cockle Town, Virginia
Pvt. William C. Corson, Co. G – 3rd Virginia Cavalry

My Dear Jennie

Pardon me dear girl for not having answered your last letter before this but I have been moving about so much in the last two weeks that I have not had the opportunity of writing. . . . I will just tell you that we have been to Hampton this week and our troops burnt the town . . . I wrote to you by Dr. Blanton and sent you a breast pin . . .

Your most devoted William

(Corson, p. 29.)

- - - - -

August 12, 1861 – camp at Bartlett's Farm
Pvt. William C. Corson, Co. G – 3rd Virginia Cavalry

Dear Miss Jennie,

. . . We have a delightful place here right on a bluff that overlooks Poquosin river. There is an abundance of good water convenient. Our boys amuse themselves at leisure hours bathing and fishing. A foraging party goes out nearly every day and brings in a load of watermelons and roasting-ears. We can buy plenty of nice fish and vegetables. There is a great deal of sickness among the soldiers at this time, particularly in Yorktown where three or four die every day. . . . Tell Mr. Caldwell he will certainly want to trade for Fancy when I get back. She out rides a revenue cutter, runs like an antelope, and jumps higher than a Kangaroo. Write soon to your devoted

William

(ed: Fancy is William's current horse and he is pleased with her abilities.)

(ed: Bartlett's farm is on the south bank of present day Harwood's Mill Reservoir. The Bartlett farm house is about a mile south of the reservoir and about three miles north of Big Bethel.)

(Corson, pp. 29–30, p. xxii.)

- - - - -

August 18, 1861 (Sunday) – Williamsburg, Virginia
Col. Lafayette McLaws, Camp of the 10th Georgia

My dear wife

. . . This morning I received a dispatch informing me that . . . the 10th La [Louisiana] would report to me for duty. The regiment is a Zouave Regiment and has a reputation for being the most lawless in existence . . . It is said that they are nearly all Frenchmen, a great many not speaking any English . . . this regiment was on Jamestown Island for twelve hours & during that time, tis said, eat up every living thing on the island, but the horses, and their own species. . . .

Tell the boys [his young sons] I have not received that letter from them as yet. And my little daughter, if she can't write she must send me the print of her foot. . . .

Your devoted husband

(McLaws, by date.)

- - - - - -

August 18, 1861 – Adams Farm, Virginia
Pvt. William C. Corson, Co. G – 3rd Virginia Cavalry

Dear Jennie,

. . . I see peace propositions are current at the north and I hope the people who have been so long duped by the Lincoln Administration are beginning to find out that old Abe is a userper and that his war is waged for the sole purpose of subjugating the South. I have no important news . . . other than to tell you that sick soldiers are getting better and that we get a plenty of Government Whisky. . . . I had the misfortune to get my forehead cut with an axe this week right badly . . . the wound is doing well and will not leave much of a scar. If I had received the wound in battle I should have been proud of it. . . .

(ed: They were on a brush cleaning detail around the campsite when a fellow soldier's axe head 'flew off the helve' and gashed William in the right temple area.)

(Corson, p. 31.)

- - - - -

August 21, 1861 – Greenmount Farm
Mr. Thomas Wynne, Farmer

Wednesday, . . . Returned from Richmond today – Goods excessively high – Found that four of my men had been ordered into
Mulberry Island to work on fortifications. Went down on yesterday.

(Greenmount Journal by month.)

- - - - -

August 23, 1861 – Ashland, Virginia
Pvt. Richard Watkins, Co. K – 3rd Virginia Cavalry

Well Darling our orders have come. Not exactly marching orders
either but to get ready to march as early as possible. And to what
point do you guess? To Johnson's Regiment between Yorktown
and Fortress Monroe . . . to act in conjunction with McGruders
[Gen. John B. Magruder] forces . . . we go with the New Kent
Troop every member of which is well acquainted with the country with all the roads and by paths. So you may expect us to pay
our respects to Gen. Wool. . . . Our company is well drilled and
well officered and tolerably armed. . . .

Please tell Mr. Bagby . . . to send my tob[acco] to Richmond as fast
as possible . . .

Kisses to my dear children and love to all.

(Send Me a Pair of Old Boots & Kiss My Little Girls – The Civil War Letters of
Richard and Mary Watkins, 1861-1865; Jeff Toalson editor, 2009, Bloomington,
p. 30. {Hereafter cited as Boots & Kisses])

- - - - -

August 25, 1861 – Camp Adams, Virginia
Pvt. William C. Corson, Co. G – 3rd Virginia Cavalry

My Dear Jennie,

. . . Do you not often think of the many games of cards and drafts
we have played together and how close I used to set to you and

how I loved to hug and kiss you. I wonder shall I ever enjoy such blissful moments again. . . .

(ed: William opens virtually every letter with "My Dear Jennie.")

(ed: Adams Ranch is near present day Oriana Road (Rt 620) about 2 miles SW of Grafton and one mile west of Harwood's Mill Reservoir. The camp is probably within one mile of the farmhouse.)

(Corson, pp. 33 & pp. xxii – xxiii.)

- - - - -

August 26, 1861 – Camp Adams, Virginia
Pvt. William C. Corson, Co. G – 3rd Virginia Cavalry

. . . I must tell you what a horrid night I spent on guard. The muskeeters swarmed around me in myriads so that I was compelled to get me a big bush to keep them off but notwithstanding I fought vigorously all the time they have bitten my face and hands till they are perfectly spotted. . . . I feel out of sorts this morning. The Yankees did not disturb us [but the muskeeters did].

(Corson, p. 35.)

- - - - -

August 26, 1861 (Monday) – camp near Williamsburg
Col. Lafayette McLaws, 10th Georgia Infantry

My dearly beloved wife

. . . There is a rumor that the enemy have landed three hundred horses at Fort Monroe, and it is believed that tis their intention to attempt forays along the coast, stealing negroes and chickens, killing cattle, and burning houses, as seems to be their practice . . .

I have heard nothing from my Generalship . . . from all accounts I think the Government . . . is rewarding politicians . . .

My regiment has not been paid off and I am afraid the new Confederacy has some agents who are desirious . . . of making money . . . I have reported the case . . . it is better not to allow such matters to go. . . .

Give love to my children and kiss them over and over . . .

Your husband

(ed: Colonel McLaws is concerned with the honesty of some C.S.A. paymasters and fears that there is corruption and theft of payroll. He notes in his letter that this was not an uncommon event during his service with the U. S. Army in the 1850s.)

(McLaws, by date.)

- - - - -

August 31, 1861 – Greenmount Farm
Mr. Thomas Wynne, Farmer

Saturday, . . . Three of my hands are still at work on the fortifications in Mulberry Island.

(ed: When the government is not able to get the quantity of workers needed by asking for volunteers they resort to conscripting the workers for a set period of time. They pay the owner and provide food and shelter for the workers if it is remote work. For remote work the County might need to supply 100 workers for 30 days. The owners would hire an overseer to go with the workers to make sure they were treated properly and returned at the end of the agreed period.)

(Greenmount Journal by month.)

- - - - -

September 2, 1861 – Greenmount Farm
Mr. Thomas Wynne, Farmer

Monday, . . . William and Moses returned home from Warwick where they have been employed, since last Tuesday week, on the fort on Mulberry Point.

(Greenmount Journal by month.)

- - - - -

September 3, 1861 – Camp Adams
Pvt. William C. Corson, Co. G – 3rd Virginia Cavalry

Dear Jennie,

Your letter of the 29th of Aug. came to hand night before last and afforded me a great deal of pleasure. I left the camp early next morning for vidette duty on Chesapeake-bay where I have been ever since till tonight. I saw the Blockade and a number of small Yankee-boats, but none of them attempted to come ashore. We have to keep a sharp look out to prevent the enemy from cutting us off. . . . no news from the Peninsula except that times are getting harder with the soldiers and musquitoes are on the increase. . . . I have no time to say more as Tattoo has sounded and my candle must be put out. . . .

(ed: In a span of less than 10 days he has found two spellings for the dreaded muskeeters or musquitoes. It is a contest in war letters whether mosquito or diarrhea is misspelled more often.)

(Corson, p. 37.)

- - - - -

September 7, 1861 – Greenmount Farm
Mr. Thomas Wynne, Farmer

Saturday, . . .Father and myself went down to Yorktown – 6 companies of the La. Regiment went below this morning – 4 companies of the 10th Georgia regiment camped out in my apple orchard late this afternoon on their way to Warwick Ct. House. Major Weems and Lt. Miller spent the night with me.

(Greenmount Journal by month.)

- - - - -

September 12, 1861 – Adam's Ranch, Virginia
Pvt. Richard Watkins, Co. K – 3rd Virginia Cavalry

My darling Mary

I reached Richmond in safety Monday and on Tuesday morning at 8 o'clock took the cars on the Richmond & York River RR for Yorktown. Reached the terminus of the road at West Point and learned to our surprise that the boat would not leave till the next day. . . . The next day (Sep 11) we reached Yorktown about 9 o'clock and hired a waggon to bring us to this place . . . Capt. Thornton's Company and the Mecklenburg Troop had gone off on a scouting expedition and would probably be absent for several days. Lieut. Redd, Sergeant Knight and about 6 privates left to guard the camp.

We are 8 miles below Yorktown but I hear that today we will be moved back one mile . . . to be more convenient to water. Yorktown is a small village and looks dilapidated. . . . The Yankees . . . do not venture more than 3 miles from Fortress Monroe. Our pickets are almost in sight of the fort.

Must close now . . . Good night . . . I love you I love you.

(Boots & Kisses, p. 35.)

- - - - -

September, 15, 1861 – City Point, Virginia
George R. Wood, deckhand, *James Buchanan*

On September 15 father took command of the transport schooner *James Buchanan* to carry stores for the Confederates and I went as a deckhand or sailor.

We anchored [for a few months] off the mouth of College Creek as a store boat to receive government stores from the steamer

Northampton at night, put the stores on board a barge [or canal boat] and poled or rowed her up the creek to Williamsburg to Captain Hope's commissary.

(Boatman, pp. 40-41.]

- - - - -

September 17, 1861 – Camp Phillips, near Adams Ranch
Pvt. Richard Watkins, Co. K – 3rd Virginia Cavalry

My own Dear Mary

. . . all is quiet and dull . . . Our duties are very light except that we have to bring water for the distance of nearly a mile and do our own cooking, the servants having gone with the majority (of the troops near Bethel Church). Ned Scott and I cooked breakfast this morning and it was pronounced by all hands a first rate breakfast. It consisted of hot flour hoe cakes, some nice fried meat, some cold ham and very good coffee. Since coming here I have commenced drinking coffee and find no inconvenience from it.

. . . I feel it was a great piece of negligence in me in not getting the measurement of the negroes shoes, but I was thinking about you and that is my only excuse. . . . get Cousin Barrett [in Richmond] who has a good deal of money in hand to buy them . . . I will also send now a sight draft by McKinney & Dupuy [where Cousin Barrett works] for $ which you can fill with any amount that you want and the bank in Farmville will give you the money. . . . Adieu My Darling I love you so much.

(ed: McKinney & Dupuy is the broker they use in Richmond to sell their tobacco, butter and grains. Richard and Mary own 22 slaves, 8 of them are under the age of 10. A constant in their letters are discussions dealing with shoes, clothing, blankets, winter coats, medicine and doctors coming out to deal with medical issues for their negro population. Mary Dupuy Watkins, Richard's wife, is the main reason that they use the family connected bro-

kerage of McKinney & Dupuy in Richmond.)

(Boots & Kisses, p. 36.)

- - - - -

September 18, 1861 – Greenmount Farm
Mr. Thomas Wynne, Farmer

Wednesday, . . . Went down to Yorktown to collect some money due Ma from the Confederate States, but was unable to get it. This is the third time I have been on the same errand and so far have accomplished nothing.

(Greenmount Journal by month.)

- - - - -

September 24, 1861 – Camp Phillips
Pvt. Richard Watkins, Co. K – 3rd Virginia Cavalry

My Darling Mary –

. . . Today Ned Scott, James Baker and I rode down to the half-way house to see our fellow troopers. Their situation is in a pretty country, very level and fertile and in full view of the Pecosan [Poquoson] River which is but an arm of the sea, quite broad and about a mile or two long. We rode down to the river, found the tide very high, the water clear, salt water of course, and saw the greatest quantity of fish of all sizes, shoals and schools of them. Not far from the bank was a man in a small boat gathering oysters . . .

We had invitations from everybody, officers and men, to dine with them each mess telling us what they were going to have for dinner. Some said fish oysters sweet potatoes, others chicken stew and pea etc. I accepted Dr. Berkeleys invitation and had peas, sweet potatoes, stewed tomatoes, & fried bacon and very nice biscuit. Ned dined with Charley Redd and our old mess. They

had chicken stew, stewed tomatoes, potatoes peas and something else which I have forgotten . . .

Oh I do wish I could see you and be with you and talk with you . . .

(Boots & Kisses, pp. 36-37.)

- - - - -

September 25, 1861 – Greenmount Farm
Mr. Thomas Wynne, Farmer

Wednesday, . . . Went down to Mulberry Island Battery in company with father to get my money for work of hands on the fort
for the month of August.

(Greenmount Journal by month.)

- - - - -

September 28, 1861 – Camp Phillips, Virginia
Pvt. William C. Corson, Co. G – 3rd Virginia Cavalry

Dear Jennie

. . . We have received shotguns from Richmond recently. I have a
fine time squirrel hunting. Several of us went out this week and
killed fifty in one day.

*(ed: Camp Philllips is not accurately located. It is probably about
three miles from Warwick Court House in the direction of Halfway
House based on notes in various letters.)*

(Corson, p. 42 & p.xxiii.)

- - - - -

September 29, 1861 (Sunday) – Young's Farm, Virginia
Col. Lafayette McLaws, Camp of the 10th Georgia

My darling wife

. . . Day before yesterday we had the usual September gales, with plenty of rain . . .

R. R. Cobb with his [Georgia] legion has already arrived, and report says that Howell is to follow & will come as a Brigadier General. I do not wish to be under any politicians, nor will I if it can be helped. Howell Cobb or any one else – I am indebted to General Magruder . . . for the honorable position I am now occupying. To his favor . . . do I owe the fortune of being in command all the time since my arrival . . . [rest of the letter is missing]

(McLaws, by date.)

- - - - -

September 30, 1861 – Greenmount Farm
Mr. Thomas Wynne, Farmer

Monday, . . . Received a check for $76 from the Engineer Department for Ma for the work of her servants on the fort at Mulberry Island Point.

(Greenmount Journal by month.)

October, November and December, 1861

The early signs of winter are in the air. Troops are starting to think about winter quarters and some even think they should go home for the winter and report back in the spring. They will be surprised when the Confederate government does not endorse this idea. The weather near Newport News, Virginia, in the words of General La-fayette McLaws, "*. . . is never good here . . . always bad, muddy and disagreable . . .*"

On October 31, in Neosho, Missouri, the Confederate legislature of Missouri met to secede from the Union. The Confederate legislators fled Jefferson City as Union troops occupied the city. The Confederate Missouri legislature will spend virtually the entire war in exile, mostly in Marshall, Texas. In mid-November a group of Confederate Kentucky legislators will adopt articles of secession and take Kentucky out of the Union. Similar to Missouri, the Confederate government of Kentucky will spend the balance of the war in exile.

General George B. McClellan is appointed General-in-Chief of all Union armies to replace the ailing Winfield Scott on November 1.

On November 7, 1861, the Union army attacks at Belmont, Missouri, across the Mississippi River from the Confederate fortifications at Columbus, Kentucky. After some initial success, General Grant and his forces are driven back to Cairo, Illinois.

On November 8 crewmen from the U.S.S. *San Jacinto* board the British ship *Trent*, in the Atlantic Ocean, and remove Mr. James Mason and Mr. John Slidell. They are enroute to Britain and France as Commissioners for the Confederacy. This is a major insult by the United States. Great Britain is outraged by the actions of Captain Wilkes in boarding a British ship in international waters and removing passengers. The opposite action, when the British were boarding and removing sailors from U.S. ships, had been one of the factors in starting the War of 1812.

Excellent progress is being made on the primary line of fortifications on the lower Peninsula. The line stretches between Yorktown and Mulberry Island using the Warwick River as the key defensive feature. Colonel McLaws has the secondary line at Williamsburg taking shape. Both lines are being built using a combination of slave and soldier labor.

Troops are building winter quarters as the cold weather approaches. Private Richard Watkins writes Mary in a December 7 note that *"the weather is so cold that we all have to sleep with our clothes on. I do not think I have taken mine off except for the purpose of changing my underwear for two months. . ."*

In late December Private Watkins writes, *"Perhaps England and the United States will get into a war that will result . . . in our independence."* On December 25 Secretary of State William Seward admits that the seizure of Mason and Slidell was an illegal act. They are sent on their way to Europe and Secretary Seward apologizes to the government of Great Britain.

(Chronicle by date.}

October, November & December, 1861

October 2, 1861 – Half-way House near Yorktown
Pvt. Richard Watkins, Co. K – 3rd Virginia Cavalry

Darling Child –

. . . Yesterday evening our company voted unanimously to spend the winter at home and enlist again for next summer and the war department will be petitioned accordingly. For the present we are doing mighty well here . . .

Is [Mr. Bagby] . . . cutting and curing [the tobacco]. If so please write me how many houses has he cut and how many are cured. . . . Tell me about the hogs . . .the sheep and the cattle and horses . . . write especially about the negroes their winter clothing etc . . .

I love you so much I want to eat you up just now.

(ed: Since virtually nothing is happening on the Peninsula, these new, and very naïve, soldiers are petitioning the government to let them go home for winter and come back in the spring.)

(ed: The tobacco is cut and hung in the tobacco houses to dry. Richard wants to know how many of his tobacco houses are full and how many are cured and ready to sell. He grows a very dark variety of tobacco on a small portion of his land in the Bush River bottom. Although he plants virtually the smallest plot of tobacco in Prince Edward County, he generates one of the highest total cash values in yield. He also imports guano to fertilize his starts following some of the farming principles of Edmund Ruffin. The blockade will eliminate his supply of guano and he will cease production of tobacco in 1863.)

(Boots & Kisses, p. 37.)

- - - - -

October 3, 1861 (Thursday) – Camp Young's Mill, Virginia
Brig. Gen. Lafayette McLaws, McLaw's Division

My Dear Wife

I am at last a Brigadier General. So you may call me General Lafayette at last. . . . My appointment dated September 25th ultimo but was not received until yesterday. . . .

. . . Give my love to all. I will write very soon in full.

Your devoted husband

Address me:

General L McLaws

Youngs Mill

via Williamsburg, Va

(McLaws, by date.)

- - - - -

October 10, 1861 (Thursday) – Camp Young's Mill, Virginia
Brig. Gen. Lafayette McLaws, McLaw's Division

My dear wife

. . . I am in the saddle nearly every day, and when night comes my time is occupied until late with office business. . . . I have but one tent for myself and one for my office . . . I [am]frequently going to bed with some persons talking & writing at my table . . . I do not like to write to my wife when anyone is about . . . I am now doing so with six or eight waiting [in the area.]

It has been raining five or six days, off and on, . . . continuously. . . . Ham and bread and coffee is all that graces my table, very often for days. I am living in a ridiculously plain manner . . . Then again someone sends me a bushel of oysters and I have a feast. . . .

I hope you have not been in want of any money . . . at the end of this month I hope to [send] . . . three hundred dollars. I have had to buy a horse, which was exorbitantly high. A good common horse selling for two hundred fifty dollars. Have had to buy a new saddle, bridle & equipment & a new uniform . . . I [need] new socks and underclothing such as drawers and flannel shirts . . .

Your devoted husband

(ed: His headquarters tent is now populated with aide-de-camps, adjutants and orderlies to accomplish the many tasks of running a division. While he is trying to go to sleep they are writing copies of his orders to deliver to the regimental officers in his command. An army runs on paperwork and the orders, reports, and requisitions never stop.)

(ed: McLaws notes in his 10/18 letter to Emily that he has under his command, at Young's Mill, the 10th Georgia; 2nd, 5th & 10th Louisiana; 14th & 15th Virginia; Montague's Battalion; 4 batteries of artillery and 4 companies of cavalry. He is charged with protecting one of the key points in the Confederate line. In addition to protecting his portion of Magruder's line he is also still responsible for completion of the Williamsburg line and the training of various commands in Williamsburg.)

(McLaws, by date.)

- - - - -

October 14, 1861 – Howitzer Camp
Pvt. James P. Williams, Richmond Howitzers

Dear Aunt Mary,

. . . Yesterday morning we were ordered off again on a scouting expedition from which we returned this morning. We went down almost in gun shot of Newport News and [Fort] Monroe again but couldn't draw the cowardly rascals out. We had two regiments of infantry, about three hundred cavalry and our battery. . . . The object of the expedition I think was, to keep the Yankees in their stronghold, and prevent their stealing the forage all around the country there, which we want for our own use . . . Last night we stopped at Young's Mill, five or six miles below here, where we laid out on the ground all night without a thread of covering. All of us thought we would freeze before morning . . . We have not commenced building our winter quarters yet . . . I am very glad to hear that Pa has such a fine crop of corn and fodder and hope it will be enough for him. . . .

(Williams, by date.)

- - - - -

October 15, 1861 – Halfway House
Pvt. Richard Watkins, Co. K – 3rd Virginia Cavalry

My own Dear Mary –

I wish you could realize how happy your letters make me. . . . let me hear how my Mary is, and how she feels, and how she looks, and what she is thinking, and what she is doing, and what she is going to do . . . Thus . . . darling I wish I could get a million letters [from you] . . .

With my whole heart I love you.

(Boots & Kisses, p. 39.)

- - - - -

October 18, 1861 – Halfway House
Pvt. Richard Watkins, Co. K – 3rd Virginia Cavalry

My Precious Wife

. . . I went out on vidette 10 miles from Camp down on Messox Point which projects out into the Chesapeake Bay at the mouth of the Back River. Tis quite a lonesome place right down in the marsh on the sea-beach . . . From that point we have a fine view of the Bay our main object being to watch the passing vessels and report if any turn their courses into Back River or begin to land soldiers on the beach. These vessels ply between Baltimore and Fortress Monroe. Just across the river the country is entirely in the possession of Yankees . . . one soldier deserted . . . and delivered himself up to me. He belonged to Company C of the 16th Massachusetts Regiment was born and raised near Boston. His name is Hartwell . . . He has been sent on to Genl. McGruder being the 4th deserter who has been sent from our camp. . . .

. . . Give love to everybody. And I know I will ever love you with my whole heart. Good bye.

(ed: A vidette or vedette is a mounted sentinel stationed in advance of the normal outposts or picket line.)

(Boots & Kisses, pp. 40-41.)

- - - - -

October 23, 1861 (Wednesday) – Young's Mill, Virginia
Brig. Gen. Lafayette McLaws, Camp of the 2nd Division

My dearly beloved wife

. . . The nights are getting quite cool, although it has been raining continuously for a week or two. In fact the weather is never good here . . . always bad, wet, muddy and disagreable, I have never been anywhere, where it rains so much. . . . My health . . . is very good. I have fine aids de camp, and three of them have been sick . . . and I am spared. . . .

Your devoted husband

(McLaws, by date.)

- - - - -

October 26, 1861 – Halfway House
Pvt. Richard Watkins, Co. K – 3rd Virginia Cavalry

. . . We are here again my own dear Mary and every thing is quiet. My little cot sits snugly in the same corner by the fire-place, by it's side my trunk, in the corner my gun and sabre, on the nail above my haversack with comb and brush. Nothing is heard of the enemy and no indication of battle. . . . Our vidette duties light and our men very cheerful.

(Boots & Kisses, pp. 41-42.)

- - - - -

November 1, 1861 – Greenmount Farm
Mr. Thomas Wynne, Farmer

Friday, . . . That portion of the fifth La. Regiment stationed in Williamsburg went below today. Five new regiments landed in Yorktown this week.

(Greenmount Journal by month.)

- - - - -

November 4, 1861 – Yorktown, Virginia
Pvt. James P. Williams, Richmond Howitzers

Dear Aunt Mary

. . . I am still here in the Hospital, but am almost entirely well and will go down to Bethel in about two days, where the rest of the company are. . . . hear that Pa had a fine crop of Potatoes . . . Ma & Nannie I reckon are very busy making up winter clothes [for family & servants]. . . . I have two blankets now and Ma said she was going to send me a comfort. I couldn't move any more than that about with me. . . . I must now close. You must write to me again soon . . .

(Williams, by date.)

- - - - -

November 9, 1861 – Greenmount Farm
Mr. Thomas Wynne, Farmer

Saturday, . . . Three soldiers stay with us tonight from the 10th Georgia Regiment. Fannie sold a ham weighing 10 lbs. to one of the soldiers this morning for $2.50.

(Greenmount Journal by month.)

- - - - -

November 10, 1861 – Camp Bethel
Pvt. Richard Watkins, Co. K – 3rd Virginia Cavalry

Darling Child:

I write you a short letter this morning because I have a good opportunity to send it. Ned Jeffreys has rheumatism & goes home to recruit . . . Yesterday evening Genl. McGruder came down with about 500 cavalry & several thousand infantry with the intention I learn of going below the pickets today to gather all of the corn, cattle etc. but a heavy rain came during the night and . . . the ground was too wet this morning for such operations . . .

(ed: The word recruit, as used in 1860s military terminology, means to replenish, repair, rejuvenate and recover. Ned is on a medical furlough to recover his health and then return to the unit.)

(ed: Rheumatism is the pain, swelling and inflammation in one or several of the larger joints. The pain can shift from one part to another. Symptoms consist of fever, white tongue, full pulse, and high colored urine.)

(ed: Treatments: Bleed the patient freely or until the pulse is sensibly affected. Purge with salts and senna. If the pain continues severe, continue to bleed again and again. The inflammation must

be reduced. In consequence of the bleeding if the patient is very weak, wrap him up in blankets, give him warm nourishing food and wine. In chronic cases the patient should be given 30 drops of laudanum (tincture of opium) with a tea-spoonful of tincture of guaiacum before bed and use flannel next to the skin winter and summer. Guaiacum is a brownish medicinal liquid from the resin of guaiacum wood and is primarily prescribed as an expectorant. The tincture probably contains around 10% guaiacum and the balance is wine or whiskey. This would be similar in makeup or percentages to a tincture of opium. Senna is a cathartic made from the dried leaves of the C. angustifolia of the genus Cassia.)

(Boots & Kisses, p. 43., Mackenzie p. 212.)

- - - - -

November 11, 1861 – Forge Road, James City County, Va.
Mr. John T. Martin. Farmer & School Teacher

The Southern ports are being blockaded by the Lincoln Government, it could not be forgotten. There is a Civil War now raging between the Free and the Slave States of this Country. It began about the 18th of April last and some great battles have been fought in all of which the South has been victorious. Coffee is now selling for 56 cents a pound, Salt $12 a sack and sugar 15 to 25 cents a pound. Bacon from 20 to 24 cents per lb., Molasses 75 cents per gallon.

(ed: "John T. Martin (1809-1881) is a James City County native. He opened a school on Forge Road and boarded with the Beal family. In fact, he married Sarah Beal in 1836 and eventually took ownership of the farm. The family often said, 'He came in the house, hung up his hat and never left.' John and Sarah's son, Enoch T. Martin, served in Company B of the 1st Virginia Artillery.")

("James City Cavalry Picket Lines" Newsletter' in February and March, 2019, page 3, Williamsburg. Historian Fred Boelt of the Cavalry wrote two historical articles on James City County featuring the Journal. The "Farm Journal of John T. Martin 1845-1861: John T. Martin is in the collection of the Library of Virginia in Richmond, Virginia. [Hereafter cited as Martin Farm Journal by date.])

- - - - -

November 11, 1861 – Hospital at Yorktown
Pvt. William C. Corson, Co. G – 3rd Virginia Cavalry

My Dear Jennie,

. . . I have been sick in the hospital with the measels ever since the day after I received your last letter. I had to ride 15 miles after night during that heavy gale and caught violent cold just as I took the measels. I came very near kicking the bucket I tell you and thought I should never see my Jennie any more . . . I have had a very hard time here in the hospital. It is the last place on earth for a man to be sick. . . . The measels affected my lungs . . . and has left me with a wretched cough which I fear I shall not recover this winter. There are about 45 patients in this hospital now and they have three to five deaths a week. . . .

(ed: Measles symptoms include inflammatory fever, dry cough, hoarseness, sneezing, watering of the eyes and running from the nose. On the fourth day, small red points break out, first on the face, and then over the body. They are in clusters . . . a little raised. On the fifth or sixth day the vivid red is changed to brown, and the eruption goes off. The eyes will be red, swollen and load- ed with tears. To help the patient the bowels may be opened with salts in addition to warm baths, and the application of mustard poultices and blisters to the feet and ankles.)

(Corson, p. 50.; Mackenzie's Five Thousand Receipts of all the Useful and Do- mestic Arts, Pittsburgh, 4th edition 1853, p. 215. [Hereafer cited as Macken- zie]).

- - - - -

November 13, 1861 – Half-way House
Pvt. Richard Watkins, Co. K – 3rd Virginia Cavalry

My own Dear Mary

Since my last letter . . . Genl. McGruder has been steadily engaged with several regiments of infantry and one of cavalry gathering corn and forage, cattle etc from the country between us and the Yankees. They go . . . every morning . . . and load 75 or 100 wagons and send them back and they are unloaded and the contents stored away, by the troops left in reserve . . . A few days ago some of the Cumberland Troop [Company G – 3rd Virginia Cavalry) were fired at across Back River by the cowardly Yankees lying in ambush . . .

It is now getting late and the wagons are coming in and I must close . . . Give love to everybody . . . especially my dear little daughters.

(ed: Richard is 35 years old, educated, and a lawyer & farmer by trade. Command quickly realized that he could write very well, knew his math and could keep excellent records. He was assigned duties as quartermaster of Company K while in training and quickly was promoted to Asst. Quartermaster for the 3rd Virginia Cavalry. The wagons are coming back and his workday is about to begin.)

(Boots & Kisses, p. 44.)

- - - - -

November 17, 1861 – Camp near Bartlett's
Pvt. Richard Watkins, Co. K – 3rd Virginia Cavalry

My Darling Mary

. . . On the morning I last wrote you I was again sent as vidette to Sawyers Swamp and again a cold northeast rain came on me . . . returning to our Camp which was then near Bethel I found to my surprise that the Troop had been moved above the Half Way house to Bartletts farm and some said we were going into winter quarters there . . . Bartlett was a wealthy famer who had left his fine house and large commodious stables & out houses and gone over to the Yankees . . . on reaching the place . . . the dwelling house was turned into a hospital and the stable into a corn house by order of Genl. McGruder and our troop in tents on a cold bleak hill side right upon the banks of the Pecosan River. . . . I forgot to tell you too that in addition to my other trials when I reached the Camp my haversack containing all of your letters was gone . . . [that] which I prized more highly than all else, could not be found . . . Charley Redd came riding up and told me that he had my haversack and had it in his trunk, And now Darling the letters are all again in my side pocket along with the nice letter that came last . . .

Good bye my own Darling . . . Love & Kisses

(Boots & Kisses, p. 46.)

- - - - -

November 23, 1861 – Greenmount Farm
Mr. Thomas Wynne, Farmer

Saturday, . . . Went to [Lebanon] church this morning. Only had seven persons present, including the preacher. The people seem as if they had no use for religion in these times of war and military commotion.

(Greenmount Journal by month.)

- - - - -

November 23, 1861 – Half way house
Pvt. Richard Watkins, Co. K – 3rd Virginia Cavalry

My Darling Mary:

. . . This is Saturday night . . .on Wednesday evening . . . I was taken quite sick from imprudent eating. Had to retire early and before nine o'clock had a violent attack of cholera morbus accompanied with a severe chill. Was really sick until midnight when a

67

dose of laudanum afforded me relief but a fever succeeded the chills and I had to remain in my bed for 24 hours. It is all over now Darling and I am again well . . .

This morning I was detailed as forager for the day and have been busy loading our wagon with wood and corn. . . . I will try to get a furlough . . . before long. Just as soon as this foraging is over and Mr. McGruder and the Peninsula get quiet.

. . . Oh I want to see you so bad it almost makes me right sick. . . . I do not feel satisfied unless I write you two letters every week. And wish that I could write more. . . .

(ed: Symptoms of cholera morbus are violent vomiting and purg-ing of bile, preceded by a pain in the stomach and bowels, heat, thirst, cold sweats, and hiccups. Laudanum is suggested either orally or by clyster (enema). The laudanum should be mixed with a mint tea. Laudanum is a 10% tincture of opium and the other 90% is usually either wine or whisky. Cholera morbus should not be confused with cholera which can be endemic and highly fatal beginning with serious watery diarrhea, cramps, and vomiting.)

(Boots & Kisses, p. 47. Mackenzie p. 206.)

- - - - -

November 27, 1861 – Half Way House
Pvt. Richard Watkins, Co. K – 3rd Virginia Cavalry

My own Dear Mary

. . . Charley Redd goes home today on a furlough in order to have tumor cut off the side of his head. It was but very small when he entered the service but is enlarging and the Surgeon has advised him to go to Dr. Mettauer and have an operation performed. We hope that it will not be a serious matter . . . As Charley is going home I will send this letter by him and he will tell you all the rest of the news. . . . Much love as usual & many kisses to my precious little girls.

- - - - -

November 29, 1861 (Friday) – Young's Mill, Virginia
Brig. Gen. Lafayette McLaws, 2nd Division

My dearly beloved Wife

The winter is coming on and I have finished the chimney to my tent . . . but as yet the weather is so moderate, no fires are required except in the mornings and evenings . . .

Write me my darling and give love to all my friends. Kiss my boys, and sweet little daughter.

Your devoted husband

- - - - -

December 7, 1861 – Half way House
Pvt. Richard Watkins, Co. K – 3rd Virginia Cavalry

My Darling Child

. . . Our Company still in tents but I, Robt. Dickinson and Mel Arvin by special permission sleep in a small room in a house near by. Our room has no fire-place but tis warmer than a tent and not so damp . . . I am writing now in Lt. Redd's tent. He is lying in a pile of straw with his bed clothes over him, complaining of a slight pain in his side . . . the weather is so cold that we all have to sleep with our clothes on. I do not think that I have taken mine off except for the purpose of changing my underclothes for two months excepting perhaps once or twice (two exceptions in one sentence!!).

. . . I need a pair of coarse heavy oversocks. Can you not make Neely knit them and send them by Frank Scott or Charley Redd

. . . Goodnight my Darling precious wife – I long to be with you.

(ed: Richard catches his double usage of exception and highlights it to Mary.)

(Boots & Kisses, pp. 50-51.)

- - - - -

December 10, 1861 – Greenmount Farm
Mr. Thomas Wynne, Farmer

Tuesday, . . . Sent William in my wagon down to Cockletown [Grafton] to carry some soldiers of the 5th North Carolina Regiment to their camp. Sold to the soldiers 9 bushels of Irish potatoes, 1 ½ bushels of sweet potatoes, 26 heads of cabbage together with some eggs, buttermilk and sweet milk.

(Greenmount Journal by month.)

- - - - -

December 14-15, 1861 – Greenmount Farm
Mr. Thomas Wynne, Farmer

Saturday, . . . Sold some fodder to the Mecklenburg Cavalry. Sold some vegetables to the soldiers of the 10th La. Regiment.

Sunday, . . . Our church being occupied by the soldiers, we had no meeting today. I understand that Gen. Magruder is moving his forces from Young's Mill to Lee's Mill and Yorktown, being in daily expectation of an attack from the Yankees.

(Greenmount Journal by month.)

- - - - -

late December, 1861 – near Yorktown
Pvt. Richard Watkins, Co. K – 3rd Virginia Cavalry

My Darling Mary

. . . my horse is so sick that he is certainly unfit for service. Has taken a violent cold, and has pneumonia or something resembling it. I fear very much that he will die and a better horse for the service I have not seen. . . .

My last letter told you of our . . . winter quarters at the Half-way House . . . but that very night orders came for us to report the next day at Yorktown and we are in tents again but protected from the weather by very thick pines so that we are . . . as comfortable as we have been for several months. . . . our vidette duties are very light and we no longer form the advance guard of the army. . . . My hopes of spending Xmas in Prince Edward with my own Dear Mary P have vanished into thin air . . .

Perhaps England and the United States will get into a war and that will result in the establishment of our independence. Most of our people seem jubilant over the prospects of such a war. But I would rejoice much more over peace without it. . . . I so earnestly hope that we may be permitted to have our own form of government and our own social institutions, and regulate our own domestic affairs. . . . The officers of our regiment have petitioned Genl McGruder to send the whole regiment home this winter on account of the scarcity of forage, and there is I learn quite a good prospect of his making this order.

*(ed: on November 8 crewmen of the **USS San Jacinto** boarded the British ship **Trent** and removed Mr. Mason and Mr. Slidell who were representatives of the Confederate government bound for England and France. This immediately started rumors of war. This event was a major insult by the United States. Great Britain was outraged by the actions of Captain Wilkes in boarding a British ship in international waters and removing passengers. The opposite action, when the British were boarding and removing sailors from U. S. ships, had been one of the key factors in starting the War of 1812.)*

(ed: The Camp rumors of the 'good prospect' of the entire regi-

ment being sent home for the winter are boosting spirits and even Richard is buying in on these rumors.)

(Boots & Kisses, pp. 53-55.)

- - - - -

December 20, 1861 (Friday) – Young's Mill, Virginia
Brig. Gen. Lafayette McLaws, 2nd Division H. Q.

It is very near Christmas and we are so far separated from each other that our letters are our only means of communication. It seems fated that we are to remain separated, although I have been all along pleasing myself with the idea that we would be together this year.

. . . The rumored hostile attitude of Great Britain towards the United States has produced great rejoicing . . . I certainly have strong hopes that Great Britain and France both will open our ports . . .

. . . I was in hopes to get a Christmas Kiss from you but our affairs are too unsettled to allow my departure . . . If I can get away I will ask for a post in Georgia as the Peninsula is not a place to long for. . . . Kiss the children for me . . .

(McLaws, by date.)

- - - - -

December 21, 1861 – Greenmount Farm
Mr. Thomas Wynne, Farmer

Saturday, . . . Dreux' Battalion [Louisiana troops] passed here this morning en route to Lee's Mill. Six of them dined here.

(ed: The journal was full and ended on January 3. No doubt Thomas started a new journal but that journal did not survive. In the spring of 1862, as the Peninsula Campaign moved toward Greenmount, Tom and Fannie, along with their families, refugeed

72

in the Danville, Virginia, area. They had a daughter born in December, 1862. Fannie died in Danville in 1864. Thomas returned to Greenmount following the war, remarried, had another daughter, taught school and farmed. He was elected Treasurer of James City County in 1895 and died in 1904.)

(Greenmount Journal by month.)

- - - - -

December 25, 1861 – City Point, Virginia
George R. Wood, deckhand, *James Buchanan*

We spent our first Christmas at City Point and it was spoiled by one of the boys taking too much of the old mellow peach brandy that had belonged to the Yankees and was confiscated and held there. The boys got permission of the depot agent to broach it. We thought it was [too] sweet and good [that] it would not make drunk come. One [fellow] played violin and bones and other instruments while singing and making Merry Xmas. I knew nothing afterward until next morning.

(Boatman, p. 45.)

- - - - -

December 27, 1861 – Broken Bridge, Virginia
Pvt. James P. Williams, Richmond Howitzers

Dear Aunt Mary,

. . . Our battery was moved from Harrod's Mill down to this place on Sunday with orders to remain here three days . . . Old McGruder expected the attack within that time, but no attack was made . . . so we remain here until further orders. We have one regiment of infantry here with us and I hope we will remain here all the winter. Our winter quarters are all here and are very comfortable houses. We hardly know whether to bring our baggage down here or not, because this is the lowest outpost . . . I suppose you all spent a quiet pleasant Christmas at home . . . I spent a very pleasant one myself considering . . . how I longed to be at home. I believe it is the first Christmas I ever spent away from home. . . . I understand we are to move from here again tomorrow to Harrod's Mill . . . give my love to Ma and Pa and to Bec and Dink. . . . I must close.

(Williams, by date.)

- - - - -

December 30, 1861 – Young's Mill, Virginia
Brig. Gen. Lafayette McLaws, 2nd Division H. Q.

My dear wife

Tomorrow will be the last day of the . . . year.

There is a steamer in our possession. One that was sunk by the scared enemy when they evacuated Norfolk. It is a first class steam frigate and is called or was called the *Merrimac*. She was raised by us and is receiving a plating if iron. She is without masts, and has a long heavy snout . . . for ramming against any vessel underwater. . . . Her speed too is very great . . . she shows but five feet out of water . . . and is covered with the heaviest iron plating. Her armaments is of the heaviest caliber, and port holes have iron shutters that open . . . as the guns are run out and close when the guns recoil.

Well this vessel is expected from her [dry] dock in a week or two . . . Her shape I will try to draw and send to Willie . . . you must bear in mind that my drawing is not of the most splendid order.

My little daughters [Laura] picture is before me and looking so sweet . . . She would laugh I know to see my long beard . . .

There are about 10 persons talking about me, making a hubbub, not at all calculated to expedite correspondence, so you must excuse errors. . . . Kiss the baby for me, do not let us quarrel

74

about the name, yet if he should be named Lafayette, he would be Lafayette McLaws Junior – think of that! . . . and then there would be Laura McLaws [my mother] and Laura McLaws Junior [our daughter] and Lafayette [Senior & Junior], four L McLawses Horrible!

(ed: Actually the camp gossip that Lafayette has written regarding the conversion of the 'Merrimac' is fairly factual. The most glaring error is her 'very great speed.' She is way too heavy for her poor engines, has a top speed of maybe 4 -5 knots, and turns like a waterlogged tree trunk. We are three months away from the attack on the Union fleet in Hampton Roads and the 'Battle of the Ironclads.')

(ed: The last paragraph shows a great sense of humor as he discusses Lafayette McLaws Junior as a possible name and then rambles on into the pitfalls of so many L. McLaws members of the immediate family and how 'Horrible' that would be. It sounds like he is leaving the naming decision up to Emily and hedging against Lafayette, Jr. or any name beginning with an 'L.')

(McLaws, by date.)

- - - - -

January, 1862

There is disappointment in the winter quarters of the 3rd Virginia Cavalry. In December they had sent a request to General Magruder to go home for the winter due to the difficulty of finding adequate forage for their horses. They propose to return to the Peninsula in the spring. Nothing has been heard regarding this request. Both armies are in winter quarters drilling, foraging, scouting, manning the picket lines and building fortifications on the Warwick Line and in Williamsburg. There will be no extended winter leave for entire commands. There will be limited winter leave for individuals.

President Lincoln is anxious for action in the western armies commanded by General Henry Halleck and General Don Carlos Buell. He speaks with his General-in-Chief on January 9 regarding the non-action and non-response to his inquiries about action against the enemy. Beseeching General McClellan to get his generals moving is ironic since McClellan is the poster boy for non-action.

On January 13, Edwin Stanton becomes the U. S. Secretary of War. Simon Cameron departs the post and becomes the U. S. Minister in Russia.

McClellan is focused on building the size and strength of the Army of the Potomac. New regiments, all over the north, are in camps learning the fundamentals of becoming soldiers. After a couple of months of very basic training, they are forwarded to the Washington, D.C., area. Pvt. Edgar Steele, and the men of the 85th New York Infantry, spend October and November near Elmira, New York, and in early December, they are shipped to Camp Warren outside of Washington to continue their training. If and when McClellan decides to advance, the 85th will be part of the invading army.

In a late January note Private William Corson, of the 3rd Virginia Cavalry, pens, *"The weather has been dreadful . . . raining nearly all the time. We have made no preparations for winter quarters as yet, and I believe will be kept in tents all the time."*

Lincoln cannot get McClellan to move or even share his thoughts and plans. On January 27, a frustrated President issues General Order #1 for all land forces to move against the enemy by February 22. On January 31, he issues Special War Order #1 directing McClellan to move against the Confederate forces near Manassas, Virginia. McClellan disregards both orders.

On January 30 an odd-looking naval vessel is launched from the ways at Greenport, Long Island, New York. Many spectators are betting the vessel will sink. The *U.S.S. Monitor* is moved to a berth at the shipyard and construction continues at a furious pace.

While it rains, snows and hails on the Peninsula, there is a serious storm brewing in the White House. Lincoln's patience is being tested to the extreme by a general who sees himself as the savior of the country while viewing the President as an impediment and annoyance.

(ed: Ways, in nautical terminology, means the timbered structure upon which a ship is built and from which it slides when launched.)

(Chronicle by date. *The Civil War Years – A Day by Day Chronicle,* Robert Denney, 1992, New York, by date [hereafter cited as Day by Day by date].)

January, 1862

January 4, 1862 (Saturday) – Young's Mill, Virginia
Brig. Gen. Lafayette McLaws, Head Qtrs. Camp

My Dearly beloved Wife

Your Christmas presents, the shirts, drawers, socks &c have been very welcomely recd. . . . The oranges are certainly a very great treat and the sausages will be magnificent for a scout. . . . My only difficulty now is about my . . . boots. My boots having now one of the toes out . . .

I have not heard from your brother, he never writes but he is within twelve miles of me at Yorktown. . . .

I keep my daughters picture open on the table before me all the time . . . I enclose my 'picture' of the Merrimac, not splendid but will give you an idea. . . .

Your devoted husband

(ed: his sketch of the C.S. Ram Virginia *[Merrimac] was not with his archived letters.)*

(ed: In a January 10th letter Lafayette wrote, "The enemy still in our front & equally noisy and demonstrative . . . one of their bands playing 'Hail Columbia' very loudly, although the night is very dark and rainy. But they are continually playing some bragadoci prank. . . . ")

(McLaws, by date.)

- - - - -

January, 6, 1862 – Yorktown, Virginia
Pvt. William C. Corson, Co. G – 3rd Virginia Cavalry

My Dear Jennie,

. . . the enemy thinking Magruder and all hands were tight [with Christmas celebrations], I suppose, sent up a scouting party a few days ago and set fire to Bethel Church, all of our forces having been withdrawn from there several weeks since. Major Phillips who was at the half way house . . . with about 50 men rode down in time to put out the fire . . . Our boys are generally well . . . Jennie I had the sweetest dream about you night before last . . . I dream of you nearly every night. I am enjoying fine health and weigh 164 pounds which is as you see (164-105), 59 ahead of you. . . . Good bye. Write soon to

Your devoted William

(Corson, pp. 56-57.)

- - - - -

January 6, 1862 – camp near Yorktown
Pvt. Richard Watkins, Co. K – 3rd Virginia Cavalry

My own Dear Mary

I thank you very much for your last . . . If you direct [mail] to Cavalry Camp near Yorktown care of Capt Jno Thornton it will be sufficient. . . . Yours was a real business letter and gave me exactly the information which I have been wishing for . . . It will not be possible to get any guano this year [for fertilizer] . . . no probability of any till the blockade is broken up . . . I notice in the papers that salt is selling cheap in Lynchburg. . . . Please tell Mr. Baker to take especial care of the young orchard . . . Tell him not to expose the negroes in bad weather & to strip tobacco as fast as possible . . . I was very glad to hear the hogs weighed so well . . . Darling in looking over my eight pairs of socks yesterday I found that everyone has a hole in it. Intended to send them home . . . but forgot. Can you send me two or three very coarse pair by the first opportunity? . . .

Give love & kisses Minnies birthday on the 19th of this month wish I could be at home then. How are Emmie and Minnie. Still growing & fattening? Good bye

(ed: Richard wrote Mary again on the 8th and started off writing Mary a love letter. Then he went into more business about hogs, cattle, not being wise to hire negroes from his sister Patty and the progress of his tobacco crop. He then wrote, "Have I not descended from the sentimental to the practical . . . Commence telling you how much I love you and find myself a few moments later writing about cattle & hogs.")

(Boots & Kisses, pp. 56-59.)

- - - - -

January 12, 1862 – Yorktown, Virginia
Pvt. William C. Corson, Co. G – 3rd Virginia Cavalry

My Dear Jennie,

. . . everything is quiet just now. Our boys are still at Jone's Farm near Young's Mill. They have been transferred over to Gen. McClaus [McLaws], as also the Charles City and James City troops. Col. Goode's command composed of the Mecklenburg and the two Halifax companies were today ordered to Mulberry Island. I took the dispatch up to Lebanon Church where they have been encamped for some weeks . . . the roads are in a horrible condition here now in consequence of the recent rains . . . my paper is nearly filled and I am compelled to close. . . . Your devoted

William

(Corson, pp. 58-59.)

- - - - -

January 14, 1862 – Camp Shields
Pvt. Richard Watkins, Co. K – 3rd Virginia Cavalry

My Precious One

. . . Snow rain and hail are falling and the ground already covered with the mixture about three inches deep. We still in tents
with our little fires built at their doors: all around the fires melting
snow & mud through which we are chased by the smoke . . . Day
before yesterday Charlie Redd & I were sent as videttes to a point
of the York River about 8 miles from here. The day was remarkably pleasant and the night one of the most beautiful that I have
ever seen. . . . The York River is about as large as the Potomac.
And our business was to sit and watch the River to see whether
any fleet was approaching. We could see the River for about 14
miles, YorkTown & Gloucester Point were in plain view and orders were being given by signal lights from Yorktown to different
points on the River the greater part of the night. . . . At one time
the Operator in Yorktown told the signal master just below us
that his negro boy had gone down the River after terrapins and
had remained so long he was fearful he was sick . . . but this sight
[signal lights] did not compare in beauty to another that we saw
which was the phosphorescent lights of the sea water. This was
something which I heard of before but had never witnessed. The
River seemed to have hundreds & thousands of lightning bugs
& glow worms down under the water and along the beach were
streams and balls of fire. It was indeed beautiful. The night was
very mild so that we could enjoy the night . . . to our satisfaction
. . . We were relieved by other videttes at eleven o'clock . . . &
returned to Camp . . . my horse is well again and but for the bad
weather would soon be as fat as ever . . . and now farewell my
precious one . . . I love you with all of my heart.

(Boots & Kisses, pp. 59-60.)

- - - - -

January 14, 1862 (Tuesday) – Young's Mill, Virginia
Brig. Gen. Lafayette McLaws, Head Qtrs. Camp

My Dear Darling

. . . I have been thinking how much better satisfied you all would have been, the children in particular, if you could have remained in Atlanta or rather . . . Marietta, where the woods are so convenient and corn was cheaper, and the Yankees were not so thick as in Augusta. . . .

Good bye my dear with a thousand kisses to you.

(McLaws, by date.)

- - - - -

January 16, 1862 – Gosport Navy Yard, Portsmouth
Asst. Engineer E. V. White, C. S. Ironclad *Virginia*

I made application for the position desired, received my appointment January 16, 1862, and two days thereafter reported for duty. . . . My position was that of junior engineer, and I was placed on the gun-deck [near the bow gun] in charge of the engine-room gong and the speaking tube, by means of which the engineers could be reached. [Captain] Buchanan and Chief Engineer Ramsey termed me their aide, and . . . I conveyed all orders . . . to the engine room both for working the engines and the sending of hot shot to the gun-deck. . . .

(ed: Asst. Engineer White [the junior engineering officer] is the only engineering officer not in the engine room. He is on the main deck right beside the Captain and Lt. Catesby Jones. He relays all engine room orders through the speaking tube. He is, in more modern naval terms, the 'engine order telegraph.' He is able to observe the events he records in his remembrances.)

(White, p. 7.)

- - - - -

January 17, 1862 – James City County, Virginia
Mr. John T. Martin, Farmer & Teacher

Salted up the pork today. Salt now sells at $10 - $12 a bushel. My cow Betty had a calf today.

(Martin Farm Journal, by date.)

- - - - -

January 20, 1862 – camp at Herrod's Mill
Pvt. James P. Williams, Richmond Howitzers

Dearest Mama,

. . . We have been very busy fixing up our beds etc. in our tents and building shelters for our horses. They suffered terribly in that cold snowy weather having no shelter whatever. . . . We are not in a house but our tent is perfectly waterproof & has a nice chimney & fireplace . . .

We have only been paid for our services up to September, so there is now due us over four months pay. . . . It is three months from tomorrow to the expiration of our time, and I will be glad enough when it comes for it seems the enemy never intend giving us a chance to fight them again. . . . What does Pa think of coming down . . . ? The trip will be worth just five times as much as it costs him. . . . The steamer *Logan* is now running regularly and there is nothing for him to do but get on the cars at Richmond or Dispatch . . . and on arriving at West Point at ten o'clock jump aboard the *Logan* which will land him at Yorktown early in the evening where I will meet him with a horse . . . The trip going & coming will not cost him altogether over about eight dollars . . . I can only give him soldier's fare in the eating line but I have a No. 1 bed for him & plenty of room. . . . I shall anxiously wait for a letter now, informing me what day he will come down. . .

(Williams, by date.)

- - - - -

January 29, 1862, Jones Farm
Pvt. William C. Corson, Co. G – 3rd Virginia Cavalry

My Dear Jennie,

. . . The weather has been dreadful here for several weeks, raining nearly all the time. We have made no preparations for winter quarters as yet, and I believe will be kept in tents all the time. We received a portion of our pay last week and will get the balance in a few days.

(Corson, p. 60.)

- - - - -

February, 1862

Shipyards, in New York and Virginia, are working around the clock to get the *Monitor* and the *Virginia* ready for action. There will be no time for training of the crews onboard their vessels. The only practice the gun crews will have will be aboard training ships. Some of the sailors recruited for the *Monitor* come onboard and suddenly realize that the entire ship, other than the turret, is underwater. They immediately desert.

Out on the western waters, General Grant and Flag Officer Andrew Foote in a combined army-navy operation push up the Tennessee River and attack Fort Henry which falls on February 6. The majority of the garrison retreats overland to Fort Donelson. Grant pursues on land and Foote moves his gunboats to the Cumberland River to support Grant. On February 16, Fort Donelson surrenders and the water route to Nashville is open. The Tennessee capital is doomed and the major manufacturing center in the state will soon be lost to the Confederacy.

If a similar type of cooperation could have been accomplished by the Union army and navy commanders at Fort Monroe, they could have quickly captured Norfolk and then begun shelling the Gosport Naval Yard, eliminating the *Virginia* as a threat.

A large group of Western Virginia counties, in convention in Wheeling, seceded from Virginia and they are admitted to the Union as West Virginia. An interesting clause is in the new state constitution. It states, *"no slave or free person of color should come into the state for permanent residence."*

Confederate Marine Private William Kline writes, *"no . . . distinguished men, . . . nor maid of honor, no bottle of wine, no brass band, . . . no great crowds to witness the memorable event"* of the launching and christening of the *Virginia* on February 17.

On the 20th Governor Isham Harris, legislators and key staff evacuate Nashville and move the state government to Memphis. Confederate troops withdraw southeast to Murfreesboro. On the 24th troops under General Buell arrive by land and troops under General Grant arrive via the Cumberland River. Andrew Johnson is appointed Military Governor of Tennessee by President Lincoln.

On February 26 President Lincoln signs legislation creating a national currency of United States paper notes. Previously the United States only minted coinage and various state banks printed their own currency.

As the month nears an end, Union combined forces are moving down the Mississippi and are approaching the first key group of fortifications at New Madrid, Missouri, and Island #10. These two points are the key positions providing upriver defense for Memphis.

Private George Englis, of the 89th New York Infantry, disembarks at Fort Monroe. He complains about the rain and mud and then notes, *"You ought to see the Contrabands here. There is so many of them of all collors and all sizes that you can have half a dozen to wait on you* [if you] *wish it."* His command will be here briefly and then they depart on the amphibious operation to capture Roanoke Island, North Carolina.

General McClellan scraps his plan for a major amphibious operation down the Chesapeake Bay with a landing at Urbanna, Virginia. He now chooses to move his army of more than 100,000 men to Fort Monroe and march up the Peninsula to capture Richmond. This invasion requires a huge number of vessels for transportation and supply. A menagerie of all types of ships is being acquired to support the operation.

(Chronicle by date; Day by Day by date.)

February, 1862

February 7, 1862 (Friday) – Young's Mill, Virginia
Brig. Gen. Lafayette McLaws, Head Qtrs. Camp

My Dear Wife

. . . The big dinner came off yesterday evening. General Magruder was there, also T. R. R. Cobb and the Colonels of the 15th VA, 2nd LA, 5th LA & numerous other officers of various grades and myself. The dinner was magnificent and would have graced a New Orleans restaurant . . . I ate all sorts of thing[s] nuts, cakes, sugar plums, and in consequence have to day something of an indigestion.

Feb 8th

General Magruder has been called to Richmond . . . [some] think it is to concert operations in connection with the steamer Merrimac which is shortly to make a trial of her skill . . .

Goodbye. Kiss the children . . . Love to all.

Your devoted husband

(McLaws, by date.)

- - - - -

February 8, 1862 – Camp Jones
Pvt. William C. Corson, Co. G – 3rd Virginia Cavalry

My Dear Jennie,

. . . I left Yorktown for West Point to look for a bundle of clothes that John Hendrick brought from home for me, but lost at that place, and as I could not find the bundle I kept on to Rd. [Richmond] to buy me a suit. The *Logan* is now running on York river and the trip is made through to Richmond in a few hours. . . . I went to the city last Saturday . . . but made a short stay coming back Sunday . . .

(Corson, p. 62.)

- - - - -

February 9, 1862 – Camp Shields
Pvt. Richard Watkins, Co. K – 3rd Virginia Cavalry

Here I am in Camp again and wanting to see you just as bad as ever and loving you just as much and more. My furlough was entirely too short . . . would you believe it there are eighteen now at home and two more going tomorrow. Since coming to Camp I have been on a 25 mile pickett once and feel very well indeed . . . I did not see Cousin Barrett [at McKinney & Dupuy] in Richmond, so you will please fill the draft with any amount you want . . . and the bank in Farmville will give you the money . . . Give a great deal of love to Mother for my nice box. It would do you good to see how we all enjoy it . . . I don't know that I shall re-enlist. I must stay with you more next year than I have this. That is certain. Am willing to enlist as a private if they will give me officer furloughs. . . . What do you think about all this. Write to me and tell me.

Good by Darling . . . Kiss Emmie & Minnie for Papa

(ed: Mary and the family got a nice surprise when Richard showed up shortly after his January 21 letter and spent the last week of January at home.)

(ed: Richard is currently 37 years old and above the upper draft age. He does not need to be serving in the cavalry. The initial Confederate draft covered men from 18 to 35. In September of 1862 it will be expanded from 18 to 45. Richard decides to remain with the 3rd Virginia Cavalry because he will conclude that he will get redrafted as the war progresses and that assumption is cor-

rect. As the need for manpower grows in 1864 and 1865 the ages will expand to 17 to 50 and finally 16 to 55.)

(Boots & Kisses, pp. 61-63.)

- - - - -

February 17, 1862 – Gosport Naval Yard, Virginia
Marine Pvt. William Cline, C. S. Ironclad *Virginia*

There were no invitations to governors and other distinguished men, no sponsor nor maid of honor, no bottle of wine, no brass band, no blowing of steam whistles, no great crowds to witness this memorable event. [the launching and christening]

(*Unlike Anything That Ever Floated – The Monitor and Virginia and the Battle of Hampton Roads, March 8-9, 1862*, Dwight S. Hughes, El Dorado Hills, 2021, p. 68 [Hereafter cited as Unlike Anything].)

- - - - -

Undated, 1862 – Gosport Naval Yard, Virginia
Mr. John L. Porter, Naval Constructor

I received but little encouragement from any one. Hundreds, I may say thousands, asserted she would never float. . . . You have no idea what I have suffered in mind since I commenced her, but I knew what I was about, and I perservered. . . . thanks to many sleepless nights and a kind Providence . . . I must say I was astonished at the success of the *Virginia*.

(Unlike Anything, p. 68.)

- - - - -

Undated – Gosport Naval Yard, Virginia
Lt. Catesby Jones, X.O., C. S. Ironclad *Virginia*

She [*Virginia*] is not sufficiently protected below the water. We are least protected where we most need it . . .

(ed: The weakest point on both the Virginia and the Monitor is the point where the top structure and the hull or bottom structure join. This is termed the 'knuckle' and is the weak point because it is not protected with armor. Constructor Porter's original design called for the knuckle to be two feet below the waterline. Evidently in his calculations he forgot to subtract the removed weight of the masts, rigging and upper decks when calculating displacement and therefore the Virginia floated too high. The unprotected hull, in calm water, sits about six inches submerged versus two feet. With wave action there will be occasion when all two feet will be exposed and one lucky shot could doom the ship.)

(Unlike Anything, p. 69.)

- - - - -

February 19, 1862 (Wednesday) – Young's Mill, Virginia
Brig. Gen. Lafayette McLaws, Head Qtrs. Camp

My dear wife

This evening a telegram announced . . . that Fort Donelson was surrendered the 16th [with] 15,000 prisoners & Generals Buckner, Pillow and (Bushrod) Johnson . . . I can scarecely credit the report of the loss of 15,000 men, but it might be so . . . I am exceedingly sorry that the beautiful city of Nashville should be under the sway of the coarse Yankee . . .

The weather is so mild that no fires are necessary, although it is continual and ever lasting rain, the whole country is flooded, the water stands in large lakes over this flat country and there is no bottom to the roads. . . .

All well. I will write you from Yorktown where I am now bound.

(McLaws, by date.)

- - - - -

February 20, 1862 – Camp Shields
Pvt. Richard Watkins. Co. K – 3rd Virginia Cavalry

My Precious Mary:

The papers of yesterday bring us sad news indeed. Our reverses in Tennessee have been very great and will probably prolong the war many years by giving encouragement to the Yankees. I still do not, cannot doubt as to the final result. . . . Justice and right must in this Enlightened age ultimately prevail and we long to be a free and happy people. . . .

This evening mail modifies the news of the Donelson disaster very materially substituting 1500 prisoners in the place of 15,000 and stating furthermore that our Generals Buckner, Pillow & Floyd have all escaped. I hope that in the end our loss may not prove even so great as 1500. . . . Everything is still quiet on the Peninsula, no appearance of an approaching fight. . . . May God in his infinite mercy preserve the lives and health of my dear little family. Farewell my precious one. Much love to all.

(ed: In a 2-23 note to Mary, "The weather down here has been very bad lately, raining nearly every day and mud without bottom.")

(ed: The fall of Fort Henry and Fort Donelson opens the Tennessee and Cumberland Rivers to the Union fleet. Nashville is doomed. The Confederacy will lose the major portion of Tennessee as a result. More than 12,000 Confederate soldiers become prisoners. General Floyd escapes with his 4 regiments by boat, Colonel Forrest and his cavalry ride out along the river bank and General Pillow with his Chief of Staff escape on a scow. General Buckner surrenders the fort, equipment and over 12,000 men to General Grant.)

(Boots & Kisses, p. 65.)

- - - - -

February 23, 1862 – Fortress Monroe, Virginia
Pvt. George M. Englis, 89th New York Infantry

Dear Family,

. . . at Baltimore . . . took a steamer for here . . . I had a very pleasant trip down the bay, the sea was quite calm. . . . It is quite warm
here. The grass and rose bushes are quite green. . . . I was not
seasick at all coming down the Bay. We are quartered here with
a verry good Company and have plenty to eat and nothing to do.
We can go out and in the Fort when have a mind to. You ought to
see the Contrabands here. There is so many of them of all collors
and all sizes that you can have half a dozen to wait on you [if you]
wish it. . . The mud is verry deep here. I can't think of anything
more at present. . .

*(ed: George is 20 years old when he enlists and he reports to
Elmira, New York, for training on October 20, 1861. George is
shown as a farmer from Spencer, New York, on his enlistment papers. He joins Company K, the Dickinson Guard, for three years
of service.)*

**(This From George – The Civil War Letters of Sgt. G. M. Englis 1861-1865; edi-
tor – Eileen M. Knapp Patch, 2001, Endicott, p. 23.)**

- - - - -

February 24, 1862 – James City County, Virginia
Mr. John T. Martin, Farmer & Teacher

Hung up my pork to be smoked. My mare "Nova" had a colt this
morning.

(Martin Farm Journal, by date.)

- - - - -

February 24, 1862 – Pr. Ed. Co. Ho., Virginia
Pvt. John J. Flournoy, Co. K – 3rd Virginia Cavalry

Cousin Dick [Richard Watkins]

. . . I can give you almost positive assurance, as far as the present company [Company K] is concerned you are their choice for Captain, in the event that Capt. Thornton no longer desires command of that Company. I want to urge you to hold on in the Co and at the proper time declare yourself a candidate, that is if you intend to reenlist. Old Berkely [Lt. Peyton R. Berkeley] is Electioneering with all his might and so is Frank Redd neither of whom I want to be Captain of that Co, not that I do not like them personally, but a good many agree with me they are not fit for leaders.

John Knight, Williams Evans, Big Harvey _____, Wm Womack, Red Spencer, Chas Flournoy, Hester Walton, and I think John Walton and Mel Arvin, and I believe George Fowlkes, Daniel Allen, Fayette Scott, & myself and I believe others that I do not know remember are all anxious I believe for your election. When I come down I will find out and let you know. We are going to try and put Stokes [2nd Lt. Stokes] in the ranks, if we can get him to reenlist.

I expect to be down the 7th March and I wish you to tell Andrew Venable to meet me in Yorktown with my horse. The weather is bad that I have not been further from home than Farmville. I was at John Knights yesterday, I think he certainly has camp fever, Dr. Dillon attends him regularly, he was able to sit up a little . . . Give my regard to all my friends.

(ed: Pvt. Flournoy is on medical leave in Prince Edward County and his home is near the Prince Edward Court House. He is returning to the unit on March 7 and wants to assure Richard that when the Company elections happen, after the reenlistments, that they want to vote him in as one of their officers. Confederate units elect their own officers at the company level. This can be good and bad, but the men now are beginning to get a feel for who would be good leaders.)

(Boots & Kisses, pp. 369-70.)

(1.

- - - - -

February 28, 1862 – James City County, Virginia
Mr. John T. Martin, Farmer & Teacher

Fast day by Proclamation of the President of the Confederate States.

 Martin Farm Journal, by date.)

- - - - -

A SOUTHERN PORTRAIT GALLERY

RICHARD CURTIS, 1864

RICHARD & MARY WATKINS--Wedding Photo, 1858

RICHARD & MARY WATKINS, circa 1890

WILLIAM CORSON, 1856

JENNIE CALDWELL, 1862

JOHN TAYLOR WOOD, 1858

March, 1862

Early spring is starting to come to Virginia. With the spring season, the Confederacy is faced with the enlistments expiring for many of their soldiers. Pvt. William Corson, of the 3rd Virginia Cavalry, writes, *"The twelve-month volunteers should to a man reenlist for the war and stand by their country now in her darkest hour."*

There are more Union successes than Confederate in the early weeks of March. Roanoke Island and New Bern fall in North Carolina. A key Union victory at Pea Ridge, Arkansas, drives the Confederate forces from Missouri and Northern Arkansas. After capturing Santa Fe, New Mexico Territory, on March 4, Confederate forces are defeated at Glorieta Pass when their rear guard and supply trains are totally destroyed and their victory is turned to defeat. This results in their complete withdrawal back to Texas.

On the Mississippi River, the forces of Flag Officer Foote and General Pope take New Madrid, Missouri, and then turn their attentions to Island #10. Foote has 7 gunboats and 10 mortar boats constantly shelling the island. Fort Pillow will be the final obstacle north of Memphis but Island #10 is the last significant stronghold north of Memphis.

March 11 sees General McClellan relieved as General-in-Chief. His sole command becomes the Army of the Potomac. President Lincoln and key cabinet members will assume the General-in-Chief responsibility.

General Grant and his armies ascend the Tennessee River and are massing around Pittsburg Landing, Tennessee, not far from Corinth, Mississippi. Confederate forces are gathering at Corinth under the command of General Albert S. Johnston.

The major event of March is the two-day battle in Hampton Roads, Virginia. On day one the C.S. Ironclad *Virginia* destroys both the U.S.S. *Cumberland* and *Congress*. The age of wooden warships ends on March 8. The *Virginia* rams the *Cumberland* after striking her with several shots from the forward gun. The bow-gunner, Seaman Richard Curtis, notes that *"the Cumberland was rapidly sinking yet her officers and men kept up the fight until she sank beneath the waters . . ."* It gets worse for the Union navy as the *Virginia* comes downstream and destroys the *Congress* and runs the *Minnesota* aground. It is a total disaster with other Union ships retreating to the protection of Fort Monroe.

The U.S.S. *Monitor* almost sinks twice while being towed to the Chesapeake Bay in rough seas and storms. She is taking on water around her turret, hatch covers, air intake pipe and her exhaust pipe. She demonstrates that she is not a sea going vessel but is only good for inland waters. Lt. Dana Greene writes, *". . . it was at once evident that the Monitor was unfit as a sea going craft."* Despite barely surviving the ocean journey and witnessing her response to heavy weather, Chief Engineer Alban Stimers files what would prove to be a totally incorrect report on the seaworthiness of the *Monitor* when he writes, *"I consider form and strength of the vessel equal to any weather I ever saw at sea."*

On March 9, the *Virginia* steams out to finish off the wooden fleet and finds the *Monitor* waiting. They battle most of the day and do no serious damage to each other. They retire to lick their wounds and make repairs. The *Virginia* comes out several times over the next month but the *Monitor* will not come out to offer battle.

John Tucker, the Assistant Secretary of War, is tasked with creating the fleet to transport the men and supplies of McClellan's Army to the Peninsula at Fort Monroe and supply them during the campaign. He leases 113 side-wheelers, ocean packets, ferry boats and excursion boats plus 276 schooners, barges and canal boats which are fitted out for animals, artillery and all types of war material. These 276 vessels will be towed by the 113 major vessels that he leases at a cost of $24,300 per day. In six weeks, starting in mid-March, this fleet moved 121,500 men, 14,592 animals, 1,224 wagons, 44 artillery batteries and enormous amounts of equipage required to support the army.[1] The Army of the Potomac is arriving. In mid-March

McClellan finally put his army in motion. The 2nd Michigan Infantry arrives on March 18. On the 20th, they march to the Hampton bridge. Lt. Charles Haydon writes, *"[Our] next move was to seize 3 or 4 oyster boats which had just landed, throw the darkies out of them & carry off the oysters."* A few days later Lt. Haydon falls prey to the local water and notes that my *"bowels are turned upside down and the contents are running out at a double quick."* Welcome to the charming environs of the swampy peninsula.

Using the Warwick River as a barrier, General Magruder has constructed a strong defensive line running between the York River and the James River. He has flooded the upper regions of the Warwick River by using a series of dams and built his defenses behind this natural moat. As General Lafayette McLaws notes, *"We have dammed up that river at various points and now the country is flooded from a point under the guns of Yorktown . . . to the James River."*

As the Union army grows rapidly by the day, General Magruder does his best to strengthen his line of fortifications and make his fewer than 20,000 men seem like a much larger force. It does not take much to convince General McClellan that he is vastly outnumbered.

(1. *To The Gates of Richmond – The Peninsula Campaign,* Stephen Sears, New York, 1992, pp. 23-24; Chronicle by date; Day by Day by date.)

March, 1862

March 2, 1862 – Cavalry Camp, Young's Mill
Pvt. William C. Corson, Co. G – 3rd Virginia Cavalry

My Dear Jennie,

. . . The twelve month volunteers should to a man reenlist for the war and stand by their country now in her darkest hours . . . About thirty members of the Cumberland Troop [Company G] have reenlisted and I presume two-thirds of the company will go in for two years or the war.

(ed: The initial enlistments are expiring and the drive is on to get the troops to reenlist for 'two years or the war'.)

(Corson, p. 67.)

- - - - -

March 5, 1862 – Young's Mil
Pvt. William C. Corson, Co. G – 3rd Virginia Cavalry

My own Dear Jennie,

. . . Have you seen Billy Price since he come home, and did you get my dogratype [Daguerreotype] sent by Macon Raine? . . . We are living very hard now. Poor beef and not enough at that, We buy a little Molasses occasionally . . . at $1.75 per gal. It rains here about 4 days in every week and the roads have no bottom. . . . Write often to your ever devoted lover

(ed: A daguerreotype is a photographic process with the image made on a light sensitive silver-coated metallic plate.)

(Corson, pp. 69-70.)

- - - - -

March 7, 1862 – Enroute from New York to Hampton Roads
Lt. Dana Greene, X.O., U.S.S. *Monitor*

We left New York in tow of the tug-boat *Seth Low* at 11:00 a.m. of Thursday the 6th of March. On [the 7th] a moderate breeze was encountered and it was at once evident that the *Monitor* was unfit as a sea-going craft. . . . The berth-deck hatch leaked . . . water came down under the turret like a waterfall . . . The waves also broke over the blower-pipes, and the water came down through them in such quantities that the belts of the blower engines slipped, and the engines consequently stopped for lack of artificial draught . . . and the fires could not get air for combustion. . . . The water continued to pour . . . down and over the smoke-stacks and blower-pipes in such quantities that there was eminent danger that the ship would founder. The steam pumps could not be operated . . . and the engine room was uninhabitable on account of the suffocating gas with which it was filled. . . . Fortunately, toward evening the wind and sea subsided, and being again in smooth water, the engine was put [back] in operation.

(ed: Good weather and bad weather continued for another day and they reached Cape Henry at the mouth of the Chesapeake Bay at 4 p.m. on March 8 and reported their arrival to the U.S.S. Roanoke at 9 p.m. She was dispatched to anchor near the Minnesota which had run aground trying to get underway to enter the fight with the C.S.S. Virginia.)

(B&L -1, Johnson & Buel – editors, "In The Monitor Turret," Cmdr. Dana Greene, executive office;, New York, 1887, p. 720-721. [Hereafter cites as B&L-Greene])

- - - - -

March 7, 1862 – Enroute to Hampton Roads
Chief Engineer Alban Stimers, U.S.S. *Monitor*

[Sea water invading the fresh air intake pipes both for the ventilation system and for the engines starved men and machines of oxygen and] the fires burned with a sickly blaze out of the ash pan doors, converting all the air in the engine room and the fire-rooms into carbonic-acid-gas, a few inhalations of which are sufficient to destroy animal life.

(Unlike Anything, p 8.)

- - - - -

March 8, 1862 – James City County
Mr. John T. Martin, Farmer & School Teacher

We have a large army concentrating about Yorktown and are expecting a great battle any day.

(Martin Farm Journal by date.)

- - - - -

March 8, 1862 – Gosport Naval Yard
Captain William Norris, Confederate Signal Corps

[Virginia] was put up in the roughest way . . . [she was] in every respect ill-proportioned and top-heavy; and what with her immense length and wretched engines . . . was little more manageable than a timber raft . . . she steered very badly and both her rudder and screw were wholly unprotected. . . . she should never have been found more than three hours from a machine shop.

(ed: Her steering combined with the fact that 4 knots is basically her top speed meant that it took over 30 minutes just to turn her around. Her turning radius is also quite large and she needs a significant area of deep water to make a turn. Unlike the Monitor which drew 10' of water the Virginia drew over 20' of water.)

(ed: Norris was an Aide-de-Camp to General Magruder who had sent him to Norfolk, in late 1861, for training in signaling using flag and balls. He will set up a Signal Corps for Magruder's troops on the Peninsula. His time in the Norfolk area, and on the Peninsula, created the opportunity for him to observe the construction

of the 'Virginia.')

(Unlike Anything, p. 19.)

- - - - -

March 8, 1862 – Hampton Roads, Virginia
Surgeon Dinwiddie Phillips, C.S. Ironclad *Virginia*

[The riverbank] thronged with people . . . most of them, perhaps attracted by our novel appearance, and desirous of witnessing our movements through the water. . . . few, if any, entertained an exalted idea of our efficiency, and many predicted a total failure.

(Yorktown's Civil War Siege, Quarstein & Moore, Charleston, 2012, p. 68. [Hereafter cited as Civil War Siege.])

- - - - -

March 8, 1862 – Hampton Roads, Virginia
Seaman Richard Curtis, Bow Gunner – C.S. *Virginia*

Great crowds lined both sides of the [Elizabeth] river cheering us on to battle, our men were ordered on deck and responded to these greetings. A little distance down the river the Confederates had placed some obstruction and as our ship was of very heavy draft . . . it took some little time in getting through, but our Pilots were equal to the occasion and slowly she steamed for Hampton Roads, we soon passed Craney Island, then Newport News was opened to our view, also the *Cumberland* and the *Congress* . . . quietly lying at anchor . . .

(History of the Great Naval Engagement between the iron-clad Merrimac C.S.N. and the Cumberland, Congress and the iron-clad Monitor U.S.N. March the 8th and 9th, 1862 as seen by a Man at the Gun. – Richard Curtis, Hampton, reprinted in 1957. [Hereafter cited as Man at the Gun.]).

(ed: Originally commissioned as the C.S.S. Merrimack on February 12, 1862, when she was launched on the rebuilt hull of the U.S.S. Merrimack she soon got a name change. Flag Officer Franklin Buchanan was designated commander of the James River Fleet

and made the new ironclad his flagship. At that time, she was renamed the C.S.S. Virginia. Many people, in error, will continue to refer to her by the name of the salvaged hull upon which she was constructed.)

(Civil War Siege, p.67.)

- - - - -

March 8, 1862 – Hampton Roads, Virginia
Lt. John Taylor Wood, C.S. Ironclad *Virginia*

From the start we saw that she [*Virginia*] was slow, not over five knots. . . . She steered so badly that, with her great length it took thirty to forty minutes to turn . . . She was as unmanageable as a waterlogged vessel.

(Civil War Siege, p. 68)

- - - - -

March 8, 1862 – Hampton Roads
Surgeon Dinwiddie Phillips, C.S. Ironclad *Virginia*

[*Virginia*] bore a resemblance to a huge terrapin with a large round chimney about the middle of its back.

(Unlike Anything, p. 18.)

- - - - -

March 8, 1862 – Hampton Roads, Virginia
Asst. Engineer E. V. White, C.S. Ironclad *Virginia*

At about 12 o'clock . . . the *Virginia* cast loose from the wharf at the Navy Yard and steamed slowly to the work of the day . . . passing through the obstruction at Craney Island, she headed directly for Newport News, where the U.S.S. *Cumberland* and the U.S.S. *Congress* lay riding at anchor. . . . Ere she reached these ships several large Men-of-War started from Old Point to the help of their sister ships; among them the *Minnesota* which grounded near Newport News point.

(White, p. 9.)

- - - - -

March 8, 1862 – Hampton Roads, Virginia
Fireman Joseph McDonald, U.S.S. *Dragon*

I shall never forget that day, nor the next, either. . . [it was bright and clear with no wind] so the sailing ships must fight as they lay. Pretty soon [about 1:00 p.m.] that great black thing, different from any vessel ever seen before, poked her nose around Sewell's Point and came directly for the two ships . . . [two small gunboats followed] just like an old duck and her brood. My, didn't orders ring out sharp, and men jump lively.

(ed: Joseph transferred from the Minnesota *to the* Dragon *hoping for better pay as a fireman and also that he would no longer be climbing the rigging as a seaman. The* Dragon *was a 92-foot steamer used as a picket boat, dispatch runner and a tug. Her total armament was a 30-pounder rifle and a 24-pounder smoothbore. After dusk the* Dragon *would be dispatched on picket duty out toward Sewell's Point to signal the fleet if the* Virginia *was slipping out at night for a surprise attack.)*

(ed: The C.S.S. Beaufort *and the C.S.S.* Raleigh *were the two "small gunboats" that followed the "old duck" toward the Union fleet.)*

(Unlike Anything, pp. 74-75, p.78.)

- - - - -

March 8, 1862 – attack on the *Cumberland*
Seaman Richard Curtis, Bow Gunner, C.S. *Virginia*

. . . when within 1,000 yards of the *Cumberland* our gun belched forth its first shot and struck the *Cumberland* just about her fore chains on the starboard side; the Capt. of [our bow gun] was

The Virginia ramming *The Cumberland*

named James Cuhill, of New Orleans, and as brave a man as ever stood behind a gun. . . . as we passed the *Congress* which was said to be a 54 gun ship [she] gave us a full broadside and it was a terrible noise . . . this broadside had no effect on the iron sides of our ship.

(ed: Gunner Richard Curtis has a view of the battle from the bow gun on the Virginia. His view is restricted to events that happen directly in front of the ship. He notes in his book that officers and sailors were at their stations and not moving around the ship. He feels & hears the broadside he mentions above.)

(Man at the Gun, p. 7.)

March 8, 1862 – attack on the *Cumberland*
Asst. Engineer E. V. White, C.S. Ironclad *Virginia*

The *Congress* was the first to fire, with a full broadside, upon our ship, followed by the *Cumberland,* and from the latter's shot the hog chain was parted and driven back into our ship, killing one man and wounding several others. . . . Reserving her fire until within easy range, the *Virginia's* bow rifle was used with terrible effect; and . . . opened a hole in the *Cumberland* large enough for a horse and cart to drive through. . . . When at probably fifty yards distance, with slackened speed, but determined purpose, we moved on and struck her [rammed] the deadly blow, . . . backing our engines . . . until we had cleared the disabled vessel. A shot from the *Congress* struck the muzzle of one of our broadside 9-inch Dahlgren guns, breaking off about 2 feet of it, killing one man and wounding a few others. . . . We then moved up the James River to a place for easy turning . . . and started back . . .

(White, p. 9.)

- - - - -

March 8, 1862 – attack on the *Cumberland*
Seaman Richard Curtis, Bow Gunner, C.S. *Virginia*

We were getting close down to the *Cumberland* . . . I heard the voice of Capt. Buchanan say "lookout men, I am going to Ram that ship." . . . I looked out of the port and just as we ramed her I saw . . . the starboard side of the *Cumberland* was lined with officers and men with rifles and boarding pikes, all ready to repel us, thinking we were intending to board her . . . then came the terrible crash and at the same time our gun was fired, adding to the terrible hole in her side . . . the *Cumberland* was rapidly sinking yet her officers and men kept up the fight until she sank beneath the waters of James River.

(ed: As the Cumberland sinks her weight breaks the ram off the bow of the Virginia before she can back away from the doomed

Union ship.)

(Man at the Gun, p.8.)

- - - - -

March 8, 1862 – Action against the *Cumberland*
Lt. John Taylor Wood, C.S. Ironclad *Virginia*

Backing clear of her [*Cumberland*] we headed up river . . . as we did so, for the first time I had an opportunity of using the after-pivot [gun] of which I had charge. As we swung, the *Congress* came in range, nearly stern on, and we got in three raking shells. She had slipped her anchor . . . but grounded.

(ed: As mentioned earlier, by Engineering Officer E. V. White, both the bow and stern pivot guns were 7-inch steel banded Brooke rifles. As the officer in charge of the aft gun, Lt. Wood will have an excellent view of any action to the rear of the Virginia.)

(Battle and Leaders of the Civil War – Vol.1, Editor Roy Nichols, New York, 1956, 'The First Fight of Ironclads' by John Taylor Wood, C.S.A.', p.698. [Hereafter cited as B&L-1, Wood].)

- - - - -

March 8, 1862 – Action against the *Congress*
Lt. John Taylor Wood, C.S. Ironclad *Virginia*

. . . we were joined by [several vessels] of the James River Squadron . . . [including] the *Yorktown,* 12 guns, Captain John R. Tucker; *Jamestown* , 2 guns, Lt. Cmdr. J. N. Barney; *Teaser,* 1 gun, Lt. Cmdr. W. B. Webb; *Beaufort,* Lt. Cmdr. W. H. Parker; and *Raleigh,* Lt. Cmdr. J. W. Alexander. . . . the gunboats *Beaufort* and *Raleigh* steamed alongside to take off the crew and set fire to the ship. Lt. Pendergrast [*Congress*] delivered his sword and colors to Lt. Parker of the *Beaufort.*

(ed: Because fire from ashore, and other locations, was hindering the evacuation of wounded and also killing and injuring Confederate sailors, Captain Buchanan ordered hot shot fired into the

Congress which quickly turned her into a blazing wreck.)

(B&L-1, Wood, pp. 699-700.)

- - - - -

March 8, 1862 – action against the *Virginia*
Lt. Austin Pendergast, X.O., U.S.S. *Congress*

{*Virginia, Patrick Henry, Jamestown & Teaser* took station 200 yards astern of *Congress*. The *Virginia* could fire broadsides and the *Congress* could only reply with two guns.] Our two stern guns were now our only means of defense . . . these were soon disabled, one being dismounted and the other having its muzzle knocked away. . . . The men were swept away from them with the great rapidity and slaughter by the terrible fire of the enemy. . . .

(Unlike Anything, p. 89.)

- - - - -

March 8, 1862 – action against the *Virginia*
Gun Captain Frederick Curtis, U.S.S. *Congress*

It was a pretty busy time aboard just then, and the men were much excited. Our little powder boy, a lad of only thirteen . . . would bring us ammunition with . . . tears streaming down his cheeks. . . . The order was then passed for us to cease firing, and our colors were struck. My gun was loaded at the time, and, although the order had been given to cease firing, I pulled the lanyard and fired what proved to be the last shot ever fired on board the fated *Congress*.

(Unlike Anything, pp. 89-90.)

- - - - -

March 8, 1862 – Observing from Sewell's Point, Virginia
General R. E Colston, C.S. Department of Norfolk

The lofty frigate, towering above the water, now offered an easy target to the rifled guns of the [*Virginia*] and the lighter artillery

of the gunboats [*Jamestown, Patrick Henry & Teaser*] . . . Projectiles hurled at the [*Virginia*] glanced harmlessly from her iron-
covered roof, while her rifled guns raked the *Congress* from end
to end . . . the latter replied gallantly . . . her decks were reek-
ing with slaughter. Then her colors were hauled down and white
flags appeared at the gaff and mainmast.

(Unlike Anything, pp. 89-90.)

- - - - -

March 8, 1862 – action against the *Congress*
Seaman Richard Curtis, Bow Gunner, C.S. *Virginia*

The *Congress* had hoisted a white flag . . . Lt. Minor, of our ship,
was sent by Capt. Buchanan . . . to take the surrender of the *Congress*; while approaching this ship men on the *Congress* and from
shore fired into the approaching boat, shooting Lt. Minor through
the body and also wounding one of the men in the boat with
him . . . Capt. Buchanan . . . ordered the pilots to place the ship
in position to rake the *Congress* which was quickly done; we lay
under her stern and pounded hot shot and incendiary shells into
her until we set her afire . . . We arrived back at Sewell's Point [in
darkness] and dropped anchor and lay there all night. The *Congress* was a grand sight, being all ablaze from her deck to her top.
Thus ended the 8th day of March, 1862, with the destruction of
two of the finest Battle Ships of the U. S. Navy.

*(ed: Seaman Curtis is part of the initial boat crew dispatched to
the Congress under flag of truce and is topside on the Virginia for
the incident above involving Lt. Minor and the second boat crew.)*

(ed: When the Congress *struck her colors, and surrendered, all
fire upon the ship and the Confederate vessels coming alongside
is honor bound to cease. However, we are early in the war, and
many non-military soldiers have no concept of the rules of war.
This leads to needless loss of life among several Confederate sailors and many sailors onboard the* Congress. *The order from Captain Buchanan to fire hot-shot into the* Congress *turns her into an*

inferno from which many Union sailors could not escape.)

(Man at the Gun, p. 9. Unlike Anything pp. 90-95.)

- - - - -

March 8, 1862 – Firing 'hot-shot' into the *Congress*
Lt. John Eggleston, C.S. Ironclad *Virginia*

Buchanan, in a ringing voice I can never forget, called down the hatchway under which I was standing: 'Destroy that = = = = ship! She's firing [under] a white flag!' It was even so, incredible as it may seem . . . Dearly did they pay for their unparalleled treachery. We raked her fore and aft with hot-shot and shell, till out of pity we stopped without waiting for orders.

(Unlike Anything, p. 94.)

- - - - -

March 8, 1862 – firing 'hot-shot' into the *Congress*
Chief Engineer H. A. Ramsay, C.S. Ironclad *Virginia*

[Two boiler furnaces were used for hot-shot] . . . they were rolled into the flames on a grating, rolled out into iron buckets, hoisted to the gun-deck, and rolled into the barrel, which had been prepared with wads of wet hemp. Then the gun would be touched off quickly and the shot sent on its errand of destruction.

(ed: There is one gun on each side of the Virginia *designated for the use of hot-shot. That gun and gun crew did all of the work that turned the* Congress *into a funeral pyre.]*

(Unlike Anything, p. 95.)

- - - - -

March 8, 1862 – escaping from the blazing *Congress*
Gunner Frederick Curtis, U.S.S. *Congress*

[crawling out of a lower gunport, hanging on a line & dropping into the water] . . . I sank well under, and on rising to the surface

120

picked up my hat and started (swimming) for the shore . . . I saw several of my comrades drown, but was powerless to help them . . . [swam nearly half a mile and crawled ashore] so weak that I was hardly able to stand.

(While Gunners Mate Curtis is swimming for his life, the U.S.S. Roanoke, Mystic and St. Lawrence discontinued their efforts to come to the aid of the U.S.S. Minnesota and turned their vessels back toward Fort Monroe and retreated, downriver, to safe haven under the guns of the fort. Confederate batteries at Sewell's Point fired some rounds to encourage their withdrawal.)

(Unlike Anything, p. 94.)

- - - - -

March 8, 1862 – evening darkness Hampton Roads
Asst. Engineer E. V. White, C.S. Ironclad *Virginia*

It now being nearly dark, and the work of transferring the dead and wounded, to be conveyed to the naval hospital, being completed, we steamed over to the buoy at Sewell's Point, and came to anchor for the night. As I was one of the . . . ones placed on first watch I . . . witnessed the grand and impressive sight of the explosion of the *Congress* later in the night – a scene too solemnly beautiful to attempt to describe.

(White, p. 9.)

- - - - -

March 8, 1862 – arriving in Chesapeake Bay
Lt. Dana Greene, X.O., U.S. Ironclad *Monitor*

. . . the *Monitor* passed Cape Henry at 4 P.M. on Saturday . . . At this point was heard the distant booming of heavy guns, which our captain rightly judged to be an engagement with the *Merrimac* [*Virginia*] twenty miles away. . . . As we approached Hampton Roads we could see the fine old *Congress* burning brightly, and soon a pilot came on board and told of the arrival of the

[*Virginia*], the disaster to the *Cumberland* and the *Congress* and the dismay of the Union forces. The *Monitor* was pushed with all haste and reached the *Roanoke* anchored in the Roads at 9 P.M.

(ed: Lt. Greene does not know that his opponent has been christened Virginia. I will place [Virginia] in brackets each time he uses Merrimack for clarity and correctness.)

(B&L – Greene, p. 721.)

- - - - -

March 8, 1862 – at anchor off Sewell's Point
Captain Franklin Buchanan, C.S. Ironclad *Virginia*

Our loss is 2 killed and 19 wounded [including myself] . . . the stem is twisted and the ship leaks. We have lost the prow [ram], starboard anchor, and all the boats. The armor is somewhat damaged; the steam pipe and smokestack both riddled; the muzzles of two of the guns shot away. It was not easy to keep a flag flying. The flagstaffs were repeatedly shot away . . . The bearing of the men was all that could be desired; their enthusiasm could scarcely be restrained. During the action they cheered again and again. Their coolness and skill were the more remarkable from the fact that the great majority of them were under fire for the first time. They were strangers to each other and to the officers, and had but a few days' instruction in the management of great guns. To the skill and example of the officers is this result in no small degree attributable.

(Unlike Anything, pp. 99-100.)

- - - - -

March 9, 1862 – alongside the *USS Minnesota*
Lt. Dana Greene, X. O., U.S.S. *Monitor*

An atmosphere of gloom pervaded the fleet and the pygmy aspect of the new-comer did not inspire confidence in those who had witnessed the destruction of the day before.

(ed: She anchored alongside Minnesota about 11:00 p.m. and Lt. Greene returned to the Monitor about 1:00 a.m. after reporting to the Captain Van Brunt of the Minnesota.)

(Unlike Anything, pp. 12-13.)

- - - - -

March 9, 1862 – Washington, D.C.
Sgt. Major Elisah Rhodes, 2nd R. Island Infantry

. . . I [have] been promoted to "Sergeant Major" of the Regiment. . . . To say that I was delighted would be very tame. . . . This morning I was mustered as Sergeant Major. . . . Tomorrow I shall receive my sash and sword. I shall mess with the officers . . .

(Robert Hunt Rhodes, editor: *All For The Union – The Civil War Diary and Letters of Elisha Hunt Rhodes,* New York, 1991, p. 37-38. [Hereafter cited as Rhodes].

- - - - -

March 9, 1862 – Casualty Report of March 8
Surgeon D. B. Phillips, C.S. Ironclad *Virginia*

Casualties of the 8th as follows: Flag-officer F. Buchanan wounded in the left thigh, a minie-ball having passed entirely through the fleshy portion, grazing femoral artery and inflicting a serious wound. Lt. R. D Minor wounded in the left side. Midshipman Marmaduke, slight wound on the arm. Killed, Charles Dunbar and _____ Waldeck. Wounded, William Burkes, seaman; John Capps, Company E, 41st Regiment; A. J. Dalton, Company E, 41st Regiment; Emerson Ivas, seaman; and John Leonard, seaman.

(White, p. 29.)

- - - - -

March 9, 1862 – in Hampton Roads

Lt. Dana Greene – X. O., U.S.S. *Monitor*

The physical condition of the officers and men of the two ships at this time was in striking contrast. The [*Virginia*] had passed the night quietly near Sewell's Point, her people enjoying rest and sleep and elated by the thoughts of their victory . . . The *Monitor* had barely escaped shipwreck twice within 36 hours, and since Friday morning, 48 hours before, few if any . . . had closed their eyes . . . or had anything to eat but hard bread . . . She was surrounded by wrecks and disaster, and her efficiency . . . was yet to be proved.

(B&L- 1, Greene, p.724.)

- - - - -

March 9, 1862 – action against the *Minnesota*
Seaman Richard Curtis, Bow Gunner, C.S. *Virginia*

Capt. Buchanan having been wounded [on March 8] the Command of the [*Virginia*] fell on Lieutenant Catesby Jones and Lieutenant Charles C. Simms. About 9 o'clock . . . everything being ready we weighed anchor and steamed toward the *Minnesota* [which had run aground the previous evening avoiding the *Virginia*] . . . at range of 1,000 yards we opened up the fight . . . the first shot passed through her side, exploding on the inside of the ship . . . and setting her on fire. The next shot went through the boiler of the Tugboat *Dragon* and exploded her boiler . . . [she] was alongside the *Minnesota*.

(ed: The Virginia *is facing the* Minnesota *in a bow-on position and therefore the only gun on the* Virginia *that is engaged is the bow gun. Therefore, Seaman Curtis has a view of the opening two shots on the* Minnesota.*)*

(Man at the Gun, pp. 10-11.)

- - - - -

March 9, 1862 – action aginst the *Minnesota*
Seaman Richard Curtis, Bow Gunner, C.S. *Virginia*

The *Minnesota* had fine gunners and many of her shots struck our Ship, one of them struck the edge of our bow port and part of it came inside . . . and badly wounded one of our men at the bow gun. Right abaft of the bow gun the Galley pipe ran through the upper deck; this pipe had been [removed creating an opening topside] and Lt. Davidson occupied this position with a pair of marine glasses . . . and reported every shot . . . and its effect on the enemy. This duel had been going on for some time when I heard Lt. Davidson say that they were leaving the *Minnesota* on a raft . . . and I saw something like a raft . . . crossing the bow of the *Minnesota* . . . Lt. Davidson came down from his post and said to the men, "by George, it is the Erricon Battery, look out for her hot work." which soon came.

(ed: The Monitor *has arrived on the scene and the battle of the ironclads is set to begin.)*

(Man at the Gun, p.11.)

- - - - -

March 9, 1862 – engaging the *Virginia*
Captain John L. Worden, U.S. Ironclad *Monitor*

At this time . . . I was approaching *[Virginia]* on her starboard bow, on a course nearly at right angles with her line of keel, reserving my fire until near enough that every shot might take effect.

(ed: The Monitor *approached to about 1/3 of a mile, altered her course, stopped her engines, and opened fire.)*

(Unlike Anything, p. 116.)

- - - - -

March 9, 1862 – action against the *Virginia*
Lt. Dana Greene – X.O., U.S. Ironclad *Monitor*

The drawbacks to the position of the pilot house were soon realized. We could not fire ahead nor within several points [degrees] of the bow, since the blast from our own guns would have injured the people in the pilot-house. . . [Also] the captain, commanding and guiding was enclosed in one place, and the executive officer, . . . fighting the guns, was shut up in another and communication between them was difficult. . .

The working of the turret was not altogether satisfactory. It was difficult to start it revolving . . . and once started, to stop it, on account of the imperfections of the novel machinery. . . When the gun was run in, the port holes were covered by heavy iron . . . [the gun crew was blind] . . . I would ask the Captain, "How does the [*Virginia*] bear?" He replied, "On the starboard beam" or "On the port quarter." . . . It finally resulted that when the gun was ready for firing, the turret would be started on its revolving journey . . . and when found [the shot] was taken "on the fly."

(ed: They had some challenges. The speaking tube between the Captain and X.O. was broken early so they had runners taking commands back and forth. Very inefficient. The marks on the inside of the turret deck to indicate starboard beam, bow, stern etc. were quickly obliterated and the gun crew had no idea in which direction they faced. It would have been comical except that it was battle and could mean life or death.)

(B&L – 1, Greene, p. 735.)

- - - - -

March 9, 1862 – dueling with the *Monitor*
Captain Catesby Jones, C.S. Ironclad *Virginia*

Monitor and *Virginia*

127

. . . Once while passing we fired a broadside at her only a few yards distant. She and her turret appeared to be under perfect control. Her light draft enabled her to move about us at pleasure.

(ed: The Virginia *has very few rounds of solid shot on board. They have various types of exploding ordnance for fighting wooden ships. On her future sorties into Hampton Roads she will have solid shot for dueling with the* Monitor *but she was under orders not to seek engagement but to protect the wooden fleet which was generally in shallow waters, where the* Virginia *could not approach.)*

(Unlike Anything, p.119.)

- - - - -

March 9, 1862 – action against the *Monitor*
Asst. Engineer E. V. White, C.S. Ironclad *Virginia*

. . . we got underway, making for the *Minnesota,* when suddenly we grounded on what is known as the Middle Ground of Hampton Roads, and there we were stuck for a considerable time. . . . the *Monitor* was discovered coming out from where the *Minnesota* lay aground . . . we opened fire . . . but with no effect and . . . the *Monitor* . . . when in good position let loose her heavy guns, giving us a good shaking up. She continued to circle us . . . throwing heavy missiles against our sides. . . . We brought guns to bear on her as she passed around. Soon, however, we were relieved by the moving of our ship . . . then . . . our commander determined to run the *Monitor* down. . . . we did run into the Monitor . . . our starboard bow drove against her and a shot from our rifle [bow gun] blinded their commander and she withdrew to shoal water near the *Minnesota.* We could not follow . . . and never again did the [*Monitor*] offer or accept battle with the *Virginia.*

By 4 o'clock we were back in the dry dock at the Navy Yard. The . . . ship was a sight to behold. You could hardly put your hand on a spot on the sides, or smokestack, that had not been battered by the shot of the enemy.

(ed: This is a very condensed version of the fight, it certainly has some of the highlights, but does not convey the time, maneuvering and the massive amount of shots and hits on both vessels during the engagement.)

(White, pp. 17-18.)

- - - - -

March 9, 1862 – dueling with the *Monitor*
Lt. John Taylor Wood, C.S. Ironclad *Virginia*

. . . she [*Monitor*] could not possibly have made her appearance at a more inopportune time . . . She appeared but a pigmy compared with the lofty frigate [*Minnesota*] which she guarded. But in her size was one great element of her success . . . The *Monitor* was firing every seven or eight minutes, and nearly every shot struck.

(Unlike Anything, p. 123.)

- - - - -

March 9, 1862 – action against the *Virginia*
Lt. Dana Greene – X. O., U.S. Ironclad *Monitor*

Once the [*Virginia*] tried to ram us; but [Captain] Worden avoided the direct impact . . . and she struck a glancing blow, which did no damage. At the instant of collision I planted a solid 180 pound shot . . . upon the forward part of her casement. Had the gun been loaded with 30 pounds of powder, which was the charge subsequently used with similar guns, it is probable that this shot would have penetrated her armor; but the charge being limited to fifteen pounds in accordance with orders . . . from the Navy Department . . .

(ed: The Monitor *is using half loads of powder (15 pounds) as a*

precaution. Remember, there had been no trials for either vessel prior to this engagement and there were concerns with a 30 pound charge and the recoil of the guns in conjunction with the damper system on the gun carriage. Would the damper system be able to control the repeated recoils during a multi-hour battle or would half loads be a more prudent move? There are dents in the back wall of the turret from recoil dampening failures when the damper was not set properly.)

(B&L-1, Greene, p. 725.)

- - - - -

March 9, 1862 – action against the *Monitor*
Lt. John Taylor Wood, C.S. Ironclad *Virginia*

The *Monitor* was well handled . . . but . . . not a single shot struck us at the water-line, where our ship was utterly unprotected and where one [major hit] would have been fatal. . . . Most of her shot struck us obliquely . . . We had no solid projectiles . . . [to damage her armor] . . . both vessels were on their trial trip, both were experimental, and both were receiving their baptism of fire.

(B&L-1, Wood, p. 703.)

- - - - -

March 9, 1862 – news of C.S. Ironclad *Virginia*
Mrs. Cynthia Coleman, Williamsburg citizen

Although we were so near the scene of the action [*Virginia* attacking the U. S. fleet], and the battle began on Saturday, the news did not reach us until Sunday just before going to church . . . Then we only heard there was a great battle going on . . .

(ed: The news was of the destruction of the Cumberland *and the* Congress. *Most likely the exact details were in error. By the time church services began on Sunday the congregation had no idea that the famous battle between the ironclads was happening while they listened to the morning sermon.)*

(Carol K. Dubbs, *Defend This Old Town – Williamsburg During the Civil War,* Baton Rouge, 2002, p.62. [Hereafter cited as Old Town].)

- - - - -

March 9, 1862 – action against the *Monitor*
Lt. John Taylor Wood, C.S. Ironclad *Virginia*

More than two hours had passed, and we had made no impression on the enemy so far as we could discover, while our wounds were slight. Several times the *Monitor* ceased firing, and we were in hopes she was disabled, but the revolution again of her turret and the heavy blows of her 11-inch shot on our sides soon undeceived us.

(ed: The Monitor *improvised a new way to load and fire her two guns. They left the gunport covers up and simply rotated the turret away from the* Virginia, *reloaded the guns in safety, then started the turret rotating again and when the* Virginia *was in the sights Lt. Greene would fire both guns. The turret would not stop rotating till facing away for a reload.)*

(Unlike Anything, p. 125.)

- - - - -

March 9, 1862 – re-engaging the *Minnesota*
Captain William Norris, C.S. Army Signal Corps

We have knocked a huge hole into [*Minnesota*], large enough to admit a wagon and four horses, driving four of her [gun]ports into one, and the carnage in and about her had been dreadful. Of the officer and crew of a steamer alongside, not one remained alive I believe.

(ed: The Dragon *was alongside* Minnesota *and Fireman Joseph McDonald was in the process of casting off the bow line when a shell from the* Virginia *hit the* Dragon *exploding her boiler ripping McDonald's right leg with shrapnel and breaking his thigh bone. He was pulled off the deck of* Dragon *and through a gun-port on*

Minnesota *where the ship's surgeon went to work. McDonald would tell people that, "his fighting was over. The long and short of it is that one of my burial places is in Old Virginia . . . where I left my leg." McDonald was lucky because several sailors on the* Dragon *were badly scalded in the boiler explosion and others drowned with the sinking vessel.)*

(Unlike Anything, p. 128 & 135.)

- - - - -

March 9, 1862 – Hampton Roads, Virginia
Lt. Dana Greene, X.O., U.S.S. Ironclad *Monitor*

My men and myself were perfectly black with smoke and powder. All my underclothes were perfectly black, and my person was in the same condition. . . . I had been up so long and been under such a state of excitement, that my nervous system was completely run down . . . My nerves and muscles twitched as though electric shocks were continually passing through them. . . I lay down and tried to sleep – I might as well have tried to fly.

(ed: Lt. Greene is in the turret and personally fired every shot from the Monitor *during the engagement. Beginning at 0845 until evening he is in a turret filled with smoke and concussive explosions. The 16 gunners serving with him were probably in very similar conditions. These thoughts were contained in a personal letter, from the lieutenant, written just after the fight.)*

(B&L -1, Greene, p.727.)

- - - - -

March 9, 1862 – returning to Gosport Naval Yard
Chief Engineer A. Ramsay, C.S. Ironclad *Virginia*

[hearing cheering and] rushing on deck, I found we were passing Craney Island on our way to Norfolk, and were being cheered by the soldiers of the battery. . . . As the *Virginia* passed up the river, trailing the ensign of the *Congress* under the stars and bars, she received a tremendous ovation from the crowds that lined the shores, while hundreds of small boats, gay with flags and bunting, converted our course into a triumphal procession.

(Unlike Anything, p. 133.)

- - - - -

March 10, 1862 – Gosport Naval Yard, Portsmouth
John L. Porter, Naval Constructor

After the engagements of the 8th and 9th . . . I put her in the dry-dock and found she had 97 indentations on her armor from shot, 20 of which were from the 10-inch guns of the *Monitor.* Six of her top layer plates were broken by the *Monitor's* shots, and none of those by other vessels. None of the lower layer of plates were injured. I removed those plates and replaced them by others. Her wood-work underneath was not hurt. Her smoke-stack was full of shot-holes. She never had any boat-davits. Her pilot-house was cast solid, and was not covered with plate-iron like her shield. . . . the conversion of the *Merrimac [Virginia]* into an iron-clad was accidental, and grew out of the impracticability of building an engine within the time at the disposal of the Confederacy, and no iron-clad, with submerged ends, was afterwards built.

(B&L-1, 'The Plan and Construction of the "Merrimac- II', by John L. Porter, p. 717.)

- - - - -

Mid-March, 1862 – Hampton Roads, Virginia
Chief Engineer Alban Stimers, U.S.S. Ironclad *Monitor*

I consider the form and strength of the vessel equal to any weather I ever saw at sea. . . . it is only the man who has studied the philosophical laws which govern flotation and stability who feels exactly comfortable in her during a gale . . .

(Stimer's improvements to the caulking around the turret and

133

"design modifications to the air intake and smoke exhaust pipes"
would hopefully solve the problems she experienced on her voy-
age to Hampton Roads. He was sadly mistaken about the Moni-
tor's seaworthiness and proven tragically wrong as the Monitor
will sink in a gale off of Cape Hatteras on December 31, 1862.)

(Unlike Anything, p.10)

- - - - -

March 10, 1862 – Washington, D.C.
Sgt. Major Elisha Rhodes, 2nd Rhode Island Infantry

3 A. M. At midnight the orders came to march, and the men are busy cooking three days rations.

8 A. M. The regiment left camp . . . and marched to Tennally Town, Maryland . . . crossed the Potomac at Chain Bridge. . . . I started out this morning very brave and determined to carry my knapsack on my back, but soon weakened and placed it in a wagon. It shall be carried for me hereafter, or I shall leave it behind me.

(Rhodes, p.59)

- - - - -

March 10, 1862 – Williamsburg, Virginia
Miss. Sally Galt, Resident

Being so near [the African Baptist Church Hospital] I do a great deal for it, indeed I call myself the Patron Saint of the institution . . . most of the ladies in Williamsburg visit the sick soldiers, but I never do, & consequently think I ought to do as much at home as I can.

(ed: Sally constantly makes jellies and custard for the soldiers at
the African Baptist Hospital. In addition, since she is the sister of
Dr. Galt who is the Superintendent of the Eastern Lunatic Asylum,
she is also able to provide additional medical supplies and other
items from the Asylum inventories.)

(Old Town, p. 63.)

- - - - -

March 13, 1862 – camp near Yorktown
Pvt. James P. Williams, Richmond Howitzers

My dear sister [Nannie]

. . . I wrote a letter to Pa asking for his advice in regard to reenlisiting . . . Not having heard from him however I determined to use my own judgement . . . We were down near Newport News on Monday on a scout and therefore I couldn't decide about it; yesterday however we returned to this place and today [our] Captain (by order of the government) took down the names of all those who were going to reenlist . . . Among the dozen going in for the war, I have the honor . . . You were right when you said you knew I was a "volunteer for the war." . . . I suppose you have heard all about the grand naval victory in Hampton Roads. Three or four of the finest vessels in the Federal navy sent to Davy Jones Locker. . . . The *Virginia* will doubtless be out again as soon as she has undergone some little repairs. . . .

(Williams, by date.)

- - - - -

March 16, 1862 – Young's Mill
Pvt. Richard Watkins, Co. K – 3rd Virginia Cavalry

My own Dear Mary

The courier is about to leave for Yorktown but I must write you a few lines. We are all in fine health and spirits. . . . Mr. Asa Dickinson promised me that he would introduce a bill [in the Virginia legislature] to exempt the overseer of widows and volunteers. I do not know whether he has or not. I have not re-enlisted yet and will not for the present. Only 15 of our troop have as yet re-enlisted. Yesterday we received 15 recruits, among them Mr. Jno Baker. Good bye my darling Mary I want to see you so bad. . .

(ed: In a 3-17 letter from Mary, "Mr Baker [the Watkins overseer] is the happiest looking man this morning that I have seen for a

135

long time [he was exempted yesterday] says he feels like going to work now." These two Bakers are different individuals.)

(Boots & Kisses, p. 68.)

- - - - -

March 18, 1862 – arriving in Hampton Roads, Virginia
Lt. Charles Haydon, Co I – 2nd Michigan Infantry

At abt. 3 P.M. we are in Hampton Roads. There are some 20 of our war steamers & gun boats anchored here. There is one English war steamer & one French, the *Gassendi,* for whose benefit our band played the Marseilles hymn as we passed. . . .

The *Monitor* is here & a most ridiculous looking craft she is. She has a flat open deck perhaps 2 feet above water but over which the waves wash continually if there is any sea at all. Abt the middle of this there is a round cylinder perhaps 10 ft. high & 20 to 25 ft. in diameter. Add a flag staff & a small steam pipe & you have all that is visible of the famous *Monitor.* Make a raft 120 ft. long in the shape of a pumpkin seed & put a cheese box in the middle of it & you will have a good picture . . . There is considerable sea running, a good many of the men are [sea] sick.

(ed: Charles was born in 1834, raised in Decatur near Kalamazoo, graduated from Michigan in 1857 and was reading law at a firm in Kalamazoo where he was a law clerk. On April 22, 1861, he enlisted in the Kalamazoo Light Guard where he was appointed to the rank of 3rd Sergeant.)

(For Country, Cause & Leader – The Journal of Charles B Haydon, Stephen Sears editor, N. Y., 1993, by date & editors comment from p. x-xi. [Hereafter cited as Haydon]).

- - - - -

March 20, 1862 – near Hampton bridge
Lt. Charles Haydon, 2nd Michigan Infantry

[Our] next move was to seize 3 or 4 oyster boats which had just landed, throw the darkies out of them & carry off the oysters. Next [the 2nd Michigan] drove some regulars crazy who were trying to guard the Hampton bridge. The boys were in 20 minutes across the river to the number of 50 & in short the fame of the 2nd had spread through the country round about before dark to such an extent that early in the m'g [morning] Gen. Wool honored us with a visit. He gave out the news that any man who was caught at any such performance would be quartered at hard labor for 3 months . .

(ed: It did not faze the men of the 2nd Michigan to steal the oysters from these Negro watermen.)

(Haydon, by date.)

- - - - -

March 20, 1862 – Alexandria, Virginia
Corporal Luther Furst, Signal Corps

The expeditions are fitting out at this place and nearly all of the Army of the Potomac is expected to leave. They are bivouacked all around Alexandria for miles. It is a beautiful sight to see the campfires at night. Last night it rained and it is pretty cold for the soldiers. They are in good spirits and a few sick. Nearly every other house is a H____ H____ [Whore House]. They are known by a flag hung out of the window.

(ed: Luther, from Clear Springs, Pennsylvania, enlisted as a private on 5/6/1861 in Co. D of the 10th Pennsylvania Infantry. They did their training in Pittsburgh. On 8/26/1861 he is transferred to the signal corps and at the end of December he is promoted to corporal and in charge of training groups of 30 men. They signaled using either a flag or a burning torch. This is not a two flag system, it is a one flag system. They were also used as mounted couriers to take messages to various generals.)

(Civil War Diary of Luther Calvin Furst, # 1-19-5-2, Slippery Rock University Archives, Slippery Rock University of Pennsylvania. [Hereafter cited as Furst]).

- - - - -

March 21 & 24, 1862 – Hampton Virginia
Lt. Charles Haydon, 2nd Michigan Infantry

We find the soldiers here & the people generally a good deal frightened since the affair with the *Merrimac* [C.S. Ironclad *Virginia*]. This pleases our men immensely, they not believing any such thing. . .

The ruins of Hampton are just across the river. I have not been there but judging from appearance it must have been a place of great beauty . . . the houses were all brick and surrounded with trees and very neat yards. The chimneys and corners are all that is left standing. . . . It was one of the oldest villages in the country . . . The burning of it was one of the most wanton and unnecessary acts . . .

(Haydon, by date.)

- - - - - -

March 25, 1862 – Young's Mill
Pvt. William C. Corson, Co. G – 3rd Virginia Cavalry

. . . Since I last wrote neither myself nor horse have had twenty-four hours rest during the [last two weeks] . . . you may imagine we are both considerably jaded. I am suffering at present from a severe cold, contracted while sleeping out in the rain . . . we have more than twenty men reported sick which makes the duties of the others very heavy. Our present camping-ground is the worst we have ever had. The mud around our quarters is knee deep and is very offensive. I fear if we are kept here much longer that Typhus-fever will prevail in our regiment. . . . we are living hard in camp. There is no coffee on the peninsula and the soldiers have to resort to parched corn for a substitute. . . . send me something good to eat by the first opportunity . . .

(ed: By 'offensive' William means that the men are not slogging all the way to the sinks (latrines) but are relieving themselves in

the mud. This increases the opportunity for a variety of diseases to impact the troops.)

(ed: Typhus can be several forms of an infectious disease caused by the microorganisms of the genus Rickettsia. Both the flea borne and louse borne types lead to endemic Typhus. Both are characterized by severe headache, sustained high fever, delirium and red rashes.)

(ed: Treatments for typhus include giving the patient a gentle laxative with six to eight grains of calomel (mercury chloride). As soon as this has operated give the patient wine or brandy. If the patient is purging give him opium while keeping the room cool and use cold compresses on the body. Bleeding, for typhus, should never be allowed. Nine times out of ten times it is fatal to the patient. Keeping the bowels open is seen as the primary option and then the use of opium to keep the patient sedated. There was no cure in 1862.)

(Corson, pp. 71-72. American Heritage Dictionary, Pamela DeVinne, editor, Boston, 1976, p. 1310. [Hereafter cited as AHD]; Mackenzie, p. 200.)

- - - - -

March 25, 1862 – Fortress Monroe
Pvt. Wilbur Fisk, Second Vermont Infantry

. . . we steamed down to Fort Monroe, and slept that night on the sandy beach, with no protection from the chilly night air except what our blankets afforded. The following day we moved on several miles farther by land, passing the town of Hampton, which the rebels burned to the ground last Summer. This village, or city was built of brick, and must have been a very elegant place, judging from the magnificence of it ruins. Nothing remains but the blackened crumbling walls – a sad commentary on the ravages of war.

(ed: Wilbur, in addition to being a soldier, is a 'field correspondent' for the Green Mountain Freeman of Montpelier, Vermont. His letters are not written home to family but rather are mailed *to the editor of the newspaper. Some 100 letters would appear in the* Freeman *and he signed them 'Anti-Rebel.' He was 'Our War Correspondent' for the* Freeman *and the letters are all archived in the Vermont State Library in bound copies of the newspapers.)*

(Hard Marching Every Day – The Civil War Letters of Pvt. Wilbur Fisk, Emil & Ruth Rosenblatt editors, Lawrence, 1983, p.16 & p. xii-xiii. [Hereafter cited as Fisk])

- - - - -

March 26, 1862 – Camp Brightwood, D. C.
Sgt. Major Elisha Rhodes, 2nd Rhode Island Infantry

This morning we left Camp . . . and . . . [at] the Sixth Street wharf embarked on the side wheel steamer *John Brooks.* Our steamer sailed down the Potomac and joined the fleet at Alexandria. I should think that there were one hundred vessels in sight. . . . Here we anchored for the night . . . the boat is crowded and the men not very comfortable. . . .

(ed: Elisha is his correct first name. The immediate reaction is to assume he is Elijah, a much more common name, which of course would be in error.)

(Rhodes, p. 61.)

- - - - -

March 27, 1862 – Young's Mill
Pvt. Richard Watkins, Co. K – 3rd Virginia Cavalry

My Dear Dear Mary

Your nice little letter of the 24th reached me yesterday . . . It is cold down here but my health is very good indeed. Yesterday we had a Regimental Inspection . . .

Have never heard whether Nat [Watkins] has returned to Glouces-ter or not. Somebody told me that he had enlisted in a company over there. Please write me about it in your next letter as I want to go over to see him. . . . Got bad news again through the papers yesterday of the defeat of Stonewall Jackson near Winchester with a loss of 200 men. Hope the Central Guards are not among the lost. . . . Please tell Mr. Baker [overseer] not to give so much attention to my place as to neglect Mothers. His first duty is to her . . .

Believe I forgot when in Richmond to take the *Examiner* as promised, but am glad now that I did, because it has turned against the administration and I think from no other cause than that the President would not appoint Floyd Secretary of War. . . . I do not consider him a good man nor can I believe that he acted right at Fort Donelson. I still have confidence in Jeff Davis and in the justice of our cause . . .

Good bye my own dear one

(ed: Mail generally makes it back and forth between Richard and Mary in 5 days or less. The Confederacy uses the railroads for delivery and the depots as the post offices. The Moore's Ordinary Depot on the Richmond to Danville Road is the post office closest to southern Prince Edward County where Richard and Mary have their farm. For most of the war the 3ʳᵈ Virginia Cavalry will be within a 125-mile circle of Richmond which aids this consistent delivery.)

(ed: Nathaniel Watkins, Richard's brother, lives in Granville County, N. Carolina, and enlisted in the King and Queen Heavy Artillery which is stationed at Gloucester Point. Richard and Nathaniel were not able to get together while only separated by one mile of the York River.)

(ed: The Richmond Examiner, *for most of the war, is an anti-administration newspaper. It should be noted that the Confederate government did not suppress or close any newspapers that were anti-administration. Freedom of the press was protected. This is*

not true in the United States where more than 200 anti-Lincoln newspapers were closed and ceased to publish for a variety of reasons.)

(Boots & Kisses, p. 70.)

- - - - -

March 27, 1862 – *John Brooks,* Potomac River
Sgt. Major Elisha Rhodes, 2nd Rhode Island Infantry

. . . we started down the river towing two schooners loaded with horses. The weather is warm and . . . delightful. We passed Fort Washington . . . and Mount Vernon . . . The rebel batteries appeared to be deserted, and a large fire was seen at Acquia Creek.

(Rhodes, p. 61.)

- - - - -

March 27, 1862 –Big Bethel, Virginia
Pvt. Wilbur Fisk, 2nd Vermont Infantry

Thursday the 27th we made a reconnoissance in force toward Big Bethel. And succeeded in driving in the enemy's pickets. We held possession of the ground that night, throwing out one company for picket guard. In the morning we 'fell back' and encamped near Newport News. We had started out with the firm belief that we were marching forward to meet the enemy, and we confidently expected victory, and falling back was the very last thing that we desired to do.

(Fisk, p. 16.)

- - - - -

March 28, 1862 – near Fort Monroe, Virginia
Sgt. Major Elisha Rhodes, 2nd Rhode Island Infantry

This morning when I turned out we were nearing Fortress Monroe, and a large fleet of war vessels, including the little *Monitor,* and transports were anchored in Hampton Roads. We landed at the wharf and marched about three miles to . . . what remains of Hampton.

(Rhodes, p. 61.)

- - - - -

March 28, 1862 – Weldon, North Carolina
Private Nathaniel Watkins, King & Queen Artillery

My dear Nannie – It is now 9:00 at night and I am still at this delightful place . . . It is impossible for us to get to Gloucester before Monday or Tuesday. The trains are entirely occupied carrying troops toward Petersburg – for the Peninsula I think . . .

Richmond – Sunday evening –

. . . Left Weldon Saturday morning at 5:00 – trains so long we were all day on the road . . . reached Richmond about dark . . . Kiss Minnie for me, tell Charlie to be a good boy . . .

Your aff husband   N.V.W.

(ed: Nat farmed and ran a classical school near Townsville, North Carolina, in Granville County. Along with other recruits he is on his way to Gloucester Point, Virginia, to join the King & Queen Heavy Artillery.)

(Nathaniel V. Watkins Papers, 39.1-W32, Box 1, Folder 2, Special Collections Research Center, Swem Library, College of William and Mary, Williamsburg, Virginia [Hereafter cited as NVW Letters].)

- - - - -

March 28, 1862 – near Big Bethel, Virginia
Lt. Charles Haydon, 2nd Michigan Infantry

Drilling same as yesterday, weather warm & fair, living hard crackers & coffee. This is a very good diet but there is a great deal of sameness abt it. . . . I have indeed no great amt of money & the rest have none at all. There is a promise of pay in a day or two.

(Haydon, by date.)

- - - - -

March 29, 1862 – Gosport Naval Yard
Lt. John Taylor Wood, C.S. Ironclad *Virginia*

[Commodore Josiah] Tattnall took command on the 29th of March. [The previous 20 days] the *Virginia* had been in drydock. The hull four feet below the shield was [now] covered with 2-inch iron. A new, heavier ram was strongly secured to the bow. Damage to the armor was repaired . . . and rifled guns were supplied with steel-pointed solid shot. Her draught [increased] to 23 feet . . . and her speed reduced to 4 knots.

(ed: They had corrected some weaknesses and magnified others (draft and speed). She was now armed with the correct projectiles to batter and potentially penetrate the armor of the Monitor.)

(B&L-1, Wood, p. 706.)

- - - - -

March 31, 1862 – Newport News, Virginia
Sgt. Major Elisha Rhodes, 2nd Rhode Island Infantry

Our tents have come, and we are in comfort again. Plenty of beef, pork, ham, bacon, etc. Yesterday I had a beefsteak and sweet potatoes. Very good living for a soldier.

(Rhodes, p.61.)

March 31 & April 1, 1862 – 5 miles beyond Big Bethel
Lt. Charles Haydon, 2nd Michigan Infantry

. . . My bowels are turned upside down & and the contents are running out at a double quick. Benson is on the sick list but I will not give in as yet. . . . If I had not been on Court Martial [duty] to day I fear I should have been obliged to go on the sick list. I got some medicine this m'g which stopped the diarhoae but I have vomited no less than eleven times today. . . .

(ed: A common remedy for diarrhea is a clyster (enema) of ipecac. This would quite often cause vomiting. Another remedy

144

is pulverized charcoal (2 oz.) boiled in a pint of milk and taken in doses of a wine-glassful every two hours. Bad water and poor sanitation are the cause and diarrhea/dysentery was the number one killer of soldiers in the war. There is no cure in 1862 and removal from the environment is seldom an option.)

(Haydon, by date. Mackenzie p. 207.)

- - - - -

March 31,1862 – Custis Farm, Virginia
Brig. Gen. Lafayette McLaws, HQ Camp, 2nd Division

My Dearly beloved wife

The country here appears quiet and the enemy have retired again . . . The Peninsula presents a very unfavorable field for operations of a large force . . . it is bounded on one side by the York and on the other side by James River. York river as far up as West Point is more properly an arm of the sea . . . If the enemy should occupy West Point then they would be within forty miles of Richmond be on a railroad which runs from that to Richmond, . . . however it is necessary to pass Yorktown . . . [where] the river narrows and is easily defended by batteries placed on the bluffs there and at Gloucester point on the other side.

. . . There is another arm of the sea called the Warwick River . . . we have dammed up that river at various points and now the country is flooded from a point under the guns of Yorktown to the head of tide water of James River. . . .

Good night my darling wife – I send you a hundred kisses.Your devoted husband

L.McLaws

I now command thirteen regiments and of course am busy all the time . . . excuse my hasty letter.
(McLaws, by date.)

NORTHERN PORTRAIT GALLERY

LT. CHARLES HAYDON, circa 1862

147

LT. DANA GREENE

carte-de-visite, late fall, 1861
Union Regimental Training Camp
Elmira, New York
Private Edgar Steele
85th New York Infantry

reverse: Weed Sewing Machine
Advertisement

PVT. WILBUR FISK, 1861

April, 1862

A continuous stream of ships and vessels of all descriptions are enroute from Baltimore and Alexandria to Fort Monroe with the men and supplies for the Army of the Potomac. McClellan is finally moving against Richmond. General Magruder at Yorktown has fewer than 20,000 Confederates to resist McClellan. General Grant has his armies near Pittsburg Landing on the Tennessee River not far from the Mississippi border. Two major Union armies threaten the South.

On the coast, Fort Pulaski guarding Savannah, Georgia, and Fort Macon guarding North Carolina's Pamlico Sound; both fall to Union forces.

On April 6 and 7 the largest battle of the war to-date is fought near Shiloh Church or Pittsburg Landing, Tennessee. General Johnston and his Confederate forces catch General Grant's men by surprise and in a day-long fight, drive them back against the river at Pittsburg Landing. Johnston is killed and General Beauregard assumes command. Union reinforcements arrive and Grant attacks on the 7th and drives the Confederates back toward Corinth. Over 3,000 men are killed, over 16,000 wounded and more than 3,500 are missing. The nation is shocked by the losses. General Halleck, Grant's superior, arrives to take field command. Grant is getting too much press for winning battles so he makes Grant his second in command and prepares to move on Corinth. It will take him a month to cover a distance that should take two or three days. General Halleck demonstrates that he can move even slower than General McClellan.

General Joe Johnston starts shifting his army from Manassas to the Peninsula to reinforce Magruder. Lincoln keeps General McDowell's army near Washington to protect the capital. General McClellan, who continues to think he is vastly outnumbered, decides to lay siege to Yorktown.

The C.S. Ironclad *Virginia,* along with vessels of the James River Fleet, steams into Hampton Roads to attack the *Monitor.* The *Monitor* will not engage so the James River Fleet captures 2 brigs and a merchantman at the Hampton wharves and takes them and their supplies back to Norfolk. The *Virginia* will make multiple sorties into the Roads during April and the *Monitor* will not give battle.

On April 16 the first Confederate Conscription Act passes Congress. Men from 18-35 years of age are subject to being drafted into the service. Some think that this will be the destruction of the fighting spirit of the Confederate army. What they fail to realize is that without bodies in the ranks, they will not be able to defend their young country.

There are small actions at Dam #1 and Wynne's Mill on the Warwick Line, but it is obvious that McClellan has no intention of a general attack.

On April 17, 1862, the Confederate Congress authorizes a fourth issue of currency. A $165,000,000 printing of $100 notes is shared by Hoyer & Ludwig, J. T. Paterson and Keatinge & Ball. The act also authorizes the printing of $5,000,000 of $1 and $2 notes. Due to a lack of coinage these bills are basically needed as change. B. Duncan receives this contract. An additional $5,000,000, of the small notes is authorized on September 17. It should be noted that many state banks issued fractional currency that is used as change along with these two small denomination bills.

The April rain is a constant on the Peninsula. The soldiers' letters are filled with comments about rain, mud, food, digging trenches and how swampy the land is around Fort Monroe and Yorktown. Private Fisk, of the 2nd Vermont Infantry, notes that, *"we are digging rifle pits in the rain and the mud. . . . hard crackers and a little meat are our only diet."* Private Reid, of the 4th South Carolina Infantry, writes, *"The country here is very low, almost at the level with the river . . . it will . . . be sickly here in the summer. . ."* Lt. Haydon, of the 2nd Michigan Infantry, states that, *"the mud a full 2 inches deep . . . tents were flooded . . . the weather is cold and misty. . ."* As the last half April approaches Magruder and Johnston have some 34,000 men opposite the 100,000 men of the Army of the Potomac. McClellan has a 3-1 advantage and continues to build trenches and bring in large guns to lay siege to the Confederate line.

(Chronicle by date; Day by Day by date; Slabaugh, pp. 48-51.)

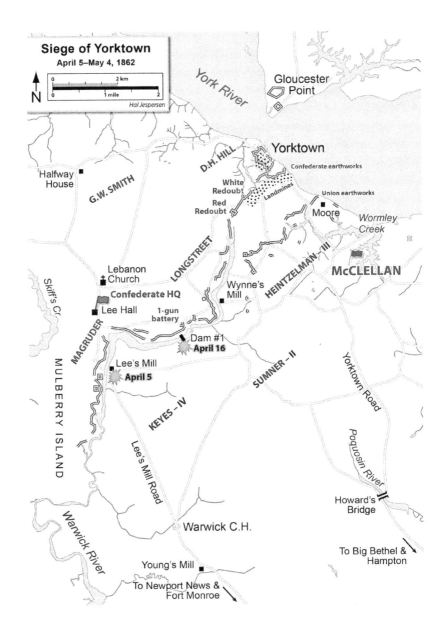

Siege of Yorktown
April 5–May 4, 1862

N

0   2 km
0   1 mile   2

Hal Jespersen

York River

Gloucester Point

Yorktown

D.H. HILL

Confederate earthworks

Halfway House

G.W. SMITH

White Redoubt
Red Redoubt

Landmines

Union earthworks

Moore

Wormley Creek

LONGSTREET

Lebanon Church

Confederate HQ

Lee Hall

1-gun battery

Wynne's Mill

HEINTZELMAN – III

McCLELLAN

Skiff's Cr.

MAGRUDER

Dam #1
April 16

Lee's Mill
April 5

SUMNER – II

Yorktown Road

MULBERRY ISLAND

KEYES – IV

Poquosin River

Lee's Mill Road

Howard's Bridge

Warwick C.H.

To Big Bethel & Hampton

Warwick River

Young's Mill

To Newport News & Fort Monroe

Map by Hal Jesperson, www.cwmaps.com

April, 1862

April 1, 1862 – Young's MIll
Pvt. Richard Watkins, Co. K – 3rd Virginia Cavalry

My own Dear Mary

... I know you are the best wife in the world. I love you too much and yet I do not feel that I love you enough ... Nearly every day we have rumors that the Yankees are advancing ... Our fortifications are getting very strong ... I thank you for the large potatoe patch which you had planted. ... the very best use that you could have made of the gardens. Darling I had to borrow a paper envelope, all our baggage was sent back to Lebanon [Church] some time ago.

(ed: A transition is starting in their letters as Mary no longer calls it 'your farm' and is now making decisions on crops to plant and not plant. Richard, showing very good judgement, supports every decision she makes and never once suggests that she should have done something different.)

(Boots & Kisses, p. 72.)

- - - - -

April 1, 1862 – Cavalry Camp, Young's Mill
Pvt. William C. Corson, Co. G – 3rd Virginia Cavalry

My Own Dear Jennie,

... We do not have any rest day or night ... our men are nearly all completely broken down. The enemy have been more annoying than ever, running in our pickets nearly every day and driving them inside the fortifications at Young's Mill. ... We have a good many on the sick list lately but no serious cases. Billy Price has returned to camp, and I learn that Js Allen reached Yorktown this evening. Have you ever received my picture.

(Corson, pp. 73-74.)

- - - - -

April 2, 1862 – Gloucester Point, Virginia
Pvt. Nathaniel Watkins, King & Queen Artillery

Dear Nannie – We reached this place yesterday evening . . . found the boys well, except slight colds . . . There is a fine prospect for a fight on the Peninsula, and I think one soon . . . about York-town, but Magruder has been reinforced and the fortifications strengthened so much I think we can repulse them with ease . . . Our officers are all good pious men . . . They are all Baptists . . . of course we have no drinking . . . write soon and a long letter. Yr husband N.V.W.

(NVW Letters, by date.)

- - - - -

April 4, 1862 – near Newport News, Virginia
Pvt. Wilbur Fisk, 2nd Vermont Infantry

Skirmishers . . . deploy something in this way: . . . if we are to deploy five paces apart the first man marches within five paces of the road and the next man within five paces of him and ten paces from the road, and so on, stretching out sometimes as far as a whole regiment will reach. To march across fields, over fenc-es, ditches, bogholes, creeks, and through swamps and almost impenetrable thickets with a heavy knapsack stropped to one's back, beside his haversack containing two days rations, a canteen of water, equipments with forty rounds of cartridges and carrying a loaded gun . . . is no easy task.

(Fisk, p. 17)

- - - - -

April 1 – 6, 1862 – Alexandria to Fort Monroe
Corporal Luther Furst, Signal Corps

. . . we received order to embark and in course of an hour all was on board and sailing down the Potomac. Our schooners were towed by the Steamer *Dan Webster.* . . . a few miles below Shipper's Point the *Dan Webster* ran aground and our schooners ran into her, damaging her bow. This occurred about dark and [by] 9 p.m. no signs of moving. . . . In shipping our horses yesterday, one of them went overboard . . . we got him out none the worse for ducking.

We were aground for 40 hours but now are enroute again for Fort Monroe. . . . ten miles beyond St. Mary's River a storm commenced to rage . . . we had to let go our horses and headed for shore to anchor till over. We had to sail back to the mouth of the St. Mary's River for safe anchorage. We stayed 50 hours. . . . Friday morning we anchored in mouth of York River awaiting a steamer to tow us to Fortress Monroe. There are a good many troops landing at this place, I believe Casey's and Hooker's Divisions. . . . a disagreeable trip . . . snowed, rained, blowed for four successive day. Our horses standing on deck of the schooner almost perished. The boys . . . in the old stinking bilge water of the vessel.

(Furst, by date.)

- - - - -

April 4, 1862 – Gloucester Point, Virginia
Pvt. Nathaniel Watkins, King & Queen Artillery

Dear Precious:

. . . Our guard duty is [easy] . . . we stand 8 out of 24 hours . . . standing 2 hours at a time, and resting four . . . stationed . . . in a fort with the York River just a few yards from me – the night was pleasant . . .

(NVW Letters, by date.)

- - - - -

April 6, 1862 – near Little Bethel
Lt. Charles Haydon, 2nd Michigan Infantry

The m'g opens very bright & fair. I slept pretty well last night. Our baggage did not come but I took the precaution to pick up a good blanket by the roadside & found it of great service. I have washed, eaten my breakfast, filled my canteen & made little preparations for whatever the day may bring forth. Our balloon is up nearly all the time viewing the enemies' works. . . . Cattle, sheep &c have been driven in from the country around & we have plenty of meat but no bread. The men are eating raw corn as substitute. . . .

(ed: The Union Army Balloon Corps is aloft observing Confederate activity at Yorktown, Dam #1 and Lee's Mill. This is the first use of airborne observation of enemy positions for reconnaissance and later to direct artillery fire. &c is a standard method of writing etc. in the 1860s. The balloons, being behind Union lines, were out of range of fire from snipers.)

(ed: Charles uses m'g for morning and abt for about. Other common abbreviations are wd, cd, & sd for would, could, and should. Each writer has a style of their own and after reading a few letters you learn their habits.)

(Haydon, by date.)

- - - - -

April 6, 1862 – Warwick County, Virginia
Pvt. Wilbur Fisk, 2nd Vermont Infantry

We are now close upon the rebel fortifications and while I am writing their heavy artillery can occasionally be heard with the prompt reply from our own batteries. The rebels are occupying strong fortifications on James river on the opposite side of the Peninsula from Yorktown and about eight miles from this place. There is a line of fortifications, connecting these two places . . .

and the rebels consider this position impregnable according to the testimony of a number of prisoners.

(Fisk, p. 15.)

- - - - -

April 7, 1862 – West Point, Virginia
Pvt. Tally Simpson, Co. A - 3rd S. C. Infantry

. . . came to West Point, a station where we took the boat, and thence proceeded to Yorktown. The day was cold, windy and rainy, so we enjoyed the river ride very little. A gale blew up some time during the night and tossed the schooner about considerably. We had three or four hundred men aboard and came within an inch or two of having a collision with another schooner . . . We reached Yorktown late at night . . . The next morning we marched seven miles to Lee's Farm . . .

(Far, far from home – The Wartime Letters of Dick and Tally Simpson, 3rd South Carolina, Guy Everson & Edward Simpson editors, New York, 1994, pp. 111-12. [Hereafter cited as Simpson]).

- - - - -

April 7, 1862 – Gloucester Point, Virginia
Pvt. Nathaniel Watkins, King & Queen Artillery

My dear wife – I've no letter from you yet . . . why can't I hear from you . . . the steamer comes day after day [from West Point] and still no letter. . . . Yankee gunboats and steamers lying in full view of us all the time . . . Our men on the Peninsula are being reinforced. . . .

(NVW Letters, by date.)

- - - - -

April 7, 1862 – West Point, Virginia
Pvt. Beaufort Buzhardt, Co. E – 3rd S. C. Infantry

. . . About 12:30 o'clock a portion of our company embarked on the schooner *Sarah Washington*. The distance . . . to Yorktown is thirty-eight miles. A cold rain set in and the wind getting pretty high all hand [except the crew] had to go in the hold . . . [At Yorktown] we anchored out in the river, the captain being afraid to come close to land for fear . . . of injuring his vessel. I got sea sick. . . we were so crowded in the hold that some had almost to sit on the others. . . . At 9 o'clock we were disembarked in a yawl boat for shore. It still continued to rain . . . unpleasant trip.

[Simpson, pp. 112-14.]

- - - -

April 7 – 8, 1862 – 2 miles of Yorktown
Corporal Luther Furst, Signal Corps

We are bivouacked along with the reserve pickets and within two miles of Yorktown and within 15 hundred yards of a strong rebel fort. . . . Our sharpshooters are lying in ambush, picking off their gunners in the fort. . . . on our journey toward Yorktown we passed through the desolate village of Hampton, the noted places of Big and Little Bethel, and are now lying along the picket line . . .

(Furst, by date.)

- - - - -

April 8, 1862 – 10 miles from 'Poquosin' river
Lt. Charles Haydon, 2nd Michigan Infantry

The clay mud is everywhere full 2 inches deep & very slippery. Many of the tents were flooded . . . it was one of the worst nights we have ever seen. . . . Each man recd 5 hard crackers this m'g. . . . It takes little to make a soldier happy. The teams have arrived bringing a pound of biscuit per man & report that coffee & sugar & salt will be here to night. This, although the mud is still deep, the weather cold & misty & wood scarce has made the men . . . as happy as larks.

(Haydon, by date)

- - - - -

April 9, 1862 – Gloucester Point, Virginia
Pvt. Nathaniel Watkins, King & Queen Artillery

Dear Nannie – I write in haste . . . since I have not heard from you
since I got here . . . the fault must be in the mails – do you direct
in care of Capt. Jno R Bagby, King and Queen Artillery, Gloucester
Point . . . We can get no reliable news here . . . I hear hundreds of
rumors every day . . . but think none are worth repeating. . . . Yr
devoted husband N.V.W.

(NVW Letters, by date.)

- - - - -

April 11, 1862 – sortie to Hampton Roads
Lt. John Taylor Wood, C.S. Ironclad *Virginia*

On the 11th we steamed down the harbor to the Roads with six
gunboats [the James River Fleet], fully expecting to meet the
Monitor again and other vessels. . . . but to our surprise we had
the Roads to ourselves. We exchanged a few shots with the Rip-
Rap batteries, but the *Monitor* with other vessels of the fleet remained below Fort Monroe in the Chesapeake Bay . . .

Observing three merchant vessels at anchor close in-shore and
within the bar of Hampton, . . . Commodore Tattnall ordered Lt.
Barney in the *Jamestown* to go in and bring them out. This was
promptly . . . accomplished under a fire from the forts. Two were
brigs loaded with supplies for the army. . . . As the *Jamestown*
towed her prizes under the stern of the English corvette *Rinaldo*
she was enthusiastically cheered [by the British crew].   We remained [in the Roads] all day and at night returned and anchored
off Sewell's Point.

*(ed: A few days later, Lt. Wood recorded, they went back down
hoping the Monitor would come out. The James River Fleet with
four small gunboats were going to try to attack and board from*

four sides . . . wedge the turret, cover the pilot house and all open-
ings with tarps, scale the turret and drop shells down the smoke-
stack. Postwar discussions with Cmdr. Greene disclosed that they
were prepared for such actions and he assured Lt. Wood that they
would have failed.)

(B&L-1, Wood, pp. 706-07.)

- - - - -

April 12, 1862 – Warwick Court House
Sgt. Major Elisha Rhodes, 2nd Rhode Island Infantry

. . . Great was our joy last night when the mail arrived, for it was
the first one for several days. We are still in front of the Rebel
forts, a distance of two miles . . . We have taken several prisoners
in our skirmishes . . . a great battle cannot be long delayed.

(Rhodes, p. 62.)

- - - - -

April 12, 1862 – Gloucester Point, Virginia
Pvt. Nathaniel Watkins, King & Queen Artillery

My dear Nannie - . . . M company is ordered out this morning,
armed with spades & shovels to make an attack on some old
breastworks which interfere with the range of some of our guns.
. . . The Yankee forces first made their appearance around Yorktown last Saturday . . . there has been heavy firing of field pieces .
. . they made a charge, on one of Magruder's batteries at Wynn's
Mill [Wynne's Mill] and lost nearly all of their regiment . . . The
Yankees are said to number 100,000 & Magruder they say has
75,000 . . . Andrew Venable, who had just come on to join the Pr.
Edward Cavalry [Company K – 3rd Virginia Cavalry] said that he
had heard Bro Dick [Pvt. Richard Watkins] had some idea of joining this company but as they wished to make him an officer it is
doubtful. . . . there was a letter from you dated 5th April – the first
letter I have received from anyone since being here . . . Your aff.
Husband N.V.Watkins

(NVW Letters, by date.)

- - - - -

April 13, 1862 – Camp Near Newport News
Pvt. Edgar Steele, Co. B – 85th New York Infantry

Dear Chum [John Debow]

As marching down to Dixie has made me quite lazy I have delayed writing much longer than usual the reason for so doing is that Sunday was my writing day and for the last two Sundays we have marched. We left Camp Warren Washington the 28th of March just at sundown marched ten miles to Alexandria laid down on the brick sidewalk the rest of the night   the next morning found me tough as ever   that was the first time I ever slept out over night   the next morn we went out of the city about two miles to wait for transports to take us down the river   the next day was Sunday and as luck would have it marching orders came to go to the landing after landing ourselves there we made out five companies of us to get aboard the *Elm City* the best boat that runs in the river   The next morning found us sailing on the Dixie   it was a very pleasant voyage being on board two nights and one day we found ourselves at Fortress Monroe then we march through Hampton the place that the rebels burnt before leaveing it   it was once a fine village inhabited by three thousand people but now it lays a heap of ruins so much for war   finely we encamp about ten miles from Fortress Monroe on the road to Yorktown   we waited there for the rest of our division   they came along however in due time   the next Sunday we went a short distance encamp again the rest of the time we have done picket duty and made roads for the Artilary as the land here is low and swampy and the rebels took up all the bridges and burnt every thing they could but the report is that we leave here tomorrow in the direction of Yorktown   there is over one hundred thousand union troops here and the report is that the rebels have nearly that number and perhaps more   it will be by no doubt the hardest fought battle of the campaign as they are so well fortified   Yorktown is about twenty miles from here we are hemed [hemmed] in on three sides by water and on the fourth by the enemy and time will show whether we stay hemed so or not and that before long already I have heard their guns and seen their tents across the river   they have sent a few shells at us but did no harm, the monortor [*Monitor*] is here in the harbor   I have also catch a glimpse of the rebel merimac [*Merrimac - Virginia*] much oblige for that paper you sent me as newpapers are out of the question here   E H Steele Washington DC 85th Regt NYV 3rd Brigade of Caseys division Company B care of Capt Clark

(ed: Marvelous detail of sailing time to Fort Monroe, the destruction of Hampton, the Gen. McClellan and Alan Pinkerton estimates of 100,000 Confederate troops [Gen. Magruder had about 25,000 in early April], and also his notes of seeing the two ironclads . . . the monortor and the merimac. Edgar will be killed in action in the battle of Seven Pines [Fairfield] on May 31, 1862.)

(ed: There is minimal punctuation, very few capitalizations, many incorrectly spelled words and Edgar quite often leaves a blank space before he begins his next thought. Edgar addressed the envelope to John Debow of Ontario Cty., NY, otherwise we would only have his 'Dear Chum' greeting.)

(ed: Also included in the envelope was a marvelous carte de visite of Pvt. Steele in uniform. Advertising on the back is for the Weed Sewing Machine Company and notes a branch office in Elmira, NY. Elmira was the muster and training point for the Regiment in August, 1861. On December 3, 1861 they departed for Camp Warren, Washington, D. C. This photo was taken in the fall of 1861 while they were in Elmira.)

(ed: Following the Seven Days Campaign, the 85th will spend almost a year in the Suffolk area of SE Virginia, then spend another year in coastal North Carolina around Kinston and Plymouth. They will join Sherman in the drive from Goldsboro, to Raleigh and finally to Durham and Greensboro for the surrender of the Army of Tennessee. They lost only 1 officer and 34 men killed or

mortally wounded in the entire war. Private Steele is one of those unlucky 34 when he dies in battle at Seven Pines on May 31, 1862. Sadly, Edgar only lived 6 weeks after writing this letter to John Debow. The 85th New York will lose 2 officers and 324 men to disease. That is a 10-1 ratio of disease vs. battle deaths.)

(Private Edgar Steele Letter, SC01325, Special Collections Research Center, Swem Library, College of William & Mary, Williamsburg, Virginia)

- - - - -

April 13, 1862 – Lee's Farm, Virginia
Pvt. Tally Simpson, 3rd S. Carolina Infantry

. . . Genl Joseph Johnston is here. I saw him myself. . . . a long mill pond is all that separates our pickets from those of the enemy. . . . Both parties are making preparation for a general engagement. We have upwards of two thousand negro men at work throwing up breast works. . . . the enemy is making railroads to transport siege guns to our lines to shell us out of the fortifications.

(Simpson, p. 114.)

- - - - -

April 13, 1862 – 4 1/2 miles from Railroad Point
Lt. Charles Haydon, 2nd Michigan Infantry

You cannot get out 20 men of this Regt. to divine services unless it be a funeral. They will play cards &c all day on Sunday, almost to a man swear beyond anything I ever heard elsewhere & steal everything they can put their hands on. Still there is a large amt of a certain kind of rude religious feeling. Perhaps it is more allied in a kind of superstition . . .

(Haydon, by date.)

- - - - -

April 14, 1862 – On board the *A. W. Schulz*
Sgt. Hamilton Branch, 8th Georgia Infantry

Dear Mother

We left . . . Richmond at 4 PM yesterday and marched down Main St. . . . We got on board this boat at 9 PM and started for Yorktown. We have passed Jamestown and are in sight of Williamsburg. . . . our destination is near Yorktown. All the boys are well. I gave Mrs. Hines a letter to mail to you.

Your loving son

Hammie

(Charlotte's Boys – The Civil War Letters of the Branch Family of Savannah, Mauriel P. Joslyn – editor, Berryville, 1996, p.111. [Hereafter cited as Branch]).

- - - - -

April 14, 1862 – Warwick Court House
Sgt. Major Elisha Rhodes, 2nd Rhode Island Infantry

. . . I made a long tramp to see the sights. I went as far as Young's Mill . . . I examined their deserted forts and was surprised to find that they had such comfortable quarters. Their old camps looked like villages with well built huts of pine slabs. The forts are . . . on a hill beneath which is a swamp. A pond was made by a dam and a gate was all in readiness to open and [flood] the swamp. For some reason the Rebels did not wait for us to attack . . .

(Rhodes, p 62.)

- - - - -

April 15, 1862 – near Yorktown
Corporal Luther Furst, Signal Corps

. . . in camp near Yorktown all day. The men were generally engaged in cleaning their revolvers and other equipment.

(Furst, by date.)

- - - - -

Mid April, 1862 – Yorktown, Virginia

[Pvt.] [S.] A. Bumgarner

Dear Brother I again write to you I hope you are all well I received unkle john's letter and was glad to hear that they were all well tell Grany ever to remember me tell unkle John I am not able to write to him but I want you to hurry and come and bring me some crout dried fruit and onions and some butter and half jug of honey or a tub of honey you may tell them at home my fare is bad and I want them to help me I will receive assistance from any source so you must help me at home as I mus live on my money at a high rate I have to give 25 cents for one little pie and 25 cents per dozen for eggs and one dollar a piece for chickens this takes money as sist us [assist us] while we are sick and save our money you had better come as quick as you can we have letters gone home that we wrote last Sunday tell them all to remember us till we come _____ bring us some dried shell beans to make some bang belly for we like it very well. You need not bring us any corn meal we have corn meal plenty Our men whipped the yankees at Yorktown Va and have taken thirteen hundred prisoners and run them off I cannot give the particulars. I am so nervous I can not write I must stop till Rash and [rations]

[S] A Bumgarner

(ed: The letter is undated. The only significant battle during the spring of 1862, near Yorktown, would be the battle of Dam #1 on April 16, 1862. The Union had 163 casualties in this failed attack but camp rumors could easily spread wild exaggerations. So, lacking better evidence I have dated this letter as mid-April, 1862.)

(ed: In line 3, crout dried fruit and onions if punctuated would read; crout, dried fruit and onions. Pickled cabbage (kraut or crout) was a staple and other pickled vegetables could also possibly fall under the heading of crout. A private was paid $11 per month and paid on the last day of the even numbered months for the previous two months service. That money does not go very

far helping a private buy food to supplement his rations.)

(ed: Mr. Bumgarner is proving a bit elusive in the military records. The Bumgarners that have been located are in units that were not at Yorktown, arrived in Virginia well after the battle or the Bumgarner in that unit enlisted after this time frame. We should assume he is in either a Virginia or North Carolina unit based on his comments about "bringing us" some items. There is also the very real possibility that he is recorded in Confederate records as a Bumgardner, Bumgardener, Bumgarden or some other spelling. More research is required.)

([Pvt.] [S.] A. Bumgarner Letter, SC00270, Special Collections Research Center, Swem Library, College of William & Mary, Williamsburg, Virginia)

- - - - -

April 15, 1862 – camp near Lebanon Church
Sgt. Hamilton Branch, 8th Georgia Infantry

We arrived at Kings Landing at 10 AM yesterday and marched to this camp which is 9 miles from the landing. We stacked arms and were told that we would have flour and bacon given us and that we must cook it up and be ready to march at dawn . . . We did . . . but did not move. . . .

(ed: The 8th Georgia has been sent to reinforce General Magruder on the Warwick [river] line. The Warwick was a sluggish stream, running through a densely wooded swamp. Originally, two dams existed at Wynne's Mill and Lee's Mill. Confederate forces built three more, flooding the stream to a hundred yards in width at some locations which greatly discouraged frontal attacks. The center of the line was at Dam #1.)

(Branch, p. 112).

- - - - -

April 15, 1862 – Gloucester Point, Virginia

Pvt. Nathaniel Watkins, King & Queen Artillery

My dear Precious - . . . Very rapid and heavy firing of big guns at Yorktown . . . yesterday two steamers came up with in about two miles of us . . . we hurried up to our guns . . . fired a few rounds at them . . . they drew off. . . .

Your aff & devoted husband   N.V.W.

(NVW Letters, by date.)

- - - - -

April 16, 1862 – near Dam # 1 –Yorktown
Corporal Henry E. Dunbar, Co. C – 3rd Vermont Infantry

My Dear Mary

Thank God I am alive yet & . . . comparatively well. We went yesterday morn up to within less than ¼ mile of the enemys works where they had 3 or 4,000 and 2 large guns . . . about 3 p.m. we threw off our Blankets and . . . started . . . and come to water . . . found it to be knee deep . . . then went in to our waists and where some crossed they went in up to their necks. The bullets began to meet us when we first got in the water . . . I got in directly behind Heath with the Flag a ball struck me on the left side of my head & partly knocked me down . . . It sort of confused me for 2 or 3 hours & that side of my head is some numb yet . . . About half of us got into their works . . . but couldn't hold it & Harrington saw . . . that we must all be killed or taken prisoner he ordered us to retreat . . . there is 22 killed 56 wounded & 5 missing . . . I crawled back to Camp & Jim built up a good fire and made me some coffee . . . I ached all night& this morn is so lame I can scarcely go, but I am alive . . .

Aff. yours, H E Dunbar

(ed: From the wording of his letter we know that Henry was in the Color Guard. The group of men carrying the colors for any unit

*were the prime target. Each company followed the flag which
served as the guide on the battlefield. Verbal communication was
virtually impossible. There was no more dangerous infantry as-
signment than being part of the color guard.)*

(*A War of the People – Vermont Civil War Letters*, Jeffry Marshall editor, Hanover, 1999, pp. 74-75. [Hereafter cited as Vermont]

- - - - -

April 16, 1862 – Near Dam #1 – Warwick Line
Corporal Luther Furst, Signal Corps

. . . the past two hours the contest has been raging. The ambulances are conveying wounded to the rear . . . General Smith's
Brigade is advancing slowly but I don't think they will take the
fort tonight. We have established a signal station and expect to
be on duty all night. . . . Four companies of the Vermont Regiment
charged the fort but were repulsed with heavy loss. It was a fool-
hardy order of General Smith, who was . . . thrown off his horse
several times during the day. We signal corps boys returned to
camp next morning.

(*ed: General Smith falling off of his horse, multiple times, is mentioned in many soldiers' letters from the action around Dam #1.
Many accuse him of being drunk.*)

(Furst, by date.)

- - - - -

April 16, 1862 – Dam #1 – Warwick Line
Cpl. Marshall H. Twitchell, Co. I - 4th Vermont Infantry

. . . on the 16th of April took part in that un-necessary sacrifice of
human life known as the battle of Lee's Mills. . . . Four companies
of our regiment commenced the fight by skirmishing down by the
creek on the right, four companies including Company I moved
out into the field and . . . started for the dam . . . to cross for

the purpose of capturing the enemy's artillery. . . . Upon our appearance in the open field it became evident to the dullest mind that none of us would be able to reach the other side by way of the dam. We threw ourselves upon the ground awaiting further orders . . . we soon received orders to get back to the woods. . . . Vermont paid 192 men killed and wounded for a reputation of bravery . . .

(Carpetbagger from Vermont – Autobiography of Marshall H. Twitchell, edited by Ted Tunnell, Baton Rouge, 1989, pp. 34-35. [Hereafter cited as Twitchell.]

- - - - -

April 16, 1862 – Dam # 1 – Warwick LIne
Private Eli P. Landers, Cobb's Legion

We did not have time to organize our regiment for the counterattack. We all run in and shot when we had the chance and never formed no line. If a man could get behind a tree it was alright. Some of the boys never fired a gun. Some lay behind logs as close to the ground as young rabbits till the battle was over. One or two of our company run back to camp but as for my part I thought I would stay till the fun was over . . . It did not frighten me as bad as I expected it would but I tell you when the bullets would whistle around my head I felt sort of ticklish.

(Yorktown's Civil War Siege, Quarstein & Moore, Charleston, 2012, p. 109, quoted from *Weep Not for Me, Dear Mother: The War Experiences of Private Eli Pinson Landers of the 16th Regiment Georgia Volunteers*)

- - - - -

April 16, 1862 – Dam #1
Pvt. Wilbur Fisk, 2nd Vermont Infantry

. . . received orders about three o'clock to march – somewhere to support the Third [Vermont]. As we emerged into the clearing, the smoke of the battle was rolling up in dense clouds . . . as our batteries vomited forth their death dealing missiles . . . We rushed past the batteries in their rear to the left, losing but one man killed, and one wounded by a piece of shell from the enemy. . . . There were other regiments ahead of us, and we were to be their support in case they attempted to cross the creek. The rebels ceased firing, and it was unknown whether they evacuated or were playing possum. As the Third and Sixth attempted to cross, they found to their cost that the enemy had a stronghold there, and were determined to hold it. The water, supposed to be about knee deep, was found to be much deeper . . . When they were in the worst possible situation, the rebels opened fire on them from their rifle-pits, with terrible effect. . . . In a few minutes squads of men were seen emerging from the woods with their wounded comrades, carrying some on their backs, some on stretchers, and other were assisted hobbling along . . . and many alas! were left that could not be recovered. . . . The men were wet to their waists, and of course every cartridge was soaked, and rendered for the time worthless. The dead were not recovered till Saturday, under a flag of truce.

(Fisk, pp. 20-21.)

- - - - -

April 16, 1862 – Camp Near Lee's Mill
Pvt. William C. Corson, Co. G – 3rd Virginia Cavalry

My Dear Jennie,

. . . We are close to enemy our lines being only a few hundred yards apart. Skirmishing is going on every day and men are lost on both sides in nearly every little engagement. The enemy's sharpshooters pick off a great many of our men. . . . I presume you have seen an account of the fight that took place . . . after the enemy came up [Dam #1]. Our troop was close but did not participate. Four companies of a Vermont Regiment, supported by several other regiments attempted to capture one of our batteries, but were repulsed with heavy loss. The enemy behaved very bravely charging through water waist deep right up to our Rifle pits. Only one company succeeded in getting through the water and nearly every man of it was killed.

(Corson, pp. 75-76.)

- - - - -

April 16, 1862 – near the York River
Lt. Charles Haydon, 2nd Michigan Infantry

Our balloon has hung all day like an evil spirit over their doomed works. It must be very aggravating to have a man just beyond their reach looking down on every move they make and telegraphing it as soon as made to Gen. McClellan. They have a balloon but for some reason it will not stay up more than 2 minutes at a time & must be more vexatious than useful.

(ed: Professor Thaddeus Lowe and the Union balloon corps use balloons filled with hydrogen. The Confederate balloons used hot air and the time aloft varied but was certainly longer than the estimates of Lt. Hayden. The combining of the surveillance with the ability to telegraph enemy movements was of tremendous tactical value. Sadly, for the Union, General McClellan made poor use of the knowledge gained.)

(Haydon, by date.)

- - - - -

April 17, 1862 – camp near Yorktown
Cpl. George French, 3rd Vermont Infantry

Dear Friends

The 3rd Vermont has won a name, but Oh! at what a cost. We fought and won but were finally driven from our position by overwhelming numbers . . .

Friday 18th P.M.

[We had] a little band of less than 200 men . . . the creek is a great hindrance to storming the rebel works . . . we moved down the slope, . . . past the pickets, . . . to the edge [of the creek] when the bullets began to whistle . . . Before us was the creek, twenty [to] forty rods in width . . . the other shore a dense woods filled with rifle pits and rebels . . . Into the water we plunged . . . pushed over logs, roots and every kind of impediment . . . we set foot on dry land . . . every rebel left the rifle pits . . . we held them . . . for a long hour waiting for reinforcements . . . a long line of rebels were coming . . . we fell back into the creek and retreated with all due haste. . . . the water boiled around us with bullets . . . of the 192 men who went into the creek 88 were killed, wounded or missing. Johnny Backum was shot through the left shoulder . . . he stands a chance to recover . . . Sgt. Holmes got a ball in the edge of his left ear – just enough to mark him. I am unhurt . . .

Good bye George

(ed: George will contract diarrhea/dysentery in June and July in the Chickahominy swamps which will eventually send him to the Fort McHenry Hospital, in Baltimore, where he will die from chronic dysentery (bloody flux) on November 4, 1862. Disease killed more men than battle and diarrhea/dysentery killed more men than any other disease.)

(ed: As the diarrhea worsens it becomes dysentery, or in the advanced stage, bloody dysentery. This was sometimes referred to as flux and bloody flux. The symptoms include, "bearing down pains, the discharge consisting of pure blood or blood and matter, sometimes resembling the shred or washing of raw flesh, a constant desire to stool and vomiting.")

(ed: Mackenzie recommends the use of clisters (enemas) to treat advanced cases. "Clisters of castor oil, with the addition of an ounce of olive oil, and twenty drops of laudanum, may likewise be injected several times a day." Laudanum is a 10% tincture of opium. The other 90% is usually either wine or whiskey. These

clisters will not cure the patient but all that opium and whiskey will make the patient oblivious to any pain and suffering.)

(Vermont History – Vermont Historical Society, Fall 1981, Vol. 49, #4, pp. 225-29.; Mackenzie, p. 207.))

- - - - -

April 18, 1862 – camp near Lebanon Church
Pvt. Richard Watkins, Co. K – 3rd Virginia Cavalry

My Precious Mary

Since my last written about 3 or 4 days ago nothing of especial interest has happened except a sharp engagement on the 16th . . . at Dam No 1 on our line of defense . . . From the most reliable information our loss was about 25 killed and about 70 wounded. After fighting more than an hour the enemy were repulsed . . . with quite heavy loss . . . Col. McKinney (Cousin Barrett's nephew) was killed while leading his regiment. . . . We have been strongly reinforced . . . and if Genl McClellan reaches Richmond by this route his picked men will have to do some very pretty fighting. Darling I see by Proclamation of Gov. Letcher that as soon as our time is out we will be immediately drafted as militia and put right back into service again, I am sorry indeed that this is so . . . The condition of the country is such as to require every man in the field who can bear arms. . . . I still think of joining the artillery with Nat. Since my last letter about one half of our company has been sick I among the rest from exposure and the irregular & poor fare but yesterday I took a large opium & ipecac pill and today some crème of tartar and feel nearly well again . . . too late to write more today . . . So good night my dear dear precious one . . .

(Boots & Kisses, p. 76.)

- - - - -

April 18, 1862 – Gloucester Point
Private Nathaniel Watkins, King & Queen Artillery

My dear wife - . . . give you our bill of fare for the day. For break-fast – coffee, nice biscuit, butter, bread, fried meat and gravy – for dinner – corn bread, beef, fried meat, eggs scrambled and raw oysters (first rate) – supper – same as breakfast with stewed oysters. We get fresh shad whenever we want it. You would be amazed to see me eat, sometimes six or eight large biscuits for breakfast . . . I can hear nothing from Bro Dick here . . .

(ed: Dick and Nat are separated by the York River. Both of the wives, Nannie and Mary, give them grief for never even trying to cross the York to see the other. The cavalry moved around but were quite often near Yorktown and Richard could have had a local row him across and he could have visited Nat at the camp of the King & Queen Artillery near the Gloucester Point fortifications.)

(NVW Letters, by date.)

- - - - -

April 18, 1862 – Custis Farm on Peninsula
Private Tally Simpson, 3rd S. Carolina Infantry

The conscription bill passed by Congress is one of the best things for the country imaginable. Many men, dead to honor, patriotism, pride, and ambition, who were going home when a battle decisive of our country's fate was expected to be fought the next day, have been detained by force. Many who had thrown down their arms when the rest were called to remain . . . returned that night or the next day of their own accord. . . . Since the Act of Congress was passed after the term of service of this brigade had expired it is thought that it (the act) does not apply to the regts composing it and that the men who have not revolunteered will be permitted to return home after the 1st of May. [Then they will be conscripted into new units] They [the men] are now, I think, much better pleased.

(Simpson, pp. 116-17 from 4-24-62 letter.)

- - - - -

April 18, 1862 – Yorktown, Virginia
Private J. W. Reid, 4th S. Carolina Infantry

I haven't the time or room to write much at present. The Conscript Bill has passed in Congress, keeping all men in service between the ages of eighteen and thirty five for three years or during the war . . . I am over 35 and will be discharged in July, if a Yankee bullett don't discharge me sooner. . . .

This Conscript Act will do away with all the patriotism we have. . . . My private opinion is that our Confederacy is gone up, or will go soon, as the soldiers themselves will take little or no interest in it hereafter. . . . Remember what I say, it will eventually be our ruin.

I am mad at the action of Congress and Jeff Davis, and I won't deny it.

We have had same pretty hard times of late. We left camp near Richmond night before last about eight o'clock and walked eight miles to the James river at Richmond, and about 2 o'clock the next morning went onboard a steamer called the *West Point* and came down river about 100 miles, landed and marched 8 miles. We are now near Yorktown and there is firing going on there now. We don't know at what moment we may be called upon to fight . . .

I am yet in tolerable spirits and as stout as a mule. I can walk fifty miles a day, swim the James river from bank to bank, can jump up and knock my heels together three times . . . and whip any Yankee this side of the Mason and Dixon line . . .

Yours as ever,

J. W. R.

(ed: Initial Confederate forces were all volunteer. It is now obvious that patriotism and volunteering will not fill the ranks. This is

the first of three different age ranges that will be draftable as the war progresses. You may hire a substitute to take your place but the laws regarding substitutes will also be changed as the war progresses. There are also exemptions for certain jobs and those slots become highly sought after to avoid military service.)

(History of the 4ᵗʰ Regiment S. C. Volunteers, J. W. Reid, Dayton, 1975, pp. 75-77 [hereafter cited as Reid])

- - - - -

April 19, 1862 – near Dam #1
Sgt. Hamilton Branch, 8ᵗʰ Georgia Infantry

The [Yankees] paid 60 men $50 apiece to cross the creek and lead their advance . . . The 60 men belonged to Companys D, E, & K of the 3ʳᵈ Vermont Regiment, about 40 of them are now lay-ing in front of our trenches . . . not 30 feet from me. We can-not burry them because the enemy are fireing at us [with] their sharpshooters all the time. . . . We are all safe yet.

(Branch, p. 115.)

- - - - -

April 20, 1862 – near Yorktown
Lt. Charles Haydon, 2ⁿᵈ Michigan Infantry

The *Monitor* and the *Merrimac [Virginia]* I see are making a great stir in the world. The latter [*Virginia*] gives the army here much more trouble than we would willingly acknowledge. The fear of it creates not a little uneasiness. If it was outside the Roads [in Chesapeake Bay] our communications at Ship Point would be de-stroyed and our operations much embarrassed.

(Haydon, by date.)

- - - - -

April 20, 1862 – Custis Farm on Peninsula

Pvt. Tally Simpson, 3rd S. Carolina Infantry

I have, with the rest of my mess, enjoyed excellent health . . . tho the fare generally has been scanty and poor, yet we have stood the marches and drills and work very well indeed. Bacon, beef, and flour are the articles of food we sometimes draw, rice once or twice, coffee we never see. We drink sassafras tea when we can get sugar.

We are still living in the open air without tents, but with little houses made of blankets, we make out very well. I am doing remarkably well with the small amount of clothing I have . . . I am fearful about keeping myself shod. My boots are giving way and no prospects for another pair.

(Simpson, p. 177 of 4-24-62 letter.)

- - - - -

April 20 – 21, 1862 – Warwick line near Yorktown
Corporal Luther Furst, Signal Corps

Yesterday and today it has been raining and the soldiers have a rough time of it. . . . I was down to Cheeseman's Point getting forage and rations.

(Furst, by date.)

- - - - -

April 22, 1862 – camp near Lebanon Church
Pvt. Richard Watkins, Co. K – 3rd Virginia Cavalry

My Dear Dear Mary

. . . We have a great deal of rain but since bringing a few of our tents we have been comparatively comfortable . . . Andrew Venable seeing my scarcity of paper very kindly presented half a quire and so I must write a little more.

Would you like to know something of our defence . . . There are some redoubts between Fort Magruder and Yorktown . . . North of Ft. Magruder sat the head of the Warwick [River] in a swamp, then comes Wynne's Mill pond, then strong fortifications at the mill, a large pond between this and Dam No. 1 another between that & Dam no. 2. another between that and Lee's Mill after passing which the river widens & deepens rapidly. Heavy guns are mounted at each of the points named above and entrenchments along the whole extend from Fort Magruder to a point far below Lee's Mill. Warwick River a mile wide at its mouth is blockaded so as to prevent enemy gunboats from entering it. Mulberry Island or Mulberry Point (it only being an island at high tide) is strongly fortified and casmated i e made bombproof. Our little Troop have been stationed all the while in a field near Lee's Mill which is called the center of the line, a little in our rear in Lee's dwelling house is Genl. Magruder who is using that as his headquarters for the present. It is a large & quite pretty brick house surrounded by green wheat fields all of which were nicely enclosed three weeks ago and promised a fine crop this summer, but the fences have been burnt up, wagons and artillery and cavalry have passed over & over them [the fields] until they are almost completely destroyed.

. . . It would not surprise me at all if he [Union General McClellan] should draw off his army and make his attack elsewhere. He may rest satisfied though that he cannot reach Richmond without a sever struggle. It cannot be taken as Nashville was.

Good bye darling write to me soon & give much love to all.

(ed: A quire is 1/20 of a 500 sheet ream. A quire is sold as 24 sheets even though the actual math would provide 25 sheets. Andrew gave Richard 12 sheets which would be a half quire)

(ed: Richard's directions are a little confusing. The defensive line began on the York River and ran to a point near the headwaters of the Warwick where Fort Magruder was located. It then runs down the Warwick past the mills, dams and ponds Richard mentions till it reaches Fort Crafford, on Mulberry Island, on the James River. The line goes entirely across the Peninsula and makes excellent use of waterways as a defensive feature for the majority of its length. See the 'Siege of Yorktown Map' by Hal Jespersen to assist with understanding the Warwick Line.)

(ed: Friendly forces were just as hard on the fences, farmland and crops as the forces of the enemy. Comments in these letters will confirm the dual army impact on farms.)

(Boots & Kisses, pp. 77-79.)

- - - - -

April 22, 1862 – Gloucester Point, Virginia
Pvt. Nathaniel Watkins, King & Queen Artillery

My dear Nannie - . . . I got a nice pair of first rate shoes in R'mond for $5.00 & a pr. of nice green pants for $8 no other clothes. . . . I wish you could have seen me sewing up my pants, which had ripped, yesterday. Had no idea I could do it half so well & it was very difficult job too, as the rip was where the pocket was put at . . . if I stay here long I may set up a tailor's shop. . . .

N.V.W.

(NVW Letters, by date.)

- - - - -

April 23, 1862 – Right Flank – The Peninsula
Brig. Gen. Lafayette McLaws, HQ 2 Division

My dear darling wife –

I read the letter of Johnny and Willie with which I am much pleased, and will answer them in a day or two. I showed them to their uncle Hugh . . . Good bye for the present. When I do not write I ask Hugh to mention me in his letters to Sallie. . . . Every one is well . . .

Kiss my little daughter and the baby and ten thousand for your-self.

Your devoted husband

(ed: McLaws' 13 regiments were divided into three brigades and several artillery units. He basically had a hodge-podge of units, he had gained the confidence of Gen. Magruder, and therefore they were lumped together as his Division. On April 16th at Dam #1 he commanded: Cobb's Brigade (6 regiments), Anderson's Brigade (2 regiments), August's Brigade (2 regiments), and 6 artillery commands: Cabell's 1st Virginia, Magruder Light Artillery, Troup Artillery, 1st Co. Washington Artillery, 2nd Co. Washington Artillery and 1st Co. Richmond Howitzers. In addition, the 32nd Virginia Infantry, was under his command but stationed in Williamsburg.)

(McLaws, by date. Yorktown's Civil War Siege, p. 159.)

- - - - -

April 24, 1862 – camp before Lee's Mill
Pvt. Wilbur Fisk, 2nd Vermont Infantry

. . . if there is anybody in the world that . . . "endureth all things," it is the soldier. All night we are employed in digging rifle-pits in the rain and mud, and the following night on picket, and then should a night occur with no duty for us to do, ten chances to one if we are not called into line at the alarm of the pickets, to repel the enemy. Hard crackers and occasionally a little meat are our only diet. . . . the boys went swimming in the James river. The trees are beginning to put out their foliage, and the grass is starting up all about. . . .

(Fisk, p. 19)

- - - - -

April 24, 1862 – camp near Yorktown, Virginia
Pvt. J. W. Reid, 4th S. Carolina Infantry

Nothing new or important. We are within a hundred yards of the house where Washington had his headquarters previous to the surrender of Lord Cornwallis. I have just returned from the place. It is a small old-fashioned house, painted white. . . . We are stationed between the James and York rivers, and not very far from either. The country here is very low, almost on a level with the river. . . . It will undoubtedly be sickly here in the summer. . . .

We have not been in the trenches on guard as yet . . . There are a few men killed about the trenches every day.

We were today reduced from a regiment to a battalion of five companies. A regiment has ten. Charles Mattison is elected Major of the battalion.

As the mail is about starting I will stop.

Yours as ever,

J. W. Reid.

(Reid, p.77.)

- - - - -

April 24, 1862 – Gloucester Point, Virginia
Pvt. Nathaniel Watkins, King & Queen Artillery

My dear wife . . . Gloucester Point is just one huge bank of sand . . . the woods around are principally pines . . . The Yankee steamers have been throwing shells at us again since I commenced writing . . .

Your devoted husband   N.V.W.

(NVW Letters, by date.)

- - - - -

April 24, 1862 – Custis Farm on Peninsula
Pvt. Tally Simpson, 3rd S. Carolina Infantry

Our men are working some, but not a great deal. Details are made to cut down timber and dig entrenchments. The Sergeant is now calling for 8 to 10 men for that purpose. . . . Many very large bass and eels have been caught. We have basket in the stream [Skiff Creek]. Caught six eels last night. . . .

(Simpson, p. 118.)

- - - - -

April 23-24, 1862 – camp near Lebanon Church
Pvt. Richard Watkins, Co. K – 3rd Virginia Cavalry

My Darling Mary

. . . We have had no skirmishing today for the first time since the advance of the enemy . . .

I am so glad my children are your children and are being brought up by you. May God in his infinite mercy long spare your life & health & their lives & health & render all of you happy . . . in this life & that which is to come is my constant prayer. Good bye, my precious darling.

(Boots & Kisses, p. 79.)

- - - - -

April 25, 1862 – Warwick Court House
Sgt. Major Elisha Rhodes, 2nd Rhode Island Infantry

. . . I borrowed the Adjutant's horse, and with Chaplain Jameson, took a ride. . . . We crossed Deep Creek and kept on until we reached Young's farm at the mouth of the Warwick River. His plantation contains some five thousand acres, and he did own

184

one hundred slaves. A large three story house stands upon a hill and the chimneys are on the outside. About a dozen cabins are clustered in the yard while a path leads down to the spring house. The house faces the river and a beautiful flower garden is in front. . . . The beach in front of the home is covered with fine black and white sand. The Rebels have some forts on the other side of the river, but although we walked on the beach they did not fire at us. . . .

(Rhodes, p. 63.)

- - - - -

April 25, 1862 – Peninsula – Right Flank
Brig. Gen. Lafayette McLaws, HQ 2 Division

My dear wife

. . . We have skirmishing all along the line all the time, . . . with casualties . . . a few killed a few wounded. The service of the troops is very severe and we have many sick.

General Magruder is fond of dress and parade and of company, conceals nothing, delights to have a crowd about him . . . He never moves from headquarters without having five or six aides and a dozen or more orderlies. . . .

General Johnston will never speak of official matters to but the person intended, dislikes to have a crowd . . . often rides alone, never with more than two aides . . . always dresses neatly and in a uniform coat – if you have business with him it is yes or no. . . .

April 26 12M.

I send five dollars to the children, to the boys for writing me and for my daughter for wishing to do it. . . .

Good bye until I have time to write again,

(McLaws, by date.)

- - - - -

April 25, 1862 – 5 miles south of Yorktown
Captain George Quimby, Co. D – 4th Vermont Infantry

We are here in the woods about 25 miles from Fortress Monroe .
. . on the Warwick creek . . . Our conveniences and accommodations are on a huge scale. Officers are allowed to carry a small
valise in which are all their worldly goods . . . We are supposed to
have two tents for the Line Officers and we have got one . . . if we
move any great distance, 4 or 5 miles . . . we have to remain two
or three days without anything . . . so if we happen to move in the
rain which the boys say always happens it makes it *agreeable* –

(Vermont, pp. 75-76.)

- - - - -

April 25, 1862 – camp near Lebanon Church
2nd Lt. Richard Watkins, Co. K – 3rd Virginia Cavalry

My Darling Mary

. . . This morning an order came from Genl. Johnston who is now
in command here that our Regiment of cavalry was to be reor-
ganized today by the election of officers in each company under
the conscription bill. I had determined not to re-enlist and being
over 35 years of age flattered myself that I could return quietly
home . . . but it seems the members . . . determined to give me
the office of first or second lieutenant. Several of them came to
me and entreated me to remain with them and take one of these
offices. . . . am therefore enlisted for two years more should the
war continue that long. This office gives me a good salary, gives
me a chance of getting furloughs more frequently . . . Besides this
the thought occurred to me that if I return home . . . I would probably be soon drafted with the militia and sent into the field again.
I hope darling that this step will meet your approval. Would certainly have consulted with you about it if I had had the time. . . .

186

tell Mother [Mrs. Watkins] & the girls that Lieut. Watkins sends his love to them. Good bye

(Boots & Kisses, pp. 80-81.)

- - - - -

April 26, 1862 – the Warwick Line
Sgt. Hamilton Branch, 8th Georgia Infantry

. . . I was very sorry to hear of the fall of Fort Pulaski [Savannah]. I never expected to hear of the fall of that Fort. I thought the men in that fort would hold out until every man was killed or wounded and that the last man would blow the fort up. But no if it is as we hear they have proved themselves poor Georgians. Mother if the 8th Ga. had of been in that fort there would have been someone killed.

(ed: Hamilton is upset that this key fort protecting Savannah would be surrendered after the opening bombardment from Tybee Island. At the very least Confederate forces could have blown up the fort after Union shelling had reduced the fortifications.)

(Branch, pp. 117-18.)

- - - - -

April 27, 1862 – Wynne's Mill, Virginia
Pvt. James P. Williams, Richmond Howitzers

Dear Aunt Mary,

. . . We have been here three weeks yesterday, lying down behind breastworks night and day most of the time in mud six inches deep . . . Yankees have a battery of four guns planted in the woods about three-fourths mile from us, from which they bombard us, all the time day and night, and we are not allowed to return the fire, and it is the most provoking thing in the world. . . . we haven't ammunition enough to be wasting any, we are reserv-

ing our fire until they make a general attack and get in closer . . .
The mail now is so irregular that it is mere chance when a letter
comes or goes straight . . . I do wish I was there too; everything
in the country, I reckon, looks so beautiful now. I say "I reckon"
because although in the country myself there is nothing beautiful
here . . . everything shows the destructive effects of grim-visaged
war. . . .

(Williams, by date.)

- - - - -

April 27, 1862 – camp near Lebanon Church
Lt. Richard Watkins, Co. K – 3rd Virginia Cavalry

My own Dear Dear Mary:

. . . Capt. Thornton has been promoted to the place of Lieut.
Colonel of the Regiment and this morning I have been promoted
again from 2nd to 1st Lieutenant of the Troop. Dr. Berkely is the
Captain. . . . Would write more but have not time now. Goodbye
my Darling. Give much love to all.

(Boots & Kisses, pp. 80-81.)

- - - - -

April 27, 1862 – Gloucester Point, Virginia
Pvt. Nathaniel Watkins, King & Queen Artillery

My dear Nannie . . . Gen Johnston commands the army, Gen
[Daniel H.] Hill the left wing resting on York River, Gen Longstreet
the center, & Gen Magruder the right wing resting on the James
River. Our lines are strongly fortified . . . the army numbers 80 to
100 thousand, well armed, with enough ammunition, . . . and a
great deal of artillery. . . . there will be some fighting here I think.
. . .

Yours N.V.W.

(ed: The Union army had over 100,000 men. The Confederate Army of the Peninsula had 34,400 men on April 7 and General Johnston noted, as he planned the retreat on May 1, that he had a total of 57,000 to withdraw in the 'face of the enemy.')

(NVW Letters, by date; *To the Gates of Richmond*, p. 48 & 60.)

- - - - -

April 30, 1862 – Ships Point, Virginia
2nd Lt. E. P. McKinney, Co. F – 6th N. Y. Cavalry

. . . When we arrived at Ship Point, on the last day of April, I found a very lively scene than I had ever before witnessed. Hundreds of vessels of all sizes and descriptions filled the harbor, many of which I had before seen in New York, New Haven and on the Sound. Steam tugs were plying back and forth, towing vessels filled with troops, horses, cannon and ammunition of all descriptions.

We came on shore in a small boat, carefully avoiding the countless moving vessels, and found the whole coast lined with troops, tents, camps, piles of cannon, cannon balls and shell, and the same activity on the water. . . .

. . . we came over to camp and found our other companies practicing all sorts of mounted maneuvers. We have been at the same kind of work ever since. . . .

(*Life in Tent and Field*, E. P. McKinney, Boston, 1922, pp. 42 – 46 [Hereafter cited as McKinney])

- - - - -

April 30, 1862 – Young's Farm, Virginia
Sgt. Major Elisha Rhodes, 2nd Rhodes Island Infantry

Monday the Rebel gunboat *Teaser* shelled our batteries near Young's Farm. . . . Levi Carr was out on picket duty last night. There is a fine peach orchard near us, but alas the peaches are

not ripe. The news of the capture of New Orleans has been received and it gives us great joy.

(Rhodes, p. 64.)

- - - - -

April 30, 1862 – Custis Farm on Peninsula
Pvt. Tally Simpson, 3rd S. Carolina Infantry

The conscript act passed by Congress is one of the best things
ever passed by a supreme body. The only misfortune is that it did
not become law a little sooner so as to include the two brigades
from South Carolina. As it is, they are not included in the act and
the Scty of War has said that, since their term of service expired
before the bill was passed, they would be mustered out upon application. [General] Johnston however, refuses to let them leave,
having obtained permission of the Secy of War to keep them. I
suppose owing to the exigency of the times. The men are very
indignant at such treatment and yield reluctantly to the military
as a supreme law.

(Simpson, pp. 119-20).

- - - - -

April 30, 1862 – camp near Yorktown, Va.
Pvt. J. W. Reid, Mattison's S. C. Battalion

As there is to be an inspection of arms this morning at 10 o'clock,
I will not have time to write much. . . . News is about as it was
when I wrote last – nothing talked of but fighting. It assuredly
will come soon. . . . Firing going on continually, but no regular
attack as yet.

. . . I wish McClelland would surrender to us and end this war. He
undoubtedly would have it to do if we had a navy on the river
below him, but as we haven't that I can't exactly say how it will
turn out. . . . Yorktown is a very old town and the York river here

190

is very wide because of the tide water. I bought a string of fish at Yorktown the other day, the first I have had in lo these many days. The next day I bought a shad, but had to give part of it for salt to salt the balance. Those who can't turn can't spin.

I must now fix up for inspection . . .

Yours as ever,

J. W. Reid.

Reid, p. 78)

- - - - -

May, 1862

McClellan is ready to start his bombardment of the Confederate lines at Yorktown. He has squandered a month and gone from having 60,000 more men than Magruder, in mid-April, to now having 30,000 more men than Johnston and Magruder combined. During the night of May 3, the Confederate forces withdraw toward Williamsburg and Richmond. The Union army is clueless. On May 4 Union forces enter empty Confederate trenches. As the rain falls the Union cavalry and infantry organize to begin the pursuit.

Missouri, Kentucky and now Tennessee are basically lost to the Confederacy. New Orleans has fallen and the Union navy has captured Natchez and is nearing Vicksburg. Coming down the Mississippi River, Union naval forces are closing in on Fort Pillow, the final Confederate fort protecting Memphis. The Union army under General Halleck will finally reach Corinth, Mississippi, and discover that the Confederates have withdrawn toward Tupelo.

On the Virginia Peninsula, the two main roads to Richmond, one from Newport News and the other from Yorktown, meet at Williamsburg about one half mile in front of the Confederate guns at Fort Magruder. In a driving cold rain, with the mud getting deeper by the hour, the Union will catch the Confederate rear guard here late on the 4th and fight a pitched battle on the 5th. Several negroes will advise the Union generals that the redoubts are empty on the Confederate left flank. Actually, there are empty redoubts on both flanks. Late in the day, General Hancock will be sent to confirm and his troops will occupy redoubt 11. If the Confederate intent had been to hold the Williamsburg Line, the loss of redoubt 11 would have been critical. Williamsburg was a delaying action and as dusk approached it had no impact on the battle. The furious fighting in the Ravine and in front of Fort Magruder (redoubt 6) stalled the Union pursuit and on the morning of the 6th, the final Confederate forces left Williamsburg heading toward Richmond.

Union burial parties are busy May 6 through May 8 burying the Union and Confederate dead. The hospitals, and many other buildings in Williamsburg, are filled with the wounded and dying of both armies.

McClellan will take 20 days to pursue the retreating Confederates 45 miles to the defenses of Richmond. Lt. Richard Watkins, of the 3rd Virginia Cavalry, will note, *"it seems right strange that Nat on foot should have retreated at a rate of 20 miles a day and we on horseback have hardly averaged four. We often march one mile a day."* The rain and storms are a daily occurrence and Cpl. Luther Furst, of the Union Signal Corps, writes, *"Today lightning struck a pine tree within twenty yards of my tent and we could feel the heat."*

As Confederate forces retreat, the *Virginia* is destroyed and sunk to avoid her capture. This opens the James River to the Union fleet and it steams upstream to try to reach Richmond by water, but are defeated on May 15 at Drewry's Bluff, ending any opportunity of taking Richmond via the river.

The United States Congress passes the Homestead Act which will provide 180 acres of land to a homesteader who will occupy and improve the land for 5 years. This will have a huge impact on the settlement of the West after the war.

As the rain continues to come down, the Union army is split by the flooded Chickahominy River. General Johnston attacks on May 31, driving the Union forces back toward the unfordable river. Late in the day, a bullet strikes General Johnston and changes the course of the war on the eastern front. General Robert E. Lee is appointed to the command of the Confederate army by President Davis.

As the month ends, the Union army is burning piles of dead horses and digging graves in the mud at Seven Pines for their fellow soldiers. Three weeks earlier they were doing the same thing at Williamsburg. Disease, especially diarrhea, is taking a toll. Lt. Charles Haydon, of the 2nd Michigan Infantry, notes his problems with ticks and lice as he writes, *". . . spend an hour every day picking off woodticks. Most of the men . . . are now becoming lousy* [infested with lice]. *I heard Prentice say this m'g that he was "going to make a desperate attempt to drive the enemy from his earthworks" meaning he hoped to get the lice & ticks out of his shoes & stockings."* The terror of battle might impact a soldier one day a month, maybe two, but the disease and pests make their lives a misery every day.

May, 1862

May 1, 1862 – near Yorktown
Lt. Charles Haydon, 2nd Michigan Infantry

The weather is cold & misty. Atlantic storms are by no means so agreeable as Atlantic magazines. . . . cannonading was very heavy last night . . . The Rebs fired pretty briskly P.M. from batteries on the right. I find that I now weigh 148 lbs., being 6 lbs. heavier than when I left Camp Mich.

(Haydon, by date.)

- - - - -

May 1, 1862 – camp near Lee's Mill
Pvt. William C. Corson, Co. G – 3rd Virginia Cavalry

My dear Jennie,

. . . An order was read in camp this evening requiring the soldiers to burn all their baggage and clothing, reserving only one change of wearing apparel and two blankets. The boys are gone to Lebanon Church this evening to select such things as they will be allowed to carry on their horses and to burn the balance. It is thought that we will evacuate Yorktown and the whole army retreat towards Richmond.

Your devoted William

P.S. I may go into a fight . . . and if I am killed remember that my last thoughts . . . will be *of thee.*

(Corson, p. 76.)

- - - - -

May 1, 1862 – Right Flank
Brig. Gen. Lafayette McLaws, Army of Peninsula HQ 2 Division

My Dearly beloved wife,

I have not received a letter from you for many days . . . I have written you very frequently, and sent the letters per special express . . . to Richmond.

The enemy are engaged in preparations for the bombardment of Yorktown. They now throw a great number of enormous shells in the place, but that is nothing to what will be done when their batteries are in place.

The news of the occupation of New Orleans . . . produced a very profound sensation . . . I do not take the desponding view of affairs as some do. . . .

Good day for today. I will try to write you tomorrow again. Give my love to all, and a great deal to my children . . .

Your devoted husband

(McLaws by date.)

- - - - -

May 2, 1862 – Kings Landing, Virginia
Sgt. Hamilton Branch, 8th Georgia Infantry

I was sent off to Richmond on sick list. I am not much sick but weak . . . I have been three days coming to Richmond. When I got to Kings Landing [Kings Mill Wharf] it was so crowded with sick that I saw there was no chance of getting off soon . . . [went on] Mac Berrien's ark . . . loaded with ammunition for Richmond . . . we stopped at Jamestown a day and night . . . I went to the ruin of the first brick church built in Virginia . . . There are some queer old tombstones . . . One reads "Here lyeth William Sherwood, born at White Chappel, near London. A great sinner waiting a joyful resurrection."

I feel a great deal better than when I left camp. My bowels are wrong and my stomach very sore. I will be all right after a few days of good eating . . .

196

(ed: In late April General Johnston sends all sick and wounded in his army to Kings Mill Landing for evacuation to Richmond hospitals. Before he slips out of his Yorktown lines to begin his withdrawal toward Richmond he wants the sick and wounded evacuated. There are over 2,500 men waiting in the rain for departure on vessels up the James River to safety. All were evacuated before the Union army got to Williamsburg.)

(Branch, pp. 121-22.)

- - - - -

May 1 to May 5, 1862 – Kings Mill Wharf, Virginia
Lt. Richard Watkins, Co. K – 3rd Virginia Cavalry

On last Friday week before the rear guard of the army took up its march, I was ordered to Kings Mill Wharf on the James [River] in charge of all sick of our Regiment. There I witnessed one of the saddest scenes ever witnessed in the army. Twenty nine hundred sick men were lying on the cold wet ground awaiting the boats. I had forty or fifty under my charge which I succeeded in getting off very soon but my orders were to remain . . . and I had to stay till Sunday . . .

(Watkins, pp. 87-88.)

- - - - -

May 3 & 4, 1862 – Yorktown, Virginia
Pvt. Milton Barrett, 18th Georgia Infantry

. . . I was at york town . . . sence then we have bin marching a little and a fighting a little. we helt our fortification til the fourth of May having everything move to our rear. we vacated the place leaving nothing behind . . . our brigade was the last to leave . . .

(The Confederacy Is on Her Way Up the Spout, edited by J. R. Heller & C. A. Heller, Athens, 1992, p.66. [Hereafter cited as Barrett.])

- - - - -

197

May 3, 1862 – trenches near Yorktown
Lt. Charles Haydon, 2ⁿᵈ Michigan Infantry

When we first came here [trenches near Yorktown) a great number of cattle, sheep, hog &c were killed all about the woods & fields, the offal of which with dead mules & horses as well as the necessary accumulation of filth abt large camps [latrines & human waste] all combine to render the air unwholesome & sometimes at night & m'g the stench is almost in supportable. This is made still worse by the low marshy nature of the ground, the heavy rains & hot sultry days which invariably follow. There is not much sickness yet but it can hardly fail to come.

(ed: With all the human and animal waste, poor sanitation, contaminated water supply and the overall living conditions it is the perfect breeding ground for diarrhea, dysentery, typhoid fever, and in the heat of summer, cholera.)

(Haydon, by date.)

NELSON HOUSE HOSPITAL -- A. R. Waud, Artist

- - - -

May 3, 1862 – Gloucester Point, Virginia
Pvt. Nathaniel Watkins, King & Queen Artillery

My dear wife – I write hastily to let you hear from me. Yesterday we were furnished with muskets & order to prepare three days provisions for a forced march – about 9 o'clk at night received marching orders . . . but . . . are still here . . . we know nothing . . . We are prepared to march at any time . . . I will write whenever I can get a letter off . . . I was with you all last night in my dreams . . . it was a happy night. – Everything was almost real. . . . I think the plan is to leave all the water courses on account of the enemy's gunboats, continue to write yr aff husband N.V.W.

(NVW Letters, by date.)

- - - - -

May 3 & 4, 1862 – Near Battery #1, Yorktown line
2nd Lt. E. P. McKinney, Co. F – 6th N. Y. Cavalry

. . . there was constant and heavy firing which was continued {into} the next [day]. . . . our troops marched into Yorktown and four thousand Cavalry and several Batteries followed the retreating enemy. . . .

We are now doing patrol duty but expect . . . perhaps in a week we shall be in Richmond.

We caught a rebel deserter tonight who said . . . they deserted Yorktown because they had positive information that McClellan had one hundred and fifty thousand troops. . . . The rebel army in constantly growing smaller and smaller by desertions, and in a fortnight I think Virginia will be cleaned out. . . .

Much love to all, from Your affectionate Son,

McKinney, pp. 46-47.)

- - - - -

May 4, 1862 – evacuation from Yorktown
Pvt. Tally Simpson, 3rd S. Carolina Infantry

. . . We evacuated Yorktown and our line extending across the Peninsula [Warwick Line]. . . . owing to bad roads and worn out teams, we were compelled to carry all of our baggage upon our backs. We traveled the whole of the first night and reached Williamsburg a while before sun up, rested a short time, and again took up the march. A large portion of the army was detained in the neighborhood of Williamsburg during Sunday, the enemy in hot pursuit. . . .

(Simpson, p. 122.)

- - - - -

May 4, 1862 – Yorktown
Corporal Luther Furst, Signal Corps

. . . loaded the wagons and started for our signal party who are following the skedaddling rebs.

(Furst, by date.)

- - - - -

May 4, 1862 – near Williamsburg
Pvt. Milton Barrett, 18th Georgia Infantry

. . . we got to williamsburg all right learning that the yankees was a going in full speed up the river aiming to out flank us at west point. our brigade was put in front and hured [hurried] to that place. . . . we marched nearly all night. . . . move on towds west point . . . landed with in six miles of that place by [Sunday] night.
(Barrett, p. 67)

(ed: An amphibious force could now head up the York River since the Yorktown and Gloucester river batteries had been abandoned. The Union objective was to get to West Point and land troops on

200

the Eltham side of the Pamunkey River and move inland to sever the Williamsburg to Richmond Road.)

- - - - -

Early May, 1862 – Kingsmill Wharf
George R. Wood deckhand, *James Buchanan*

We were ordered to Kingsmill Wharf, about four miles from Williamsburg, to assist with the evacuation. We took a load of flour [and] sugar. We had orders to destroy all we could not get on board the schooner. On the wharf was a nice barrel of New Orleans molasses, and as it would be destroyed if left and it was food that I was always fond of, I rolled it aboard. It was marked "Blassinham, Williamsburg."

At Jamestown we took on several barrels of whiskey and Capt. Barlow's battery of artillery of Richmond [the Metropolitan Guards, Tenth Battalion, Virginia Heavy Artillery]. Going up[river] the soldiers knocked the bung out of a barrel of whisky and sucked the whisky out . . . until many of them were drunk. Brother Billy, who was a member of the Wythe Rifles and had been disabled at Yorktown, was taken up to City Point.

. . . We arrived at Richmond about daylight [on May 4].

(Boatman, pp. 47-48.)

- - - - -

May 4, 1862 – rear-guard near Williamsburg
Pvt. William C. Corson, Co. G – 3rd Virginia Cavalry

My Dear Jennie,

. . . the Cavalry arm has to pass in covering the retreat of a large army like ours . . . General Stewart's [Stuart] Brigade was the last to leave closely pressed by the enemy's cavalry and infantry and came near being surrounded before we reached Williamsburg.

Often we suffered for water and were not allowed to leave the ranks long enough to ride a hundred yards to a spring or branch.

(Corson, p. 77.)

- - - - -

May 4, 1862 – Williamsburg, Virginia
Pvt. J. W. Reid, Mattison's S. C. Battalion

. . . On Sunday, the 4th, we traveled about twelve miles. My battalion passed Williamsburg about 4 miles and put up for camp. The enemy was close behind our rear guard all day, and late in the evening there was a considerable skirmish with them near Williamsburg. About an hour after dark we were sent back below Williamsburg on picket guard, after traveling all day and the night before. It was a very dark night, cloudy and drizzling rain. We nearly ran into the enemy's lines before we knew it. Three men were put at each post, with orders to stay awake all night, and for one of us to crawl out toward the enemy's lines and find out, if possible, their position. I crawled out to a fence about one hundred yards . . . two or three times through the night . . . I could distinctly hear them talking but . . . could see nothing. . . .

(Reid, pp. 79-80)

- - - - -

May 4, 1862 – near Yorktown
Lt. Charles Haydon, 2nd Michigan Infantry

Early this m'g came news that Yorktown was evacuated. . . . At abt 4 P.M. we left & moved out through Yorktown. [The Confederate works] were very formidable, far surpassing any of our works on the Potomac. There were a large number of guns still mounted & the fields were covered with tents & hastily abandoned stores . . . New made graves were abundant. The stench abt the camp was intolerable. The ground, roads & in fact every place were filled with torpedoes [land mines]. Several men were killed . . . guards were placed all around to warn abt them. We camped 2 miles above Yorktown.

(Haydon, by date.)

- - - - -

May 4 to 6,1862 – near Williamsburg
Lt. Richard Watkins, Co. J – 3rd Virginia Cavalry

On Sunday [4th] I left for Williamsburg in company with detachments from various companies who had been sent to the Wharf to forward commissary stores. When within a few miles of Williamsburg an aid of Genl Stewart [Gen. J. E. B. Stuart] came by at full speed saying that his entire command has been cut off including our regiment. . . fortunately before going far we met the General and all were safe. . . The next day [May 5] the battle commenced . . . and raged until sundown. . . . The next day [May 6] we commenced our march again and have been right closely pursued . . . It can hardly be called a pursuit for we travel only 3 or 4 miles a day and the enemy very often in sight. . . I must close for want of more time . . . Oh I do want to see you too bad . . . much love to all.

(Watkins, pp. 87-88.)

- - - - -

May 5, 1862 – Williamsburg, Virginia
Pvt. J. W. Reid, Mattison's S. C. Battalion

. . . Just at daylight the enemy commenced snapping caps on their guns – to dry the tubes, I suppose. I will admit I never felt so nervous in my life. . . . I never shall forget the bursting of those caps.

A little after daylight they attacked . . . We held our ground as long as possible . . . until about 7 o'clock when they came in overwhelming numbers as to force us back on our main lines, a distance of about six hundred yards. I lost all my clothing and blankets. In falling back we had a slanting hill to go down and when we got to the foot of it our artillery opened fire over our heads. . . . We took a circuitous route, so as not to be in the way of the artillery, finally got around and went into the fort [Fort Magruder] near the main road into Williamsburg.

(Reid, p. 80)

- - - - -

May 5, 1862 – Williamsburg, Virginia
Corporal Luther Furst, Signal Corps

. . . enroute early this morning, rain coming down in torrents. . . . we came near Williamsburg and then halted, the fight raging fiercely. The enemy took one of our batteries and drove our left wing [Hooker's Division] about a half mile. It commenced to look a little blue . . . the contest was fierce, but our boys gained the day. We camped for the night near the battlefield, the rain still pouring down in torrents. . . .

(Furst, by date.)

- - - - -

May 5, 1862 – Williamsburg, Virginia
Cpl. Joseph B. Laughton, 38th New York Infantry

. . . To tell the truth John, when I first came on the field at a double quick tramping over the dead of the whole day & hearing the cries of the wounded & dying . . . & surrounded on all sides by the enemy I came near fainting but . . . as soon as our line came to the 'charge' & I saw the enemy retreat back it filled me with new courage & I thought no more of fear . . .

(ed: Joseph is a color bearer with the 38th New York.)

(To The Gates of Richmond – The Peninsula Campaign, Sears, New York, 1982, p. 78. [Hereafter cited as Gates of Richmond])

- - - - -

May 5, 1862 – afternoon at Williamsburg
Lt. Charles Haydon, 2nd Michigan Infantry

. . . we moved to the right across the road & . . . moved forward into a thick pine slashing in which the fight was raging . . . "gray coated chaps" started to come down a little open space toward us. Our men fired on them, killing 7 . . . others dodged behind logs and about 20 minutes of very sharp firing from perhaps 200 on a side ensued. . . . more than 30 balls struck within 5 feet of me and several within a foot. The enemy fell back & we pursued them . . led by Gen. Kearney to the edge of the slashing. The enemy then opened on us with shot, shell and canister . . . we lay down on the ground & I only saw one man killed. . . . We lay there till after dark . . . I had . . . become so chilled by the rain & exhausted . . . that legs and arms were cramping. . . . We had now driven them entirely out of the woods . . . we were relieved after dark by the 40th N.Y. . . . but [my] Regt. except abt a doz. men in the darkness of the woods could not be found. . . .

(ed: This is the Union counterattack led by Gen. Kearney's troops against the Confederate forces that have driven through the 'Ravine' and battered the troops of Hooker to a frazzle. Kearney was able to drive the Confederates back through the 'Ravine' and restore the Union line. This was the main part of the battle of Williamsburg and produced the vast majority of the casualties.)

(Haydon, May 5.)

- - - - -

May 5, 1862 – Fort Magruder, Wiliamsburg, Virginia
Pvt. J. W. Reid, Mattison's S. C. Battalion

We remained in the fort amid a storm of shell, cannon and musket balls . . . The fighting was going on all this time to our right and left without a moment's intermission. The noise was deafening. The sight was sickening. A continual roar was going on the full length of our line. Oh, the slaughter that was made that day – the slaughter of human beings, brother against brother.

The fort, as I have said, was on the main road, and it was here that the heaviest attack was made, but the nine pieces artillery we had in the fort and the infantry backing it kept the enemy at a distance all day. Two or three times . . . they attempted to charge and drive us out of the fort, but were just as often repulsed with heavy loss.

Reid, pp. 80-81)

- - - - -

May 5, 1862 – Williamsburg, Virginia
Pvt. Newton Camper, Co. D – 11th Virginia Infantry

. . . in this battle we advanced thro' the woods (The Ravine) and into a clearing driving the Yankees into the woods beyond the clearing. Here the Company remained until night closed the contest. . . . John Carper and John Maury were killed at our front line and Lt. James was wounded. . . . (also) Killed: Wm. Bower, Tine Kessler, Edward James. Wounded: Lt. J. T. James, 2nd Lt. J. H. Camper, George Loop, and Dr. Carper . . . Dr. Carper and George Loop afterward died from the effects of their wounds. Jno. Maury was killed while on retreat through the fallen timber [Ravine], and was left on the ground.

(ed: The 11th Virginia lost more men killed at Williamsburg than in any other battle during the entire war. Their total loss of killed and wounded made Williamsburg their second worst battle behind Seven Pines which will also be in May, 1862. Williamsburg: 31 KIA, 93W; Seven Pines: 30KIA, 115W. Gettysburg is in third with 18KIA, 99W.)

(A Sketch of the Fincastle Rifles, Newton Camper, 1979, Fincastle, p. 6-7. Compiled from a series of articles by Mr. Camper in the *Fincastle Herald* beginning in July, 1891. [Hereafter cited as Newton Camper]; The 11th Virginia Infantry, Robert Bell, Lynchburg, 1985, pp. 60-61.)

- - - - -

May 5, 1862 – Redoubt 9 - Williamsburg, Virginia
Pvt. J. W. Reid, Mattison's S. C. Battalion

At this juncture in the affair our battalion was taken out of the fort [and were moved further left to redoubt #9 to watch the left flank] . . . we were ordered to storm a fort [redoubt 11] the enemy were in possession of up to our left. [Hancock's brigade had captured the empty redoubt toward the left end of the Confederate line] We made a bold but unsuccessful effort to drive them out, and being repulsed, filed off into a strip of woods somewhat out of range of their guns. Just after this a whole brigade of ours made a charge but were driven back with considerable loss. [This was Early's brigade and primarily the 5th North Carolina and the 24th Virginia] About the time the brigade made its unsuccessful charge night came on and ended the slaughter.

(ed: Following the brief Union counterattack after their blunting of the assaults of the 5th North Carolina and the 24th Virginia, the regiments of Early and Jenkins formed a defensive line in the area of redoubt 10 to secure the left flank of the Confederate forces. This was formed in the growing darkness and the Union did not attempt a night assault on the Confederate position.)

(Reid, p. 81.)

- - - - -

Night of May 5, 1862 – Williamsburg, Virginia
Pvt. Newton Camper, Co. D – 11th Virginia Infantry

In the night . . . Co. D was relieved and sent to Fort Magruda [Magruder], a short distance to the rear. Here the men spent a miserable night. Having left their baggage in Williamsburg on the morning of the battle, the men were without blankets or protection of any kind from the weather. More than this, they had no fires, and were standing in mud and water, in many places over their shoe-tops . . . the officers shared the toils equally with the men.

(Newton Camper, p. 7.)

- - - - -

Night of May 5, 1862 – Redoubt # 10 – Williamsburg
Pvt. J. W. Reid, Mattison's S. C. Battalion

. . . I was completely broken down . . . my clothing was wet, my body nearly frozen, and in this condition we were again ordered on guard . . . orders came to go to an ordnance wagon about 300 yards off and draw cartridges . . . I got a hundred pound box for my company . . . It was now about two o'clock . . . about 8 o'clock the next morning I awoke refreshed, and in a short time we re-sumed the march, . . .the enemy following close in our rear.

(Reid, pp. 83-84.)

- - - - -

May 5, 1862 – Wren Building Hospital, Wiliamsburg
Pvt. Randolph A. Shotwell, 8th Virginia Infantry

What a strange metamorphosis was this peaceful abode of science and learning [Wren Building on William & Mary campus] into a veritable chamber of horrors, where every turn of the eye revealed some shocking spectacle of human misery . . . As I ascended the stairway my foot struck some object, and a man passing at that moment with a light . . . showed me a pile of legs and arms that had been amputated and thrown on the landing of the stairway, that being the only place unoccupied by the wounded.

(150 Civil War, Strange Metamorphosis by Wilford Kale, p. 40.)

- - - - -

May 5, 1862 – Forge Road, James City County
Mr. John T. Martin, Farmer & School Teacher

Finished planting corn [on May 3]. A rainy day and memorable on account of it being the day the battle was fought in Williamsburg in which several thousand of the Southern Troops encamped on the front part of my farm and in other [neighboring farm fields].

(Martin Farm Journal, by date)

- - - - -

May 6, 1862 – Williamsburg, Virginia
Pvt. Newton Camper, Co. D – 11th Virginia Infantry

On the 6th of May began the memorable march from Williamsburg to Richmond. Much rain had fallen and the roads were deep with mud. For three days, and without rations, the wearied troops painfully trudged along through the mire. . . Artillery and baggage wagons would sink into the mud and remain to be dragged out by . . . man and beast. By many [Company D] soldiers this march is thought to have been the most painful of any made during the whole war.

(Newton Camper, p. 7.)

- - - - -

May 6, 1862 – Williamsburg, Virginia
Mrs. Cynthia Coleman, Resident

How could [our] little band of badly clothed, badly fed patriots who foot-sore and hungry plough through mud and water on to Richmond [withstand] this great army with all its warlike appliances in gallant array?

(ed: She has seen the condition of the withdrawing Confederates and now is seeing the columns of Union soldiers as they march through town in pursuit.)

(Old Town, p. 224)

- - - - -

May 6, 1862 – Williamsburg, Virginia
Lt. Charles Haydon, 2nd Michigan Infantry

. . . We are now bivouacked near Williamsburg. Victory was with us but dearly won.

When I went back from the front last night I found the woods and roadside strewed with dead & the moans & cries of the wounded could be heard on all sides. They were scattered around among logs & brush so it was almost impossible to get at them . . . All our wounded are supposed to be found and cared for & our dead by this time (3 p.m.) buried. Those of the enemy most of them will be buried today. Their loss must exceed ours. Thirty were in one pile, 65 in another, 150 in another this morning that had been collected for [mass] burial. In passing over the field from which they were taken I saw without search 13 bodies which were not collected. Their dead are also lying along the road & in the street of Williamsburg at which place there are 600 of their wounded.

(ed: Union casualties totaled 2,283 and Confederate casualties were 1,682. This reflects killed, wounded and missing.)

(Haydon, by date.)

- - - - -

May 6, 1862 – Williamsburg, Virginia
Pvt. William P. Holland, Co. G – 11th Virginia Infantry

. . . we resumed our retreat without any further trouble with the Yankees. As we went back through Williamsburg, we passed near the lunatic asylum. Some of the inmates were out in the yard, and some of our men called out, "We'd like to swap places with you." "We've tried it out there and we like it better in here," some of them answered. One old man, however, upstairs at a window, replied, "I wish to the lord I could, but they won't let me out."

(Recollection of a Private, William Preston Holland, 1936, reprinted 2009, Rocky Mount, p.12 [Hereafter cited as Holland])

- - - - -

May 6, 1862 – Williamsburg, Virginia
Dr. John M. Galt II, Superintendent, Eastern Lunatic Asylum

At eight o'clock . . . the army came by the Asylum, I went out & addressed the Colonel, telling him I was the Superintendent & I supposed that this house [in addition to the Asylum] would be included in the protection. He simply smiled & observed that he would attend to this.

(ed: Dr. Galt was a brilliant and compassionate Superintendent. He revolutionized the treatment of the mentally ill and treated them with human dignity. Cruel restraints were replaced with calming medications, therapeutic activities, and beautiful grounds for strolling and relaxation. The Union forces immediately banned him from the hospital and his patients on May 6 and Dr. Galt died a few days later, possibly from a heart attack or an overdose of laudanum.)

(Old Town, p.228; 150 Civil War, Dr. Galt & The Lunatic Asylum by Joli Huelskamp, p.54.)

- - - - -

May 6, 1862 – Wiliamsburg, Virginia
Corporal Luther Furst, Signal Corps

The St Mary's and Williams College [William & Mary] of this place is a fine institution . . . We bivouacked on the campus for the day and the college building was used for a hospital. I passed over the battlefield this morning which was strewn with wounded and dead. We are gathering them up as soon as possible and providing for them as best we can. Lt. Daniels received 15 [Confederate] surgeons under a flag of truce this morning who came in to take care of their sick and wounded. . . .

(ed: It was very common, during the war, for the losing or with-drawing side, to either leave or send surgeons, doctors and assis-tants to help with the care of the wounded. They reported to the senior medical officer and normally worked where needed. They normally did not divide by Union and Confederate. They would quite often share supplies, provide morphine or other items since the doctor requesting was also treating their soldiers. The medi-cal staff would be returned under a flag of truce afterwards.)

(Furst, by date.)

- - - - -

May 6, 1862 – Williamsburg, Virginia
Cpl. Marshall H. Twitchell, Co. I -4th Vermont Infantry

. . . after the battle of Williamsburg a detail was made from our regiment with orders to report to the surgeon of the hospital in the field for duty. I was in command of the detail and, marching to a large barn, halted my men and went in to report. At the side of the door as I passed in I saw amputated limbs thrown together, reminding me of stove wood beside the farmhouse door. I re-ported to the surgeon and asked for instructions. He said, "Go into the field, bury the dead, and bring in the wounded. Do not bring in men who are about to die. Let them die there."

(ed: The 4th Vermont has still not really received their baptism of fire and they are just beginning to be exposed to some of the harsh realities of war.)

(Twitchell, pp. 36-37.)

- - - - -

May 6, 1862 – Williamsburg, Virginia
Mrs. Harriette Cary, Resident

All is quiet [as darkness approaches], and being assured of pro-tection by two sentinels placed at our door . . . under the degrading yoke of Yankee despotism.

(Old Town, p. 237.)

- - - - -

May 6, 1862 – Forge Road, James City Cty., Virginia
Mr. John T. Martin, Farmer & School Teacher

A fine day and also a large number of troops [Confederate] encamped for the night in the same location killing our cattle, hogs
and fowl.

*(ed: These troops, and those mentioned in Mr. Martin's May 5th
entry, are Confederate troops. The Union Army will appear in his
upcoming entry of May 8th. Depredations of property and even
normal destruction such as trampling of fields by troops, horses
and wagons, fences being torn down for firewood and orchards
being raided were compounded by troops killing chickens, hogs
and other livestock. Farms were impacted by both armies and
the owners seldom got any compensation with claims filed with
either army.)*

(Martin Farm Journal, by date.)

- - - - -

May 7, 1862 – Eltham's Landing
Pvt. Milton Barrett, 18th Georgia Infantry

. . . we scouted a round un tell on the night of the sixth we learnt
from our picets that a large number of Yankees had landed near
West Point early on the morning of the [6th]. we march a few
miles towards the river. gen Hood . . . was in front a looking wher
to form his line of battle a yankee picket fiard at him but mist him.
the yankee was shot down on the spot. two company of the forth
Texas ws depoed as cromishers [was deployed as skirmishers] and
was throwing the yankees about right. the 18th Georgia was place
in rear of the artilry to defend hit, the other three Texas reg. ad-

vance [on May 7] thrue a strip o wood and was soon ingage with doble ther number. . . we are expecting nother fight soon. we have fell back out the reach of the gun boats on the chickhomey [Pamunkey] rivor. i remain your effecnate brother tel death

Milton

(ed: Hood held the 18ᵗʰ Georgia in reserve and attacked with three Texas regiments and the Hampton Legion. His aggressive reconnaissance hit the Union advance and drove it back toward their gunboats. The battle at Eltham blunted the attempt to cut the Confederate line of retreat and the withdrawal toward Richmond continued.)

(Barrett, pp. 67-68.)

- - - - -

May 7, 1862 – Williamsburg, Virginia
New York Daily Tribune, traveling correspondent

. . . The second line of Rebel defenses above Yorktown consisted of 13 formidable earth forts, within sure artillery range of each other. One of them, Fort Magruder, was of great strength. Fort Magruder and most of the key forts were in front of General Heintzelman and on his left . . . [there are] abandoned wounded in forts, in cornfields, in churches, record offices, colleges, hospitals . . . What of the abandoned dead? They strewed the woods, they were in fields, along the fence lines, on the edge of timbered portions and near the forts. Burial parties worked all day Tuesday [6ᵗʰ] and the labor begins again this morning . . .

(ed: They were buried in groups by Union burial parties. The Confederate dead in a variety of mass graves and the Union dead with wooden identification markers for those that were known, and the soldiers simply wrapped in blankets in shallow graves. In 1864 and 1865 the Federal government began exhuming the bodies of the Union soldiers and relocating them to the Nation-

al Cemetery in Yorktown. Many of the wooden markers did not survive for two years and those soldiers also became 'unknown.' The Confederate dead were never exhumed and remain on the battlefield. No doubt a few Union soldiers also remain on the battlefield.)

(The New York Daily Tribune, Saturday, May 10, 1862, p. 4, col. 1 & col. 2, "The Battle Near Williamsburg Revisited." By an un-named correspondent attached to Heintzelman's Division. Grave information from 'A History of Fort Magruder' by Jeff Toalson which was presented at a Battle of Williamsburg Anniversary Celebration on May 2, 2021. A copy of this footnoted document is in the collection of the Swem Archives at the College of William and Mary and attached as Appendix 3 in this work.)

(ed: See the May 21 letter of Sgt. Robert Johnson, of Co. H – 8th New Jersey Infantry, on the topic of the burial of Union soldiers.)

(ed: Union soldier Robert Knox Sneden created a wonderful selection of watercolors of the battlefield in early May, 1862, when his unit was in Williamsburg. Many of his paintings show burial sites of both Union and Confederate soldiers with notations. In one of his sketches of Fort Magruder he notes the site of 300 Union graves near the southwestern bastion of the fort. The Virginia Historical Society has his entire collection.)

(ed: The 104th Pennsylvania Infantry collected 96 dead of the 5th North Carolina Infantry from the field in front of Redoubt 11. They carried them in and stacked them, in a group near or inside of the redoubt. Their mass grave was probably in the muddy moat but could be inside the redoubt. No doubt they dug the mass grave as close to the stacked bodies as possible.)

(Old Town, pp. 225-27.)

- - - - -

May 7, 1862 – Williamsbug, Virginia
Sgt. Major Elisha Rhodes, 2nd Rhode Island Infantry

. . . It rained hard all night [4th] and we lay in the mud and water but felt happy for now was our turn to chase and Rebels turn to run. Early Monday morning [5th] we moved towards Williamsburg and about noon we began to hear the roar of cannon and rattle of musketry. . . . we arrived under fire at about 4 P.M. Here we were placed in the reserves . . . and took position in the edge of a piece of woods about six hundred yards in front of Fort Magruder. . . . as day began to break [6th] Major Viall and myself crawled toward the fort. . . and walked up the glacis and looked into an embrasure. Behold, the fort was deserted. . . . The ground was covered with dead men and horses. . . . The field presented a horrible appearance and in one small spot I counted sixty dead bodies. . . . Our Cavalry are now in pursuit. . . .

(Rhodes, pp. 64-65.)

- - - - -

May 7, 1862 – near Olive Branch, Virginia
Cpl. Patrick Lyons, 2nd Rhode Island Infantry

The Cavalry being about two miles in advance of us came up with the enemies rear guard of about 1000 Cavalry at a place called Olive Branch . . . we were ordered to unsling Knapsacks & load & immediately deployed to the right & left of the road as skirmishers – arriving at Olive Branch we found the Cavalry & Artillery in line of Battle in a large clearing near a house, but the enemy retreated and the Cavalry rode back after our Knapsacks . . . In the house . . . we found a woman & her son, they had a lot of Confederate Money which our men bought of them to be sent home as Souvenirs . . . another house was owned by a minister named Taylor but nobody remained in it and our men ransacked it of everything of any value. We were informed that the enemies rear guard left here at 3 ocl. Our Cavalry drove in a lot of cattle & sheep which were slaughtered immediately for the troops & while in the act of cooking our shares we were ordered to fall in, it being then 6 ocl. P. M. & marched forward . . . marched about two miles when we were halted & camped for the night in a wheat field.

(James City Cavalry *'Picket Lines'*, March 2020, p. 3, an article on Olive Branch Christian Church by Fred Boelt quoting from *A Soldier's Log* a privately published diary of Patrick Lyons that was printed in Providence, RI, in 1988.)

- - - - -

May 7, 1862 – Williamsburg, Virginia
Bruton Parish Hospital
Miss Delia Bucktrout, 16-year-old nurse's aide

[To a wounded Union soldier begging for water she said,] "Remember, this is our land. We did not ask you to come here and fight. I give you the water, but if you were well I would gladly kill you."

(Old Town, pp. 241-42.)

- - - - -

May 8, 1862 – sortie in Hampton Road
Lt. John Taylor Wood, C.S. Ironclad *Virginia*

. . . Having completed our engine repairs on May 8th . . . we heard heavy firing and in going down the harbor found the *Monitor,* with the *Galena, Naugatuck,* and a number of heavy ships, shelling our batteries at Sewell's Point. We stood directly for the *Monitor* but as we approached they all ceased firing and retreated below [Fort Monroe]. We remained for several hours in the Roads . . . and finally the Commodore, in a tone of deep disgust gave the order, "Mr. Jones, . . . take the ship back to her buoy."

(B&L-1, Wood, p. 709.)

- - - - -

May 8, 1862 – Forge Road, James City Cty., Virginia
Mr. John T. Martin, Farmer & School Teacher

The Federal or Northern Army made their appearance in the neighborhood on their way to Richmond burning . . . the woods, and the fences, stealing horses, breaking up furniture and running off many of the slaves. Great disturbance and ruin prevades the county.

(Martin Farm Journal, by date.)

- - - - -

May 8, 1862 – Mangochick Church
Pvt. Nathaniel Watkins, King & Queen Artillery

King William County, Virginia

My dear wife - . . . we reached this place yesterday (Wednesday) evening after a forced march of 100 miles from Glost. Point. It was one of the most remarkable marches of the war. We left the Point Saturday night at 8 O.C. and marched 40 miles by 7 O.C. Sunday evening . . . We have since marched almost 20 miles a day over good sandy roads & are resting today, in 9 miles of Hanover C.H. . . . our destination. Our boys have stood it like old veterans . . . haven't lagged behind and are in fine spirits . . . Of course the artillery companies more armed like infantry, but Col . Crump has given our company four field pieces, and we are preparing to take charge of a light battery as soon as we can get them more pieces. . . I had been sick with dysentery for a week before leaving the Point . . . For three days I have nothing to eat but biscuits . . . a good many of the Eastern Shore militia and a good many Glouces- ter volunteers (about 10 of our company from these two places) have deserted. A good many [of them] are forced to leave their wives & children behind and when I think of this and how they bear it, I can't help but feeling pained . . . Hanover C.H. is about 15 miles from Richmond on the RR.

(ed: The famed 'Foot Cavalry' of Stonewall Jackson seldom did 40 miles in a day and these artillerymen, who never marched at all, could never march 40 miles in one day and certainly could never do it without stragglers. The mileage to Hanover C.H., go- ing through West Point is approximately 77 miles. Maybe in 1862 with wandering dirt roads it could have been 23 miles further. If

they were able to march 20 miles a day with their field artillery and baggage that would have been quite an accomplishment.)

(ed; The watermen of Gloucester, from the lower Peninsula and the Eastern Shore, enlisted to protect their families and homes from the invading Yankees and were alienated by the withdrawal. When Johnston withdrew up the Peninsula from Williamsburg more than 80 men deserted from the 32nd Virginia Infantry. They were all in companies raised in the lower peninsula and were mostly watermen.)

(NVW Letters, by date; *32nd Virginia Infantry*, Lee Jensen, 1990, Lynchburg, p. 3 & pp. 159-72. See also Appendix 3 in this book.)

- - - - -

May 8, 1862 – Williamsburg, Virginia
Lt. Charles Haydon, 2nd Michigan Infantry

. . . I was compelled to go on guard duty today at Williamsburg. It is quite a place, half as large as Kalamazoo & like that the site of the State Insane Asylum & a college. . . . Business is suspended. One can buy nothing . . . The inhabitants have plenty of provisions for their prisoners & wounded of whom large numbers are here confined. . . . This is a very old but pleasant place containing many things of interest if one had an opportunity to look about.

(Haydon, by date.)

- - - - -

May 9, 1862 – Williamsburg, Virginia
Pvt. Wilbur Fisk, 2nd Vermont Infantry

It rained till midnight. In the morning we moved and encamped in the woods near the battle-field. . . . In company with a friend, I visited the battle-field where there were many of the dead still unburied. One can hardly refrain from shedding a silent tear over the last resting place of these brave men. I saw as many as a dozen buried side by side in one grave [1ˢᵗ Regiment, Excelsior Brigade], all from one company. Perhaps in other places there were even more . . . and now a simple shingle with their name marked on it tells the traveler where they lie. But the saddest sight of all was to see wounded men still alive and uncared for. I saw a man wounded in the head, a clot of brains marking the spot where he was hit. He was leaning back against some logs, in a partially upright posture, still breathing, though apparently unconscious. I might multiply descriptions of these horrors if it were pleasant to write of them, but it is not.

(Fisk, pp. 25-26)

- - - - -

May 10, 1862 – 17 MIles W. of Williamsburg
Lt. Charles Haydon, 2ⁿᵈ Michigan Infantry

We camped an hour before sundown in an oat field 17 miles from Williamsburg. . . . we are near the rear of the army . . . We are now from 40 to 45 miles from Richmond & our advance is probably 15 miles nearer.

Our loss (in the Regt.) on the 5ᵗʰ as near as can be learned is 18 killed, 39 wounded & a few missing.

(ed: The official casualties for the regiment were 17 killed, 38 wounded, and 5 missing. His report is quite accurate which is the exception rather than the rule.)

(Haydon, by date.)

- - - - -

May 10, 1862
New York Daily Tribune

Gen. Jamison has been appointed Military Governor and Provost Marshal of Williamsburg.

(New York Daily Tribune, May 10, p. 4 [Hereafter cited as NYDT.)

- - - - -

May 10, 1862 – near new Kent Courthouse, Virginia
Corporal Luther Furst, Signal Corps

. . . It is 6 a.m. and I am lying beside my horse awaiting orders . . . This is a fine country, very level. Nearly everybody has left, leaving house and home with niggers, horses and furniture, granaries filled with corn, everything is in a deplorable condition. We now gather all our forage as we advance. The cattle, hogs, and colts are running at large and our men confiscate all they want. . . . We have captured mules and horses which we use.

(Furst, by date.)

- - - - -

May 10, 1862
New York Daily Tribune

May 7 report by our correspondent:

As the enemy passed out of Williamsburg, on the north side . . . they left the Churches, the College, the Court House – all public buildings – filled with their wounded. Their ambulances and hospital wagons went out full also. . . . I saw 82 wounded men lying upon corn husks in the tobacco barn nearest Hancock's ground [Custis Farm barn and Redoubt #11].

(NYDT, p. 8.)

- - - - -

May 10, 1862 – Richmond, Virginia
John B. Jones, Clerk, C.S.A. War Department

The President's family have departed for Raleigh and the families of most of the cabinet to their respective homes . . .

(*Rebel War Clerks Diary*, John B. jones, New York, 2 vols., 1935, by date [Hereafter cited as RWCD]).

- - - - -

May 10, 1862 – West of Williamsburg
Pvt. Wilbur Fisk, 2nd Vermont Infantry

We resumed our march early in the morning, and pushed on till early afternoon, this time halting in the orchard of a staunch secessionist. Hard crackers, and but a limited supply of them, were the only contents [of our haversacks]. No meat, salt or fresh, and no butter or cheese. . . .

Those that had the materials made coffee in their tin cups to eat with their crackers . . . Under these circumstances, you will hardly blame the boys for being tempted to capture some of the "Virginia rabbits" that were squealing about in the woods near by, apparently common property. There were some good suppers eaten . . . that night, which may possibly diminish the inventory of property on the estate of this man . . . who served in the rebel army.

(Fisk, p. 27.)

- - - - -

May 10, 1862
New York Daily Tribune

The steamship *Ocean Queen*, from Yorktown [arrived in New York city] with 800 invalid and wounded [Union soldiers] last evening after a 30 hour passage. News of their approach was telegraphed from Sandy Hook.

(NYDT, p. 8.)

- - - - -

May 11, 1862 – New Kent
Lt. Richard Watkins, Co. K – 3rd Virginia Cavalry

My darling Mary

I am away out here in the woods hardly know where riding around every day watching the Yankees and sleeping out in the pines at night sometimes eating two meals a day sometimes only one and never three. Sometimes sitting on my horse all day at other times one half of the night, always moving with no means of writing letters and no regular courier or post office. . . . I have no time to write more tonight. It is late and I must be in my saddle at 3 ½ - will send this by John Knight's boy and hope it will reach you. Will always write when I can get a chance. . . . Love and kisses to all. . . .

(ed: This letter was not in ink and not in Richard's normal neat writing style. It was in pencil, hastily scrawled, and in places impossible to read. Mary will comprehend that it is very difficult to write a letter when your horse is moving. I certainly reached that conclusion as I tried to transcribe Richard's text.)

(ed: Richard's letter was carried by John Knight's servant who was probably going to Prince Edward County to get fresh horses. Of the 300 letters of Richard and Mary's that survive, I would estimate that 30% were mailed. The rest were carried by rotating preachers, men going back and forth on horse details, men going & coming from furloughs, and various other persons who might visit the camp and return to Prince Edward County. Mary's covers (envelopes) always show the Moore's Ordinary [railroad depot] return address. Richard sent Mary's letter back home in bundles when one of the men was going home on a horse detail or the preachers were rotating. Mary saved all of their letters and preserved a remarkable history. These 300+ letters were donated to the Virginia Historical Society in 1928 and sat quietly for 80 years waiting for me to transcribe and publish them in Send Me a Pair of Old Boots & Kiss My Little Girls – The Civil War Letters of Richard and Mary Watkins, 1861-1865.*)*

(Boots & Kisses, pp. 88-89.)

- - - - -

May 11, 1862 – camp near Pamunkey River
Sgt. Major Elisha Rhodes, 2nd Rhode Island Infantry

. . . We followed to this place and are now awaiting orders. Food is scarce, and all that we have to eat is the cattle killed by the way. No bread or salt in the Regiment and I am most starved.

(Rhodes, p. 65.)

- - - - -

May 11, 1862 – Williamsburg, Virginia
Pvt. Lyman A. Dickey, 2nd New Hampshire Infantry

Dear Mother

. . . We had a hard fight and this time we are the concores [conquerors]. I was not hurt but came very near it three or four times by having shells explode close to me. I had one rifle ball put through my clothes. I took one prisoner in the engagement – our boys are in fine spirits. We lost 107 killed and wounded. The Rebs are the worst set of lookin men I ever see . . . It is my opinion that the war will soon be closed. . . .

(150 Civil War Sesquicentennial: Virtue, Valor & Sacrifice: Yorktown-Williamsburg-Jamestown & West Point – edited by the *Virginia Gazette*, Williamsburg, 2012, p. 40. [Hereafter cited as 150 Civil War].

- - - - -

May 11, 1862 – James River, Virginia
George R Wood, deckhand, *James Buchanan*

. . . Our *Virginia* could not be taken up James River on account of the draft . . . so was blown up [on May 11] at Craney Island. . . . After the ship was blown up the balance of the fleet – *Patrick Henry, Thomas Jefferson, Beauford, Raleigh, and Teaser* - went up the James and anchored under the guns of Drewry's Bluff.

(ed: The James Buchanan, *the Wood's schooner, was confiscated*

by the Confederate government and used in a pontoon bridge across the James River above Drewry's Bluff. This gave easy passage for Confederate troops and supplies back and forth across the James River to support the fortifications and defenses on both sides of the river.)

(Boatman, pp. 47-49.)

- - - - -

May 11, 1862 – White House on the Pamunkey
Corporal Luther Furst, Signal Corps

. . . I have just been up to the advance picket now at the White House (rebel Colonel Lee's plantation) [actually a Custis plantation from his wife's family]. It is the nicest farm I ever saw, situated on the Pamunkey River. There are about 50 niggers, as many mules and oxen left behind and all faming utensils. The darkies were very kind to us and gave us corn cake, eggs, and fresh herring. . . They catch many assortment of fish here, in large seines. There are 900 acres in farm. The niggers all want to be free and ask me if they had to go to work or not. The Rebel pickets are in sight. It is now nearly dark and I am sitting on my horse a mile this side of our camp waiting on the Lieutenant, who is off to the left hunting a Signal Station. . . . Our soldiers throw away blankets, overcoats, knapsacks and hundreds could be picked up along the roads where they marched [coming to New Kent Courthouse].

(Furst, by date.)

- - - - -

May 11, 1862 – Craney Island, Virginia
Asst. Engineer E. V. White, C.S. Ironclad *Virginia*

We [tried] to lighten the ship enough to let her draw four or five feet less [so we could go up the James to Richmond]. We learned about 12 o'clock Saturday night that we could not get up the river, and now nothing was left but to destroy the ship. . . . She was then run aground on Craney Island [the guns had already been removed and sent to safety], and the work of destruction commenced. . . . I was one of ten selected to destroy the ship, and held the candle for Mr. Oliver, the gunner, to uncap the powder in the magazine to insure a quick explosion, and, necessarily, was among the last to leave her decks . . . the conflagration was a sight ever to remember. . . . Our crew landing Sunday morning, May 12, at about 4 o'clock . . . marched to Suffolk . . . took the train arriving in Richmond . . . and were ordered to Drewry's Bluff.

(White, p. 19.)

- - - - -

May 11, 1862 – aground off Craney Island
Chief Engineer H. A. Ramsay, C.S. Ironclad *Virginia*

Still unconquered we hauled down our drooping colors [and] . . . with mingled pride and grief, gave her to the flames.

(Unlike Anything, p. 138,)

- - - - -

May 11, 1862 – Aground off Craney Island
Asst. Engineer E. A. Jack, C.S. Ironclad *Virginia*

Flames issuing through the port holes, through the gratings, and smokestack . . . the conflagration was a sight ever to be remembered.

(Unlike Anything, p. 138.)

- - - - -

May 11, 1862 – Charles City County, Virginia
Lt. Richard Watkins, Co K – 3rd Virginia Cavalry

My own Dear Mary

I have only time to write a very few lines this morning by a gentleman going to Richmond. It is the very first opportunity I have had since we commenced our retreat from Yorktown nearly a fort-night [two weeks] ago. I have undergone very great privations and exposure and passed through a fiercely fought battle but God in his infinite mercy still spared my life and health . . . I have been able to perform my whole duty on this perilous retreat. Have remained with the troop all the time in the extreme rear of the army [rear guard] . . . We are now on the Chicahominy [Chicka-hominy River] near the Long Bridge about twenty miles of Rich-mond. No members of our troop has been killed, for although we were on the battlefield . . . in view of the contending forces with bombs bursting . . . and Minnie balls in great abundance passing over our heads yet we were not called into direct action. . . .

(ed: When Richards states that he has, "remained with the troop" he refers to Company K of the 3rd Virginia Cavalry which is The Prince Edward Troop or more formally the Prince Edward Dragoons.)

(Watkins, pp. 87-88.)

- - - - -

Mid May, 1862 – near the Chickahominy
Pvt. William P. Holland, Co. G – 11th Virginia Infantry

One night we were not far from the Chickahominy River. It was rainy, some of the wagons had stuck in the mud and all were be-hind, and we tried to keep on going as there was no good place to stop. There was a long deep mud hole in the road, and I be-lieve every other man that went by got in it. There was just light enough for the next man to see the one before him had stepped in and to avoid it; then the man next to him would get in it, and so on, till I believe every other man in our regiment – and maybe some others – had stepped in that mud hole. I got in up to the knee. It rained continually. One man declared his hat got moldy on his head.

Holland, p. 12.)

- - - - -

May 12 -13, 1862 – White House Landing, Virginia
Sgt. Major Elisha Rhodes, 2nd Rhode Island Infantry

Left camp in the evening and marched to White House Landing
on the Pamunkey River. Here we found three gun boats, and
we feel more comfortable. . . . 13th – This is historic ground for
in yonder house George Washington was married. From this
house Colonel Wheaton has procured a fine black saddle mule.
We are now within twenty-four miles of Richmond. . . .

(Rhodes, pp. 65-66.)

- - - - -

May 13, 1862 – 18 miles below Richmond
Pvt. Tally Simpson, 3rd S. Carolina Infantry

[The night of May 5] we again commenced the retreat and
marched four or five miles from town. . . . we kept up the retreat slowly, taking care not to lose any baggage, wagons, artillery
or men. I am sorry to say however that the enemy captured a
great number of our stragglers and sick. I never saw men suffer
so much in all my life. They were half fed & marched almost to
death. Some regiments actually received [raw] corn on the cob
for their rations. You can guess by that how scarce rations were. I
stood the trip remarkably well, with the exception of my sore feet
from which I suffered very much. . . . We are five miles from the
Chickahominy River. . . .

(Simpson, pp. 122-23.)

- - - - -

May 13, 1862 (Tuesday) – camp 8 miles above New Kent C.H.
Brig. Gen. Lafayette McLaws

My dearly beloved wife,

Our army is at a stand in and about this place, recuperating . . . from our fall back from the Peninsula . . .

Our government has now committed itself to a policy of concentration . . . if our armies can be fed there is every reason that victory . . . will crown our efforts. . . .

My warmest love to all.

(McLaws, by date.)

- - - - -

May 13, 1862 – New Kent County
Pvt. Nathaniel Watkins, King & Queen Artillery

My dear Nannie – . . . we are now in the Army of Peninsula . . . somewhere in New Kent County . . . in a nice old field . . . doing finely. We staid at Hanover CH one day to rest . . . Our Company has been temporarily divided, one half (including our boys) being detailed to take charge of four field pieces . . . and the other half armed with muskets . . . Until today I was as dirty & black as you ever saw . . . today I took a nice bath & put on . . . clean clothes. . . . There are about 65,000 [Confederate] men on the Peninsula, I have this from good authority. Have seen & heard nothing fm Bro Dick . . . I shall write whenever I can . . .

(NVW Letter, by date.)

- - - - -

May 13, 1862 – City Point, Virginia
George R. Wood, deckhand, *James Buchanan*

. . . the flag of truce boats, *Northampton,* Captain Hicks, and *Curtis Peck*, Captain Barnes, returned from the lower James where they had taken a load of Yankee prisoners [for exchange], passed the U. S. fleet at Harrison Bar and [as they passed] City Point said the Yankee fleet is coming.

(Boatman, p. 51.)

- - - - -

May 14, 1862 – Camp Tyler - near Chickahominy
Pvt. J. W. Reid, Mattison's S. C. Battalion

When I wrote my last letter, on the 11th, we were on the march. We continued marching day and night until we reached this place. We have had a dreadful time of it. . . . I have gotten so used to fighting that I do not mind it much.

I bought three pounds of manufactured tobacco last night, the best I ever saw. I am chewing it now. It rained all night last night. . . . put up my oilcloth and kept myself dry. I let Rufus McLees stay with me. He is sick.

I am almost bomb proof, but if it foreordained that I shall die to-day, tell your people that Jesse died at his post. . . . Firing continues. Yours as ever,

(Reid, pp. 84-85.)

- - - - -

May 14, 1862 – Richmond, Virginia
Mr. John B. Jones, Clerk – War Department

Our army has fallen back to within four miles of Richmond. Much anxiety is felt for the fate of the city. Is there no turning point in this long lane of downward progress? . . . The enemy's fleet of gunboats is ascending the James River, and the obstructions are not complete . . .

(RWCD, by date.)

- - - - -

May 14, 1862 – 'still in this cursed oat field'
Lt. Charles Haydon, 2nd Michigan Infantry

We were considerably troubled by gnat & mosquitoes. Woodticks are however our greatest annoyance. It is impossible to keep clear of them. The night was perfectly quiet & very warm. The roads are dusty.

(Haydon, by date.)

- - - - -

May 14-15, 1862 – near Drewery's Bluff, Virginia
George R. Wood, deckhand, *James Buchanan*

Rogers [Commander of the Union squadron] asked for a pilot [at City Point]. He offered as much as $1,000 in gold to one pilot. They could not do it. They had pledged their word to Governor Letcher to aid this state. He said he would not force any one. He had pilots but they had not been up the river for years. He left at 1 o'clock [on May 14th] with *Galena*, flagship, *Seminole, Aroostook, Naugatuck and Monitor,* and at 4 anchored at Varina or Aiken [Landing] on the James. The next day he was before Fort Darling [Drewry's Bluff] and made a big fight but was beaten off badly damaged.

(Boatman, pp. 52-53.)

- - - - -

May 15, 1862 – Drewry's Bluff
Lt. Dana Greene, U.S. Ironclad *Monitor*

Probably no ship was ever devised which was so uncomfortable for her crew, and certainly no sailor ever led a more disagreeable life than we did on the James River, suffocated with heat and bad air if we remained below, and a target for sharp-shooters if we came on deck.

(B&L-1, Greene, p. 729.)

- - - - -

May 15, 1862 – Richmond, Virginia

Mr. John B. Jones, Clerk, War Department

The enemy's gunboats, *Monitor, Galena,* etc. are at Drewry's Bluff, eight miles below the city, shelling our batteries, and our batteries are bravely shelling them. The President rode down to the vicinity this morning and observed the firing. . . . Joyful tidings! The gunboats have been repulsed! A heavy shot from one of our batteries ranged through the *Galena* . . . making frightful slaughter, and disabling the ship . . . the whole fleet turned about and steamed down the river. . . .

(RWCD, by date.)

- - - - -

May 15, 1862 – Cumberland landing on Pamunkey
Lt. Charles Haydon, 2nd Michigan Infantry

We were called up at 4 A.M. Marched at 6. Did not march more than 4 or 5 miles, are now bivouacking on a large flat near Cumberland Landing on the Pamunkey River. There are here some 30 sail vessels & a large number of steamers & tugs.

(Haydon, by date.)

- - - - -

May 15, 1862 – Forge Road, James City County
Mr. John T. Martin, Farmer & Teacher

More rain and planted some cotton and watermelon seed.

(Martin Farm Journal, by date.)

- - - - -

May 15, 1862 – Dr. Macon's farm
Corporal Luther Furst, Signal Corps

. . . encamped at the Macon Farm about two miles from Lee's Farm. It commenced raining last night and has been raining all

day. We manage to keep dry by fixing up shelters with our pon-
chos . . . We confiscated eight chickens today and had a fine dinner.

(Furst, by date.)

- - - - -

May 16, 1862 – Macon Plantation
Sgt. Major Elisha Rhodes, 2nd Rhode Island Infantry

Wednesday we left the White House and came to this place, a
distance of three miles . . .This farm is owned by a Dr. Macon .
. . Property is respected as much as it was in Washington. Even
the generals sleep out of doors, and the rights of people are respected. The men living here are surprised at this, as they were
told the Yankees would destroy everything. The female portion
of the population are very bitter and insult every soldier . . .

(Rhodes, p.60.)

- - - - -

May 16, 1862 – Cumberland Landing
Lt. Charles Haydon, 2nd Michigan Infantry

Nothing has surprised me more than the astonishing & incom-
prehensible stupidity or untruthfulness of newspaper reporters
as shown by their accounts of the battle of Williamsburg. I have
seen several & among all hardly a single statement was true.

Handcock's [Hancock's] brigade fought in the open field, [late
in the afternoon] made a brilliant charge, did excellent service
& lost perhaps 300 [100] men. Of this I have read many different accounts & it is spoken of as constituting nearly the whole
battle. As a matter of fact the greater part of the fighting was
on the left where the loss was from 1600 to 1800 & the battle
continued more than twice as long. This is hardly mentioned. . . .
Gen. Heintzelman & McClellan say that we saved the army from

defeat.

(ed: The Divisions of Hooker and Kearney bore the brunt of the battle out in the Ravine and the open land in front of Fort Magruder and Redoubts 7, 5 and 4.)

(ed: See the May 21ˢᵗ letter of Sgt. Johnston of the 8ᵗʰ N. J. Infantry on the same subject.)

(ed: As noted earlier, the Union losses were 2,283 men killed, wounded and missing. Hancock's Brigade was exactly 100 of that total. Hooker's Division, fighting in the 'Ravine' and in front of Fort Magruder, incurred almost 70% of the total Union casualties. Hooker, Kearny and Heintzelman were infuriated by all the praise lavished on Hancock for capturing 2 empty redoubts and repulsing one poorly coordinated Confederate attack just before sunset.)

(Haydon, by date. & Gates of Richmond, pp. 82-83.)

- - - - -

May 16, 1862 – Richmond, Virginia
Mr. John B. Jones, Clerk, C.S.A. War Department

McClellan is entrenching – that is, at least, significant as a respite.

(RWCD, by date.)

- - - - -

May 17, 1862 – Mount Airy on Pamunkey River
Corporal Luther Furst, Signal Corps

I am sitting on my horse scribbling these few lines. The farm that we have just left at Mount Airy is the finest tract of land I ever saw with 500 acres in one field of wheat, corn, oats and clover growing and now the soldiers are picketing their horses in it. The barn was filled with tobacco of which the soldiers confiscated tons of it. . . . I understand the U. S. is taking an inventory of all rebel goods which I suppose will be confiscated. Today is extremely hot and the pores are gushing forth their briny sweat profusely.

(ed: Luther wrote all of his entries in pencil and they have held up surprisingly well over time. Often ink will fade quite badly where- as pencil does not seem to encounter the problem.)

(Furst, by date.)

- - - - -

May 17, 1862 – On the way to Richmond
[Pvt] George [   ], 3rd Vermont Infantry

Dear Father

. . . I tell you we have not yet been paid, & are not likely to be for a long time . . . I was out of money & . . . out of paper, stamps & envelopes. [Enclosed] is an ambrotype if I can raise any way of doing it up securely. The picture was taken last winter at Camp Griffin [3 miles from the Chain Bridge near D.C.]. The case is some what damaged by getting damp in my knapsack. . . .

But this chasing of rebels is tiresome business. I am growing wea- ry of camp life and long to be free from it. If we can only corner & bay them up at Richmond we may yet soon be free but I am fearful they will escape. . . . Meantime I hope the box of sugar is on the way am awful hungry for a taste. I do hope that before another sugar season [maple sugar & maple syrup season] we shall have this cursed war closed up. . . .

Remember me to all friends & write soon & often.

George

(ed: George wrote a great 10 page letter but did not mention his last name or the names of any men in his Company and did not name his Regiment or Regimental commander. The fact that he

was in the morning assault indicates that he was a member of the 3rd Vermont. Colonel Breed Noyes Hyde commanded the 3rd Vermont at Dam #1. The 3rd sent 192 men across the Warwick to attack the One-Gun Battery. George indicates in his letter that he participated as close support in the assault and was in the water but did not cross the creek. The quotes above are from the portion of the letter dealing with the pursuit of the Confederate army after Williamsburg.)

(Vermont Brigade Letter – Dam #1 dtd. 5-17-1862; SC01698, Box 116, Folder 1, Special Collections Research Center, Swem Library, College of William and Mary, Williamsburg, Virginia. Assistance from J. Michael Moore at Lee Hall in determining, that based on George's comments, he would have been in the 3rd Vermont.)

- - - - -

May 18, 1862 – White House on Pamunkey River
Pvt. Wilbur Fisk, 2nd Vermont Infantry

The [troops thoughts on] the inevitable negro question: The boys think it their duty to put down rebellion and nothing more, and they view abolition of slavery in the present time as saddling so much additional labor upon them before the present great work is accomplished. Negro prejudice is as strong here as anywhere and most of the boys would think it a humiliating compromise to the dignity of their work to have it declared that the object of their services was to free the repulsive creatures from slavery, and raise the negro to an equality with themselves. I verily believe if such a declaration was made to-day a majority would be inclined to lay down their arms and quit the service in disgust. . . . They [the negroes] were dirty and ragged and probably as a perfectly natural result were ignorant and degraded but they seemed to understand that all this commotion has a connection with them . . .

(Fisk, p. 26.)

- - - - -

May 19, 1862 – west of White House
Pvt. Wilbur Fisk, 2nd Vermont Infantry

To-night we are encamped in an oak woods, whose rich foliage protects us overhead while huckle and blue berries just in full bloom make a beautiful carpet underneath. The whipowill is singing merrily on a branch over my head and as we are to start again in the morning at precisely four o'clock I am reminded that it is time to seek repose.

(Fisk, p. 30.)

- - - - -

May 20, 1862 – Chickahominy River
Corporal Luther Furst, Signal Corps

. . . we advanced about five miles and Lt. Daniels and the pickets have been at Chickahominy swamp.

(Furst, by date.)

- - - - -

May 20, 1862 – camp near Bottom's Bridge
Lt. Richard Watkins, Co. K – 3rd Virginia Cavalry

My own Dear Mary

We are again within fifteen miles of Richmond. Still in the rear of the Army watching the movements of the enemy, almost always in sight of them. We sleep in the woods with our horses saddled, and remain in the ranks all day from daylight till dark . . . a majority or at least half of the troop are on sick leave . . . I think that McClellan has shown plainly that he is not a great general. . . . I am ashamed to say that Charley Redd . . . [is] trying to get a substitute. It is a shame. . . Please write to me at once . . . Love to all.

(ed: A person is allowed to hire a substitute to take their place in the service. A contract is signed between the two individuals. The substitute must be presented to the command and be accepted by the commanding officer as a fit and dependable replacement before the contract is binding on all parties. The contract usually involves a cash or property payment (cattle, grain or chickens) to the substitute. Sometimes the substitute agrees to serve to pay off a financial debt he owes the other individual.)

(Boots & Kisses, p. 91.)

- - - - -

May 20, 1862 – Dr. Macon's Farm
Sgt. Major Elisha Rhodes, 2nd Rhode Island Infantry

Saturday night we left Macon farm . . . We have had a tedious march. Every night wood was placed under our wagons ready to light and destroy them if the enemy should surprise us. The men . . . wear their equipment day and night, and we have resorted to all kinds of tricks to deceive the Rebels. Sometimes at night we build fires in all directions to lead them to believe that a large force was following them. . . . Yesterday our Cavalry captured a [wagon] train with one hundred barrels of flour and fifty mules. The plantations . . . are deserted but show that this was before the war a delightful country.

(Rhodes, pp. 66-67.)

- - - - -

May 20, 1862 – 'Glenwood', near Richmond
Brig. Gen. Lafayette McLaws, Division Headquarters

My dear wife,

Your letter of the 6th inst. was received yesterday. By directing to Richmond our communication with each other is rapid . . . I am afraid that some of your letters have fallen into the hands of the

Yankees . . .

You can have no idea how our presence has given confidence to the people in Richmond. Before our arrival there was panic among all classes. . . .

I . . . have in my command 18 regiments, although my rank does not entitle me to it. . . . I suppose there will be a reorganization and my command, of course, will be reduced. . . .

It is about time for Willie and Johnny to be writing to me again, and longer letters than before . . . Give my love to Laura and give a thousand thanks for the socks she sent me. I am now commencing to wear cotton socks . . . I send you a rough draft of my report of the engagement in front of WmsBurg on Sunday [May 4].

L.McLaws

(ed: Lafayette is staying at 'Glenwood' which is the home of a Mr. Stubbs. Late in May, on the 23rd, in recognition of his services on the lower Peninsula, Lafayette is promoted to Major General.)

(Mclaws, by date. *Generals in Gray,* Ezra Warner, Baton Rouge, 1950, p. 204.)

- - - - -

May 21, 1862 – near New Kent Courthouse
Lt. Charles Haydon, 2nd Michigan Infantry

. . . I had a dish of strawberries to day. They sell at one dollar per qt. Butter is 60 cts. per lb., cheese 40 cts. & other things in proportion. . . .

(Haydon, by date.)

- - - - -

May 21, 1862 – near 'Pamunky' River
Sgt. Robert W. Johnson, Co. H – 8th New Jersey Infantry

Dear Sis –

Your 2nd letter of the 17th came at hand soon after I wrote you, and I am happy to hear you have received the money.

We are now within 21 miles of Richmond, and perhaps we will be in the City before you receive this. A Flag of truce was brought in yesterday as we where marching to our present encampment but I have not learned what it was for. There was two of them bearing it, one a Col. and the other a Major they were dressed in Grey Uniform, and blind folded. I give you a full account of the battle [Williamsburg] in my other letter therefore it will not be necessary to say much in this. I believe I did not tell you the Rebels had a Fort . . . covering about one acre of land with two Guns mounted (or rather dismounted). On this [unmanned] Fort [Redoubt 11] is where Hancocks Brigade won so much praise on a charge. It is all very nice for a lot of fresh men to come in when the Battle is at an end, and make a "gallant charge" thereby winning the praise of all the papers. Dont you think so. . . . After we had cleared the woods of killed and wounded we set it on fire, and as the fire ran over the dry twigs (the wood and leaves had all dried off now) and through the woods, now and then a Torpedoe would explode, which the Rebels had planted for us. I believe I have not given you a description of Williamsburg yet. Before the breaking out of the war there was about 2000 inhabitants in it. There is several Hotels in it and Stores of every description. There is also a Court House and Insane Asylum. The town is beautifully situated on a level tract of land and about 2 miles from the James River. But to change the subject. It will be an utter impossibility to procu[re] those bodies I think for they are decayed a great deal by this time, and then they where not buryed in coffins for we could not get them. Even the Officers where buried the same as the men no distinction in death. Our Officers where are not elected yet and I do not know who are candidates. Capt. Henry is acting Col. he being the Senior Officer, the Lieu. Col. being sick. I am very sorry to hear that Joe is sick but I hope he will recover in a few days.

I received the postage stamps you sent me . . . When you write again tell me how Mother is . . . and how Grand Mother is and Grand Father and all the Folks. . . .

As I said before, keep the shop for I have presentiment we are going to be home again before long. Latest news is Richmond is being evacua[t]ed, our Cavelry has been out on a scout and brought in the news. I don't know wether it is so or not, but hope it is.

Write soon, Yours &c

Robert W. Johnson

(Letter of Sgt. Robert W. Johnson, SCO1349, Special Collections Research Center, Swem Library, College of William & Mary)

(ed: The 1860 Census shows Robert with a sister Maria (age 17) and a sister Mary (age 13). Maria would have been 18-19 years old when he wrote the above letter and therefore, as his oldest sister, she would seem to be the likely recipient of this letter.)

(ed: You can certainly feel the contempt for the praise being heaped on Hancock's Brigade, by the press, for their glorious assault and capture of the unmanned Redoubt #11. Hooker's Division had been part of the heaviest fighting in the battle of Williamsburg in the area of 'The Ravine' and the land in front of Redoubts 3 thru 7. After the capture of the empty redoubt Hancock did repulse a piecemeal counterattack by 2 Confederate regiments just prior to nightfall.)

(ed: A normal Union infantry regiment has 10 companies and 1000 men. The 8th New Jersey had 38 officers and 851 enlisted men. They averaged, at the start of the conflict, slightly less than 89 men per company. During the war they lost 9 officers killed (K) or mortally wounded (MW) and 1 officer died of disease. 167 enlisted men were K or MW and 109 died of disease. In addition, they also lost men with amputated limbs, other service ending wounds, medical discharges, deserters, transfers to the Pioneer Corps, Hospital Details, Courier duty, etc. etc. In 1864 they became a Battalion and were consolidated with other units to form a new command. Some Union states did not send reinforcements to regiments, instead they created new regiments. New Jersey did not send reinforcements whereas the state of Vermont sent reinforcements. The Confederacy sent reinforcements to try to replace the losses of the regiments. Different manpower philosophies. See Appendix 1 for additional information on this subject.)

(ed: The 1860 Monmouth, N. J., census report shows Robert as a 21 year old clerk/salesman in some type of mercantile establishment. Robert was born in 1839 and joined Co. H on 9-14-1861 as a Sergeant. The Regiment will serve under General Joe Hooker at Williamsburg, Seven Pines and during the Seven Days Campaign. Robert will survive and muster out of the service at the end of the war.)

(ed: Robert has a marvelous writing style, tells great stories with interesting details and has several interesting writing traits. He does not always use periods and other punctuation. Were is always written as where and whether is written as wether. He will write both don't & dont and he uses &c which was the normal way to write etc. in the 1860s.)

(National Park Service – U. S. Civil War Soldiers 1861-1865 Records, Ancestry. com, Provo, UT., M550, roll 12: Copy of Penison Application detail at Ancestry Pension Application; U. S. Federal Census 1860, Ancestry.com, Provo, UT., for Monmouth, N.J.)

- - - - -

May 21, 1862 – Cold Harbor crossroads
Corporal Luther Furst, Signal Corps

. . . I am now halted at crossroads at Cold Harbor and 12 miles from Richmond. . . .Last night where we camped we cut down a bee tree . . . but it was too early and they had no honey. . . General Stoneman [Union Cavalry] order Signal Captain Fisher and party to the rear today.

(Furst, by date.)

- - - - -

late May, 1862 – near the Chickahominy
2nd Lt. E. P. McKinney, 6th New York Cavalry

Our squadron was ordered up the Peninsula to the Chickahominy to picket the railroad that carried supplies for McClellan's Army from White House to Savage Station. . . .

While on picket duty the officers had a hard time to get enough to eat. The enlisted men had their rations issued to them, but the officers could not draw rations. They had to buy their supplies and there was no commissary in reach from whom we could buy. We bought some from the inhabitants. When they wouldn't sell we 'borrowed." I have a vivid recollection of sitting up one night till past midnight trying to cook a tough old guinea hen. . . .

(McKinney, pp. 54-55.)

- - - - -

late May, 1862 – Richmond, Virginia
Pvt. Tally Simpson, 3rd S. Carolina Infantry

. . . Richmond is quiet . . . the President is determined to defend it to the last. McClellan is steadily advancing and will make a desperate attempt to capture the city. . . . If Johnston waits for the enemy to make the attack the fight may be delayed some time, for it will takes weeks for him [McClellan] to make preparations . . . I scarcely think our General will wait . . . but while the enemy is making arrangements . . . he will sally forth and give battle.

(Simpson, p. 124.)

- - - - -

May 23, 1862
New York Daily Tribune

The following list [240 soldiers mainly from New York and Pennsylvania] of sick and wounded men who came from the extreme advance of McClellan's Army. They were at West Point on Tuesday [18th] and fell from the ranks from fatigue and sickness; a few were wounded. They were 28 hours coming from Baltimore [on a] freight train [to New York City].

(NYDT, p. 12.)

- - - - -

late May, 1862 – north bank of the Chickahominy
Cpl. Marshall H. Twitchell, Co. I – 4th Vermont Infantry

From Williamsburg we moved up . . . in front of Richmond and took position on the north bank of the Chickahominy. In our advance we made twenty miles in one day. This we thought, at the time, something extraordinary; we then had a poor knowledge of our travelling powers or what would be done by us in the future. It was here that the "gray back" joined the regiment and with the persistency of an old veteran stayed with us during the war.

(ed: "Gray back" was a nickname used in both armies for lice. They infested the clothing of the soldiers and with the sanitary conditions and the fact that uniforms and clothing were seldom washed the lice were a constant companion.)

(ed: To quote Pvt. Sam Watkins of the 1st Tennessee Infantry, "Every soldier had a brigade of lice on him, and I have seen fellows so busily engaged in cracking lice, that it reminded me of old women knitting." Your clothing, bedding and even the campground, if you had been there for a few days, was infested with lice. You needed to boil everything but that was not possible. So, the soldiers would sit around warming their clothing over the fire, some

lice would pop to the surface, and they would crack them with their fingernail (split them in two). Great skill was developed in using the heat of the fire or the soldier scorched his clothing.

(Twitchell, p. 37.; Company Aytch – A Memoir of the Civil War, Sam Watkins, Nashville, 2011, p. 55.)

- - - - -

May 23, 1862 – Richmond, Virginia
Pvt. Tally Simpson, 3rd S. Carolina Infantry

. . . scurvy is in some of the regiment. Magruder has ordered that a detail be made from each company to gather vegetables for the soldiers, they being a preventative. The names of the plants are these: wild onions, lamb's quarters, potato tops and other which I forgot. . . I do not relish the onions . . . the other, I am afraid, will be worse.

. . . The other day I feasted on a mess of fried onions, and today we had for dinner some fresh butter and a delicious quarter of mutton. The butter only cost $1.00 per pound and the qr of mutton $2.30.

(ed: The symptoms of scurvy include bleeding of the gums, teeth loose, spots of various colours on the skin, debility, pale countenance and bloating. The pulse will be small, quick and intermitting. In its advanced stage the joints swell and blood bursts out from different parts of the body.

Treatment: Give the patient plenty of fresh vegetables such as spinnage, lettuce, beets, carrots, and scurvy-grass. This with oranges, lemons, sugar, and spruce beer . . . are generally sufficient to cure the complaint. Nitric vinegar is strongly recommended for the same purpose.)

(Simpson, pp. 125-26. Mackenzie p. 217.)

- - - - -

May 23, 1862 –Richmond, Virginia
Mr. John B. Jones – Clerk, C.S.A. War Department

Oh the extortioners! Meats of all kinds are selling at 50 cts. per pound; butter, 75 cts.; coffee, $1.50; tea, $10; boots, $30 per pair; shoes, $18; shirts, $5 each. Houses are rented for $500 last year, are $1000 now. Boarding from $30 to $40 per month.

(RWCD, by date.)

- - - - -

May 24, 1862 – New Bridge on the Chickahominy River
Sgt. Major Elisha Rhodes, 2nd Rhode Island Infantry

. . . Just as we reached a bridge over a creek bang goes a gun [cannon], and a shot struck within ten feet of me. I thought my time had come and stood stupidly waiting for it to explode. But it proved to be a solid shot. Soon the shells were flying all around us . . . It has rained nearly all day, and we are wet and uncomfortable. The Negroes are queer people and seem to understand the war. They leave for Fortress Monroe as soon as they can get to our rear. Strawberries and peas are ripe, and we get a few occasionally. . . . found we were near a town called Mechanicsville. I went into town. The houses were riddled with shot fired from both sides . . .

(Rhodes, pp. 67- 68.)

- - - - -

May 25, 1862 – near the Chickahominy
Lt. Charles Haydon, 2nd Michigan Infantry

Reveille was at 4 A.M. & we left camp at 6 A.M. Two hours later we crossed the Chickahominy, a narrow, deep, sluggish stream at Bottom's Bridge. Soon after crossing we filed into the woods & halted for dinner.

(Haydon, by date.)

- - - - -

May 26, 1862
New York Daily Tribune

Capt. Joseph Gartoh informed our reporter that the Chesapeake Hospital, . . . 3 miles from Fortress Monroe, contains 600 patients, half of whom are Confederate soldiers. In the United States Hospital there are 100 men belonging to the regular service [Union]. The Hygea Hospital has 200 patients.

The steamers *John Tyler,* the *Vanderbilt* and *Kennebeck* are ready to depart with large numbers of sick and wounded [for various Northern hospitals in Baltimore, Philadelphia and New York.]

(NYDT, p. 8.)

- - - - -

May 26, 1862 – 6 miles from Richmond
Pvt. Nathaniel Watkins, King & Queen Artillery

My dear wife – Our brigade is now stationed about 6 miles from Richmond . . . I can't help hoping & thinking that the war will not last longer than five or six months - & will try to stand it for that length of time, but if it continues longer I will make every effort to get out of the army. . . . if I was ever placed in an infantry contrary to my wish . . . I would substitute . . . mail is just starting so I must close. Yraff husband N.V.W.

(NVW Letters, by date.)

- - - - -

May 27, 1862 – near Mechanicsville, Virginia
Corporal Luther Furst, Signal Corps

Up at 3 a.m. received orders to put up three days rations. . . . by daylight on our way to report to the head of the Signal Corps, Major Myer, rain pouring down in torrents. We then received sealed orders and left with Porter's Division. . . . We proceeded as far as Hanover Courthouse . . . our flag signaling has saved our guns from [firing] on our own men. . . . we reached the railroad bridge and set fire to it, the [purpose] of our movement . . .

(ed: Albert J. Meyer developed a series of codes using a single signal flag, lantern or torch system during his service on western Army posts in the 1850's. This was not a semaphore system which uses two flags. In 1858 the Army convened a board headed by Lt. Col. Robert E. Lee to evaluate and conduct field tests of Meyer's concept. The field tests were successful and he was appointed Chief Signal Officer of the U. S. Army in 1859. 1861 found Major Meyer at Fort Monroe, under General Butler, training signalmen. Then under Gen. McClellan, in the Army of the Potomac, he put his signalmen into action. He won brevet promotion to Lt. Colonel at Hanover Court House and Colonel at Malvern Hill for the success of his signalmen in aiding the army.)

(Furst, by date. Wikipedia and Library of Congress sites on the Signal Corp and Albert Meyer.)

- - - - -

May 27, 1862 – camp 3 miles from Richmond
Pvt. William C. Corson, Co. G – 3rd Virginia Cavalry

My Dear Jennie,

. . . We brought up the rear of the entire cavalry force and ours was the last squadron that crossed the Chickahominy at Camp Bottom's bridge. We are now only three miles from Richmond still doing heavy picket duty . . . Our army is done falling back now and we are waiting for the enemy. . . .

May 28

. . . I am glad to know you received my picture at last. If you recognize the picture, I am sure you would not know the original now . . . All of my clothes were burnt at Yorktown and I have only one suit of unmentionables and those I had to wash myself in a branch and wait until they dried in the sun. [Since he was naked maybe he also took a bath in the branch] I had my head sheared yesterday so close that a fly slips up if lights on it. Capt. Isbell says I look like a blue hog badly cleaned. . . .

I fear you will never be able to read this letter as I have the worst pencil I ever saw. You deserve much credit for your home made envelope.

(ed: William probably had his head 'sheared close' to help with the continual battle with lice.)

(ed: You will also note that the 3rd Virginia Cavalry is crossing at Bottom's Bridge two days after the 2nd Michigan Infantry. This is a bit confusing. Dating error by one or the other? One of them perhaps crossing at a different point?)

(Corson, pp. 78-79.)

- - - - -

May 27, 1862
New York Daily Tribune

Certain parties have obtained a contract for raising the *Merrimac* [*C. S. Ironclad Virginia*] . . . sunk by the Rebels in the Elizabeth River. It is presumed that the chief purpose in raising the *Merrimac* is to supply the demand for mementoes . . . which exists in regard to that vessel.

(NYDT, p. 1.)

- - - - -

May 27, 1862 – 6 miles from Richmond
Pvt. Nathaniel Watkins, King & Queen Artillery

My dear wife - We are still at the same place . . . drawn out in line . . . under arms an hour & half in a hard rain . . . ordered to cook three days rations. Sunday . . . marched some four miles down the road and drawn out in line of battle . . . then rested again . . . we will be fed on ship crackers which I like very much . . . Kiss the children . . . N.V.W.

(NVW Letters, by date.)

- - - - -

May 28, 1862 – Hanover Court House, Virginia
Sgt. Major Elisha Rhodes, 2nd Rhodes Island Infantry

. . . the Rebels had repaired the track and the Cavalry scouts reported that a train was coming from the direction of Hanover. We put some artillery in position and as the cars came around a curve we sent a polite message to stop in the form of a few shells. . . . There were four cars with ammunition and other stores. We destroyed the track by tearing up the rails. Huge piles of ties were made and the rails laid across. When the fire reached the rails they bent of their own weight . . . and became useless. . . . I procured a fine pair of new gray pantaloons. . . . the place where we destroyed the train is called Atlee Station.

(Rhodes, p.68.)

- - - - -

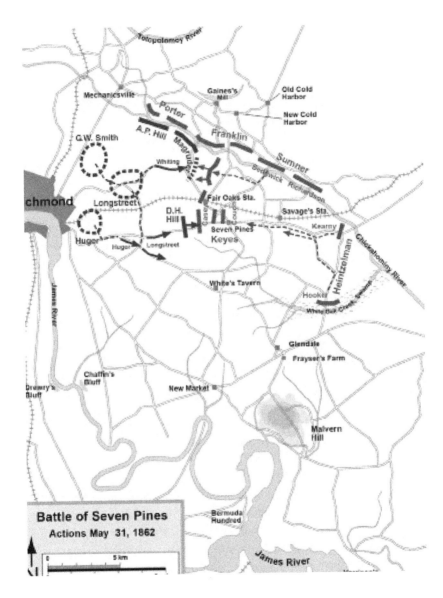

Battle of Seven Pines
Actions May 31, 1862

0   5 km

Map by Hal Jesperson, www.cwmaps.com

251

May 29, 1862 – Richmond, Virginia
Sgt. Benjamin Porter, Co. E – 11th Alabama Infantry

Mrs. M. A. Porter

I seat myself to write an offended mother. I am a fraid I think I have been very negligent in writing to you. . . . I expect you have all heard about the retreat or evacuation of York Town I was not on the march myself it was then I was sick & I was sent to Richmond [to Chimborazo hospital].

I joined my company on the way. They had a very hard time of it. They subsisted on parched corn for a day or so at a time & hardly that. The roads was so bad we could not get our supplies for seven days. . . . I was to see Frank but poor fellow he is now in the hand of the enemy. He was taken sick and was sent to Williamsburge to the hospital about a week before the retreat from that place & was not able to walk and was left behind. . . . all the company was sorry to see him left behind. . . .

. . . The yankey army is in five miles of us at this time & we are expecting a fight soon. Our men are waiting very impatiently . . . I was sorry to hear of the surrender of New Orleans. I hear it said that our great little city Mobile will share the same fate . . .

Ma I beg you to let no one see this. It is so badly writin I am out of practice & have no form. Dear Ma you must always prey for me.

your son B. F. Porter

(ed: Mobile did not fall till the very end of the war. The Union fleet led by Admiral Farragut captured the two main forts guarding the main channel into Mobile Bay but the city of Mobil did not fall until the second week of April, 1865. Blockade runners still ran in and out of Mobile using other channels.)

Prey for Us All – The War Letters of Benjamin Franklin Porter, 11th Alabama, Ellen Williams, Mobile, 06, p.33 [hereafter cited as B. F. Porter]).

- - - - -

May 30, 1862 – camp this side of Chickahominy
Corporal Luther Furst, Signal Corps

. . . still lying in camp within 5 miles of Richmond . . . Today lightning struck a pine tree within 20 yards of my tent and we could feel the heat . . . the thunder showers are very heavy . . .

(Furst, by date.)

- - - - -

May 30, 1862 – 5 miles below Richmond
Lt. Richard Watkins, Co. K – 3rd Virginia Cavalry

My own dear Mary

. . . I am now sitting right down in the middle of the road in the midst of a swamp. The enemy about a mile below us . . . yesterday our company on pickett took five prisoners. It seems right strange that Nat [Richard's brother] on foot should have retreated at the rate of 20 miles a day and we on horseback have hardly averaged four. We often only march a mile a day. . . holding our horses by the bridles. They have been saddled the whole time of our retreat . . . I lost no clothes at all . . . I had only one blanket with me and on the battlefield at Williamsburg in the midst of a hard rain gave that to a poor wounded soldier . . . Would be glad if you could send me one of my blankets if you have a chance. . . . By the by you ought not to show my love letters to Ma . . . Kiss my dear children for me & give love to all . . .

(ed: Pvt. Nathaniel Watkins and the King & Queen Heavy Artillery were forced to abandon their works at Gloucester Point, losing their heavy artillery, and flee on foot toward Richmond. Without artillery they will be used as infantry in the battle of Seven Pines.)

(Boots & Kisses, p. 93.)

- - - - -

May 30, 1862
New York Daily Tribune

From Fortress Monroe, Wednesday, May 28:

SIX NEGROES SHOT – QUIET RESTORED

Quite a disturbance took place in Norfolk last night, it is said to have been occasioned by a Negroe shooting Corporal John Brooke, Company C, 99th New York Infantry. The disturbance became general and the greater part of the company was engaged. Three negroes were killed and two or three wounded. Six ringleaders were sent to the Rip Raps to-day; many others were arrested but released. All is quiet now.

(NYDT, p. 1.)

- - - - -

May 31, 1862 – Richmond, Virginia
Mr. John B. Jones – Clerk, C. S.A. – War Department

The great storm day before yesterday . . . has so swollen the Chickahominy as to prevent McClellan's left wing from retreating, and reinforcements from being sent to his relief. The time is well chosen by General Johnston for the attack. . . .

(RWCD, by date.)

- - - - -

May 31, 1862 – camp near Richmond
Private William Holland, Co. G – 11th Virginia Infantry

It rained hard [last night] and I waked up in my tent to find that my feet were in water. [That morning] we were ordered out to march. We didn't know where. I had felt ill that morning, and had been excused from duty, but before my company had started, I felt somewhat better, so I thought I ought to go on with the others. I took my place in ranks and went on. We left our blankets and knapsacks at the cook camp and we saw Col. Houston and A.A.G. of the Division, G. M. Sorrel talking together. Then we saw Sorrel take the road toward the enemy. We knew then that we were in for it.

(Holland, p. 13.)

- - - - -

May 31, 1862 – Fair Oaks Station [Seven Pines]
Col. W. W. H. Davis, 104th Pennsylvania Infantry

. . . The night of the thirtieth of May will long be remembered by the old Army of the Potomac on account of the fearful storm that prevailed. The rain fell in torrents; the lightning flashed with unusual vividness and the thunder was fearful. It would have required no great stretch of the imagination to believe a great battle going on between the opposing armies.

The 104th opened the battle of Fair Oaks [May 31] and was the first to receive the overwhelming shock of the enemy. . . . Three hours had elapsed since the regiment had gone into action and more than one third of our men had fallen . . . reinforcements did not arrive . . . no order was given to retire but we were literally pushed back by the superior force of the enemy . . . The regiment lost all its camp equipage and baggage . . . and most of their personal effects. . . . the enemy was kind to our wounded . . . they carried a number of the men to the shade of an old building . . . and supplied them with crackers and water. . . .

(The Civil War – Volume 1 – The American Iliad, Otto Eisenschiml & Ralph Newman editors, New York, 1956, p.191. {Hereafter cited as Iliad.])

- - - - -

May 31, 1862 – Stumpy Camp, near Richmond
Private Newton Camper, Co. D – 11th Virginia Infantry

. . . The troops were ordered to prepare two days rations . . . day began to dawn . . Soon the whole army was in motion back on the Williamsburg road, destined for a place called Seven Pines, about six miles from Richmond.

. . . our Brigade, commanded by Gen. Kemper, filed to the right, to remain as reserves. About 4 PM orders came to hurry forward . . . in taking proper position the Brigade was compelled to march a distance of five hundred yards across the line of battle, in the face of galling fire . . . when our brave boys reached their post many of their comrades had fallen. . . the Company swept on to the charge . . . they drove the enemy out of their trenches and hurled them back on their main line. Then falling back to the captured trenches they remained till night ended the conflict. . . . About 9 o'clock the Company moved a mile to the right and did not engage in the fight the next day. . . .

(Newton Camper pp. 7-8.)

- - - - -

May 31, 1862 – near Seven Pines battlefield
Pvt. Milton Barrett, 18th Georgia Infantry

. . . i am well hoping thes hasty rote lines may find you [well]. . . . on 31 day of may we was orderd to the chickahoma swamp. gen. Longstreets division was all ready ingage with the emney. at one oclock our brigade was call into action and order to sport those brigade that was all ready closely ingage. . . . a heavy rain had fel on Friday night and the swamp full of water. we had to waid some places waist deep. we routed the yankees from ever pershion that took . . . we capture 26 peces of artilar two hundred barrels of whiskey military stoers and so forth. the fight lasted tel dark. . . . we have purcesion of the yankees camps and had drove them back three mile. . . . we move all of the wonded we could find . . . i must close for the wont of paper.

your effecnate brother

Milton

(ed: Milton describes day one of the two-day battle of Seven Pines with his very unique writing style. The 18th Georgia was mostly held in reserve on May 31 and June 1 but a good part of May 31 they spent standing in the swamp.)

(Barrett, pp. 69-70.)

- - - - -

May 31, 1862 – Seven Pines battlefield
Pvt. James T. Petty, Co. B – 17th Virginia Infantry

Finding him weak [a wounded soldier of the 105th Pennsylvania] from his wound [I] wouldn't talk to him myself, and prevailed on the few around to preserve a little silence . . . all seemed to have sympathy for him in his helpless condition – having eased him as best I could by a change of position, left him to be cared for when the ambulance arrive.

(*The 17th Virginia Infantry*, David Riggs, Lynchburg, 1980, p.35. [Hereafter cited as 17th Virginia]).

- - - - -

May 31, 1862 – Seven Pines battlefield
Corporal Luther Furst, Signal Corps

. . . since 1 p.m. there has been a big fight on. . . . it is now dark and still raging furiously. I have been unwell, since our last tramp to Hanover, with a diarrhoea caused by the swamp water. Kay's [Casey's] Division was attacked and driven back with the loss of 14 pieces of artillery . . .

(Furst, by date.)

- - - - -

Afternoon, May 31, 1862 – Seven Pines battlefield
Pvt. William P. Holland, Co. G – 11th Virginia Infantry

I had gone on with the others some distance. I don't know how far, when I felt something of a shock. I thought at first a bullet had struck the musket in my hand and I looked and saw blood and found that my right thumb had been shot. The bullet had come from the left, and I don't think it missed my body by more than two inches. I got a comrade to help me fix my arm in a sling. He said, "If I were in your place I'd go to the rear." And I did so.. . .

I went on to a field hospital, about two miles off. . . . I got to the field hospital, and as no one was ready to attend to me then, I sat down on a fence to wait. . . . a Mr. Archer, told me to get up be-hind him . . . invited me to spend the night at his house and took me to what was called the "Ladies Hospital" where my thumb was dressed by Dr. Garnett who expressed the opinion that it should be cut off. I would not agree. . . "

(ed: The 'Ladies Hospital" quite possibly could be Robertson Hos-pital which was run by Captain Sally Thompkins. She was the only woman in charge of a hospital in Richmond.)

(ed: William got a medical furlough and returned to his Company in October when they were near Winchester. He could not hold a musket, so after some temporary duty he was assigned duty as a Quartermaster where he served for the balance of the conflict.)

(Holland, p. 14)

- - - - -

May 31, 1862 – west of the Chickahominy
Lt. Charles Haydon, 2nd Michigan Infantry

We have to spend an hour every day picking off woodticks. Most of the men owing to our mode of living & the want of clean clothes are now becoming lousy [infested with lice]. I think they got most of them from Secesh blankets picked up at Williamsburgh. Benson & Seward are both well supplied but I have thus far escaped. I heard Prentice say this m'g that he was "going to make a desperate attempt to drive the enemy from his earthworks" meaning that he would try to get the lice & ticks out of his shoes & stockings.

(Haydon, by date.)

- - - - -

May 31, 1862 –Near Seven Pines battlefield
Lt. Charles Haydon, 2nd Michigan Infantry

. . . General Heintzelman . . . ordered us to deploy, act as a guard & arrest everybody we found retreating [from the battlefield]. Within an hour we had arrested more than 1000 men. We were kept here till long after dark.

To be there seeing wounded men, cowardly stragglers with their doleful stories . . . and rascally lies, the disabled artillery & all the debris of the battlefield while the combat was going on in front & our comrads engaged was the most . . . discouraging duty I ever performed. I would rather go in ten battles than suffer the anxiety of another day like this.

(Haydon, by date.)

- - - - -

May 31, 1862 – Seven Pines battlefield
Sgt. Wm. Randolph Smith, Co. F – 17th Virginia Infantry

Lights are seen glancing to and fro across the field . . . some upon hospitable . . . intent, but the greater portion in search of booty. Knapsacks & haversacks are emptied of their contents and overhauled. All that is valuable is stored away . . . the dead that strew the ground are examined; if a foe his pockets are . . . rifled.

(17th Virginia Infantry, p. 34.)

- - - - -

June, 1862

On June 1 the battle resumes. General Robert E. Lee is now in command of the army. Private Reid, of Mattison's South Carolina Battalion, is surprised and writes, *"General Johnston is badly wounded, . . . who will succeed him . . . it is said it will be R. E. Lee. I know but little about him. . . . They say he is a good general, but I doubt his being better than . . . Longstreet."* Sgt. Benjamin Porter, of the 11th Alabama, penned the following thoughts to his Ma, *". . . we drove them from there own redoubts & they left all there canons & tents, provisions, knapsacks, haversach & infact everything they had. . . . Our Regt. Suffered very mutch . . . I do not know how many wer killed . . . I want you to prey for me all the time for preyers are of great youse . . ."*

Rain and mud continue to dominate army life around Richmond. McClellan gets some reinforcements, but not enough to meet his needs for his vastly outnumbered army. In his mind, the only solution is to build trenches and lay siege to Richmond. Lee adds to the Richmond trenches to counter McClellan. This will allow a smaller number of his men to hold McClellan in place so that the Confederate army can assume the offense.

Fort Pillow falls on June 4 and two days later, in a naval battle at Memphis, the Confederate fleet of cotton-clads is defeated and Memphis falls to Union forces. Only the Confederate fortifications at Port Hudson, Louisiana, and on the cliffs at Vicksburg, Mississippi, keep the Union from gaining total control of the Mississippi River and cutting the Confederacy in half. It will take 13 more months for

General Grant to capture Vicksburg and deliver one of the decisive victories of the war to the Union.

Burial parties are working to bury the dead at Seven Pines. Lt. Charles Haydon, of the 2nd Michigan, notes on June 5, *"the dead whom are still unburied are now nearly decomposed . . . details are sent out daily to burn the dead horses . . ."* Private J. W. Reid, of Mattison's South Carolina Battalion writes home, *"there is a great deal of sickness in our army, and soldiers are dying at the hospital almost daily."*

General J. E. B. Stuart takes a portion of his cavalry to check out the right flank of McClellan's army. He ends up riding completely around the Union army and brings Lee the key information that the right flank is vulnerable. Out in the Shenandoah Valley, in a span of 33 days, Stonewall Jackson will march and countermarch his small army, fight six battles against four Union generals while marching over 400 miles. When the dust settles he has all four generals and their troops in full retreat. The Valley is clear of Union troops and no significant reinforcements will be sent to McClellan. Jackson's men now board trains to transport them toward Richmond to join Lee. Lee will still have 20,000 fewer men than McClellan but McClellan certainly would never believe that was the situation.

General Lee changes the name of his army from the Army of the Peninsula to the Army of Northern Virginia. The Peninsula Campaign has ended and the Seven Days Campaign is set to begin.

June, 1862

June 1, 1862 – battlefield near Richmond
Lt. Richard Watkins, Co. K – 3rd Virginia Cavalry

My dear dear Mary I write simply to let you know I am well. Our company is at the rear of the Army doing the most disagreeable of all work, catching stragglers from the Army and sending them back. Yesterday afternoon for five hours a fierce battle was fought . . . a large number of killed and wounded on both sides . . . Our men forced the enemy back, took two batteries, all their tents, camp equipage, ammunition and still hold their position, some sharp fighting this morning & preparedness for a great deal more . . . Genl Johnston is wounded . . . Poor Charley Redd . . . yesterday brought out a worthless substitute . . . Capt. Berkeley . . . refused to take him and properly too. Oh tis a shame not a single Redd is now with the company all sick without exception – Have heard nothing from Nat [Richard's brother] Genl Rhodes brigade has been in the fight but I do not know whether Nat is infantry or heavy artillery since retreat. If in the infantry he had in all probability been in the engagement. . . . Mr Dickinson is about to leave and I must close to send this by him to Richmond. Goodbye dear one

(ed: In this letter, when Richard mentions working in the rear, he is not the rear guard between the two armies but behind the attacking Confederate army collecting stragglers.)

(Boots & Kisses, pp. 93-94.)

- - - - -

June 1, 1862 – Richmond, Virginia
Pvt. Nathaniel Watkins, King & Queen Artillery

My dear wife - . . . I had a spell with a good deal of pain . . . [came] to Richmond for a few days . . . my sickness was caused by the passage of gravel from the kidney . . . which the surgeon says is very common. I am now well again & will report back to my company tomorrow. . . . You will see in tomorrow's paper of a fight on the Chickahominy . . . [where] we have whipped the Yankees terribly . . . Our company lost 5 killed & 26 wounded (only 1 mortally) . . . They entered the fight with 58 . . . nearly half killed & wounded . . . Yr devoted husband N.V.W.

(ed: Nathaniel had reported to the Confederate hospitals in Richmond. His unit fought under General Robert Rodes, as infantry, in the battle of Seven Pines and was battered pretty badly.)

(ed: Kidney stones or 'gravel' and Bladder stones could be major problems. The symptoms are deep seated pain in the small of the back, urine high-colored and small in quantity, voided with pain and sometimes bloody. The suggested treatments include putting the patient in a warm bath, a grain of opium every two hours will be useful, strong coffee without milk or sugar, and twenty drops of turpentine on a lump of sugar every half hour. Small quantities of warm barley water can help soothe the system following the turpentine. Blisters should never be applied. When the pain is somewhat subsided the bowels should be opened with castor oil.)

(NVW Letters, Box 1, Folder 3, by date. McKenzie p. 208.)

- - - - -

Collecting Bodies & Burning Horses at Seven Pines,
A. R. Waud, artist

265

June 1, 1862 – Richmond, Virginia
Mr. John B. Jones, Clerk, C.S.A. War Department

The ambulances are now bringing in the enemy's wounded as well as our own.

(RWCD, by date.)

- - - - -

June 2, 1862 – Richmond, Virginia
Sgt. Benjamin F. Porter, Co. E – 11th Alabama Infantry

My Dear Ma, I doubt not that you have heard of the battle on the Chicahomany swamp on the 31st of May & lasted till dark on the 1st of June. The swamp is . . . flat country & on the 30th of May the heavyest rain fell that I ever saw. The mud was half leg deep nearly all the time & when we wer not in the mud we wer wadin up to our nees in the water.

This was a very wis movement of our Generals, for the River was over flowed & all the bridges was washed away & ther was only a part of ther forces on this side of the River & we completely drove them from there own redoubts & they left all there canons & tents, provisions, knapsacks, haversach & infact everything they had.

Our Regt. Suffered very mutch . . . I am sorry to say we lost one man before we got in two hundred yards of the redoubt. . . . Walter E. Winstanly was wounded in the abodoman & died on yesterday & was buried as deasently as could be expected . . .

. . . I do not know how many wer killed & wounded yet. . . . We suffered very much from colde & weriness.

. . . I want you to prey for me all the time for preyers are of great youse to us. . .

B. F. Porter

(B. F. Porter, pp. 34-35.)

- - - - -

June 2, 1862 – Chickahominy Swamp
Corporal Luther Furst, Signal Corps

. . . We now have bridges built across the Chickahominy on the right.

(ed: The heavy rain had washed out most of the bridges across the Chickahominy so it was impossible for most of May 31 to get reinforcements to Casey and the other Union troops on the Richmond side of the river. Crossings at Bottoms Bridge and Grapevine Bridge were the first ones opened and then as Luther notes they were able to repair the other crossings.)

(Furst, by date.)

- - - - -

June 2, 1862 – near Richmond, Virginia
Pvt. J. W. Reid, Mattison's S. C. Battalion

. . . the night of the 30th of May a tremendous rain fell, and it was reasonable to suppose that the Chickahominy would be very much swollen, and as it was understood that a dvision or two of the enemy were on this side of the river, it was also very reasonable to suppose that they could not recross to the other side . . . of the stream. Neither was it probable that they could be reinforced. This, I believe, is the reason the attack was made by General Johnston.

. . . General Johnston is badly wounded. I don't know as yet who will succeed him, but it is said it will be R. E. Lee . . . I know but little about him. They say he is a good general, but I doubt his being better than . . . Longstreet. . . .

We got a great many provisions of all kinds in their camps – bacon, flour, sugar, coffee, and almost every other kind of dainty, besides several barrels of whiskey. . . . Among other things I got, and by the way, not before I needed it, was a new hat, new for me, but somewhat frazzled by its original owner. It fit me to a fraction. . . .

(Reid, pp. 91-92.)

- - - - -

June 2, 1862 – near Seven Pines battlefield
Lt. Charles Haydon, 2nd Michigan Infantry

There was heavy firing all night in the direction of Richmond which was to some extent continued during the day. A great battle had been fought but we know very little of the result. . . . Our loss [of our 7 companies in the battle] is now known to be 57 [10 dead and 47 wounded]; that of the Brigade 450 [464].

(Haydon, by date.)

- - - - -

June 3, 1862
New York Daily Tribune

General Casey's Division which met a disaster at the Chickahominy River, was composed of the following regiments from [New York]:

56th N.Y. Infantry (Sullivan and Orange Counties)

81st N.Y. Infantry (Oswego and Rome)

85th N.Y. Infantry (Allegheny and Southwestern Counties)

92nd N.Y. Infantry (Potsdam)

93rd N.Y. Infantry (Albany, Saratoga & Washington County)

96th N.Y. Infantry (Plattsburg)

98th N.Y. Infantry (Malone and Lyons Counties)

100th N.Y. Infantry (Buffalo)

Governor Morgan has confidence that the disaster is not attributable to the fault of the officers or the men.

(ed: In subsequent issues the paper will publish casualty reports.)

(NYDT, p. 1.)

- - - - -

June 3, 1862 – near Richmond, Virginia
Lt. Richard Watkins, Co. K – 3rd Virginia Cavalry

My darling Mary

I wrote you last Sunday just after the fearful battle . . . Most of our regiment were engaged in gathering up arms left on the battlefield and one company with others in the disagreeable business which I have mentioned. It is shameful and at the same time amusing to hear the various excuses given by men for leaving their companies. One man had cramps in his feet, another said he was a raw recruit and had not been drilled enough to know how to fight, some were lying in the shade unable to walk but when told that our army might fall back they left to walk rapidly to the rear. . . . Fortunately for me I have not been required to go over the battlefield . . . I knew I would suffer greatly at the sight of the dead & wounded . . . changing the subject I saw Nat this morning he has been right sick and was unable to be on the battlefield . . . he looks better than I expected to find him, is a little reduced in flesh but not more so than the majority of our soldiers. His company was in the hottest of the battle, charged the enemy battery and after taking one turned the guns upon them and gave them five rounds before they could get out of sight . . . Out of 58 in [his] company 5 were killed and 28 wounded. . . . I love you more and more. And now must close in order to get this off today. Good bye dear one. Much love to all.

(ed: Weapons are collected on every battlefield following the engagement. They are forwarded to various CSA arsenals and manufacturing facilities where they are repaired and refurbished for return to the supply system. Captured Union weapons, in addition to weapons purchased overseas and run through the blockade are the major sources of small arms for the Confederacy. Manufacturing capacity of CSA arsenals is totally inadequate to meet the demand for rifles and pistols.)

(Boots & Kisses, pp. 95-96.)

- - - - -

June 3, 1862
New York Daily Tribune

Arrival of Prisoners: The steamship *Star of the South* from Fortress Monroe arrived Monday morning [June 2] with 540 prisoners . . . for Governor's Island.

There were not two prisoners dressed alike . . . wretchedly clad in dirty rags. Such a variety of caps, coasts and pants . . . some in shirt sleeves . . . several were barefoot . . . a few had knapsacks, some had quilts or horse blankets. . . . There were about a dozen negroes [among them] dressed in similar style . . . The Rebel officers, including lieutenants, of the prisoners, numbered fourteen.

(ed: The officers were from the 28th, 37th, and 18th North Carolina Infantry and 5th Louisiana Infantry.)

(NYDT, p.3.)

- - - - -

June 3, 1862 – Richmond, Virginia
Mr. John B. Jones, Clerk, C.S.A. War Department

Gen. Lee henceforth assumes command of the army in person . . .

(RWCD, by date.)

- - - - -

June 3, 1862
New York Daily Tribune

The Battles Before Richmond – Dispatches from Washington assure us that the whole army has advanced [since the battle of Seven Pines] and is now within four miles of the Rebel Capitol. The fall of Richmond is henceforth a matter of days – perhaps hours only. We will be disappointed if the Stars and Bars were over it another Sunday.

(NYDT, p.4.)

- - - - -

June 4, 1862 – Seven Pines Battlefield
Pvt. William C. Corson, Co. G – 3rd Virginia Cavalry

Dear Jennie,

. . . I was not allowed the honour of taking part in the fight of the 31st May and 1st of June. Our Reg. was drawn up in line of battle near by the scene of carnage, but out of sight. The dead and wounded being carried by us all day. We were on the battlefield early on the morning of the 1st to assist in removing the wounded and taking off the arms and ammunition left on the ground by the enemy. I rode all through the Yankee camp and . . . supplied myself with coffee, sugar, cheese, whiskey etc. It was a desperately hard fought battle . . . . Our brave fellows fought like tigers and drove the Federals from their works capturing all their artillery,

271

tents, wagons, provisions and . . . a large quantity of arms and ammunition. . . .

(Corson, pp. 80-81.)

- - - - -

June 4, 1862 – Mechanicsville, Virginia
Sgt. Major Elisha Rhodes, 2ⁿᵈ Rhode Island Infantry

We are still in this position and appear to be on the right of the Army. . . . We have not tents and our blankets are wet most of the time. . . . Several of the men are sick and some have died, but my health is good. . , , Tomorrow will complete my first year in the Army and it has been one of hardships, but . . . [I] want to see . . . the Union restored and peace again in our land.

(ed: Elisha enlisted at age 19, with his widowed mother's per-mission, in July of 1861. Four years later he will depart the regi-ment as a seasoned soldier of 23 and the Colonel commanding the 2ⁿᵈ Rhode Island Infantry. He will marry Caroline Pearce Hunt of Providence, Rhode Island, on June 12, 1866, and they will have two children. He took leadership of the Frederick Miller firm which was a supplier to woolen mills. He formed Dunham & Rhodes Co. and traveled the south and west expanding the business, work-ing with many war veterans, supplying goods and equipment to cotton and woolen mills. He will die at the age of 75 on January 14, 1917.)

(Rhodes, p. 69. & vii to ix.)

- - - - -

June 4, 1862
New York Daily Tribune

General McClellan's Sister and Nephew:

Mrs. English, sister of General McClellan [was in Mobile, Ala-bama] . . . Her husband is a wealthy planter, and lives on the Ala-bama River. Young English, the General's nephew, has gone to

Corinth to fight for the South . . .

Fortress Monroe, June 2, 1862:

The change in the command of this department which has been announced to the public via telegraph, took place today. General Dix arrived in the morning boat from Baltimore and immediately published orders [officially taking command].

(ed: General Wool took leave of the department having commanded at Fortress Monroe for the past nine months.)

(NYDT, p. 1 & p.12.

- - - - -

early June, 1862 – Golding's Farm, south bank of Chickahominy
Cpl. Marshall H. Twitchell, Co. I – 4th Vermont Infantry

Soon after the battle of Fair Oaks [Seven Pines] we moved to the south bank of the Chickahominy, taking position at Golding's Farm . . . During the nineteen days we were in position [here] . . . a man without diarrhea seemed to be an exception. I was one of the exceptions, which I attributed to my drinking no water, always coffee or tea made of water which had been boiled.

(ed: Marshall is correct that boiling the water is the answer. Unfortunately, Dr. Joseph Lister, and his germ theory is still in the future. So, whether it involves surgeons operating with dirty hands and non-sterilized instruments or infantrymen failing to boil their water the results are the same. The filthy Chickahominy water probably tastes awful and Marshall boils it and makes coffee hoping to kill the taste. He has no idea he is killing germs.)

(Twitchell, pp. 37-38.)

- - - - -

June 5, 1862 – Seven Pines Battlefield
Lt. Charles Haydon, 2nd Michigan Infantry

It rained hard all night but the weather is now cooler . . . The dead of whom many are still unburied are now nearly decomposed or consumed by maggots. Details are sent out daily to burn dead horses & bury so far as may be the human bodies. At first great holes were dug [for the horses] into which numbers were thrown but the stench soon became so great that they could not be moved.

(Haydon, by date.)

- - - - -

June 5, 1862 – Richmond, Virginia
Lt. Richard Watkins, Co. K – 3rd Virginia Cavalry

My own dear Mary

We are now only one mile from Richmond . . . actually resting but still without tents and yesterday (my birthday) I arose with my clothes very damp, my blanket wet, with the prospect of . . . sitting about on stumps . . . taking the rain. . . . I had a real treat and what do you suppose it was . . . A letter right fresh from your own hand written on my birthday and received on the evening of the same day. Really I almost felt as if I were with you and could hear your voice. . . .

Well our Col gave me leave this morning to get my horse shod [in Richmond] . . . and while that is being done I have stolen off to Cousin Barretts office . . . and I find that McKinney & Dupuy are owing me Four Hundred and Thirteen dollars. This is in their hand subject to your orders at any time . . .

I cannot write more at present. Was exceeding sorry to hear of Dr. Woolton's death . . . I sent your letters by Mr. Haskins along with the candy [for Emmie & Minnie] . . . I would give anything for a furlough but cannot expect one till the fate of Richmond has been decided . . . Again good bye. Many kisses for the little girls . . .

(ed: Richard turned 37 on his birthday and Mary has her birthday

coming up on June 21 and she will be 23.)

(Boots & Kisses, pp. 97-98.)

- - - - -

June 6, 1862 – Seven PInes Battlefield
Lt. Charles Haydon, 2nd Michigan Infantry

A few dead remain unburied. They are so bloated as to burst open the legs of their pants & the sleeves of their coats. Their features are entirely obliterated . . .

(Haydon, by date.)

- - - - -

June 7, 1862 – across the Chickahominy
Pvt. Wilbur Fisk, 2nd Vermont Infantry

It seems after much debating, that [the U. S.] Congress has refused to pass the Emancipation Act, but the Provisional [U. S. Military] Governor Stanley of North Carolina, without stopping to debate at all, has not refused to close the schools in that State for colored children, nor to return runaway niggers to their masters, providing the master will take the Oath of Allegiance. Simplified to the comprehension of our soldiers . . . only swear allegiance when you are caught, dear rebels, and we will return you your niggers. Why won't the rebels appreciate the wondrous magnanimity of our government?

(ed: There are U. S. Military Governors in all Confederate territory that is controlled by the U. S. Military. The outer banks of North Carolina; Norfolk, Hampton, Fort Monroe and Yorktown, Virginia; and Northern Virginia around Alexandria, Arlington and Fairfax. New Orleans and portions of S. Louisiana along with significant portions of Tennessee would come under Military Governors as the war progressed. These Military Governors uphold United States law. The Runaway Slave Act is U. S. law, therefore

275

in U. S. controlled Virginia a runaway slave will be returned to his owner. The same is true in Maryland, Kentucky, Missouri, New Jersey and Delaware. If a runaway slave came from the C. S. A. portion of Virginia he would not be returned but treated as contraband seeking freedom. This is just one example of blurred lines that are obviously confusing.)

(Fisk, p. 33)

- - - - -

June 7, 1862 – Near Seven Pines Battlefield
Pvt. Nathaniel Watkins, King & Queen Artillery

My dear Nannie - . . . Our men have been withdrawn and the enemy now occupy the same entrenchments from which they were driven – and I don't know any great advantages that we gained, except their commissary & tents, and 500 prisoners and some artillery. . . . They were magnificently armed & equipped – had nice tents, barrels of oranges, lemons, ground coffee, whiskey, &c. – their haversacks, knapsacks, canteens, cooking utensils, uniforms, and all the furniture of a soldier were such as I have never seen in our army. Our men got a good many things - I drank some fine Yankee coffee this morning which Sam Graham put in his haversack as he passed through their tents. . . . Yr aff husband N.V.W.

(NVW Letters, by date.)

- - - - -

June 7, 1862 – Camp near Richmond
Pvt. J. W. Reid, Mattison's S. C. Battalion

. . . there is a great deal of sickness in our army, and soldiers are dying at the hospital almost daily. A man of my company, Rufus McLees, died at Richmond on last Wednesday. He is the man I took under my oilcloth one rainy night during the march from Yorktown. His brother was killed at Seven Pines the other day. They were good boys, the sons of Jeff McLees, and well liked in the company.

(ed: In one week the McLees family lost two sons. It is possible that this will be the first letter received in the neighborhood advising of their deaths. The Captain of their Company will write a letter but along with his other duties he may not have written the initial letter about a son being killed at the battle of Seven Pines.)

(Reid, p. 94)

- - - - -

June 7, 1862 – across the Chickahominy
Pvt. Wilbur Fisk, 2nd Vermont Infantry

Occasionally a sutler come into camp, and forthwith a rush is made for the "goodies," regardless of the extravagant prices demanded. Cheese at fifty cents a chunk, pies as large as a common saucer, and perhaps a little too thick to read fine print through, a quarter, and other thing accordingly. A hungry man could invest five dollars for a dinner at one of these establishments and scarcely do justice to his appetite.

(Fisk, p. 33.)

- - - - -

June 9, 1862 – near Richmond
Pvt. William C. Corson, Co. G – 3rd Virginia Cavalry

My Dear Jennie,

I wrote to you from Richmond last week at which time I was quite sick. I am now nearly convalescent and have returned to my company . . . I am still feeble. There is a great deal of sickness in our regiment, one in every four on the sick list. . . . I had to pay $1.50 for as many strawberries as I could eat, in Richmond the other day. . . .

(ed: The 3rd Virginia Cavalry, not just Company G, has over 1/5 of their men out sick and they also have many broken down horses

and many cavalrymen home on 10 day remounting furloughs to get replacement horses. This total manpower loss seriously impacts the ability of the Cavalry to function. Company K, the Prince Edward Troop, has so many men sick, and on remount furloughs, that they did not participate in the June and early July operations of the 3rd Virginia Cavalry.)

(Corson, p. 83.)

- - - - -

June 10, 1862
New York Daily Tribune

Report from Fortress Monroe of June 8:

Dr. Curtis who accompanied the [Steamer] *Louisiana* states that 4000 wounded have been sent from White House [on the Pamunkey River near West Point] and more are to come. . . . another steamer load on the way to this place.

Dr. Cuylor is making arrangements to enlarge the hospital accommodations, besides the new General Hospital at Newport News, will proceed with [a] New Point Comfort [Hospital] . . . with the view of occupying the large hotel and cottages there, [which will] materially increase the hospital accommodations in the vicinity.

(ed: Dr. Cuylor is also aggressively recruiting and hiring permanent surgeons, doctors, nurses and other staff.)

(NYDT, p. 8.)

- - - - -

June 10, 1862 – camp on the Chickahominy River
Maj. Gen. Lafayette McLaws, McLaws Division

My dearly beloved wife,

. . . John Gibson had two balls through his clothes in the late fight

[Battle of Seven Pines], but was not touched in the flesh, escaped entirely unhurt . . . although the ball holes looked as if they . . . must have gone through his leg. . . .

The news come to us of the successive victories gained by [Stonewall] Jackson over our enemies . . . General McClelland in the meanwhile . . . keeps throwing up intrenchments . . . The Northern papers are so full of lying reports . . . Their statements of the fights about Richmond are ridiculously false, for in no instance have we been worsted . . . whenever we have met the enemy they have been easily driven before us. . . .

My dear wife I very much long to have you once more in my arms. . . . Our forces and those of the enemy cannot long be kept apart, one or the other must be attacked – it is not improbable that we will be the attacking party . . .

Mutton is fifty cents per pound – sugar is difficult to obtain and all things are so exceedingly high . . . people must be content to live . . . without . . . luxury of any kind.

Give my love to all . . . I send you enclosed One hundred dollars.

L.McLaws

(ed: Lafayette penned a note at the bottom: "This letter was Mislaid and Not Mailed – I however Send it July 7/62   LMcL". Even though not mailed on time all of the information relates to June, 1862.)

(McLaws, by date.)

- - - - -

June 11, 1862 – near the Chickahominy
Corporal Luther Furst, Signal Corps

. . . Everything you buy here is very dear, butter $1.00 per pound, milk $ .25 quart, onions $ .50 per dozen, bread $ .25 per pound and everything else in proportion. I am still unwell . . .

(Furst, by date.)

- - - - -

June 11, 1862 – Drury's Bluff, Virginia
Pvt. Nathaniel Watkins, King & Queen Artillery

My dear wife [Nannie]

. . . We have been taken out of the Chickahominy swamps and . . .
are on the bluffs of the James River . . . The greatest objection to
moving from our old resting place yesterday, was that Bro Dicks
Regt was camped about 300 yds from us & we had been allowed
to be together a great deal . . .

NVW

*(ed: Nat and his fellow soldiers are again a Heavy Artillery Unit
down at Drewry's Bluff and Chaffin's Bluff defending the river approaches to Richmond. The brothers will not cross paths again
during the war. Richard will stop in Nat's camp at Drewry's Bluff
in 1864, when the 3rd Virginia Cavalry is in the area, but Nat was
not in Camp and Richard left him a note.)*

(Boots & Kisses, p. 99.)

- - - - -

Mid-June, 1862 – outside of Richmond
Lt. E. P. McKinney, 6th New York Cavalry

When McClellan's Army went to the Peninsula, General Magruder was sent by Lee to delay his advance toward Richmond. He
had a small force compared to McClellan, and doubtless if he had
been pushed would have got out of Yorktown a month earlier.

The pursuit of Magruder as far as the Chickahominy took nearly a
month, whereas it should have been accomplished in a few days.

Former QM Aldis O. Brainerd, 5th Vermont Infantry
Dear Sister –

I received your kind letter. I found that the hardships of the QM [Quartermaster] department would be rather hard for me as we were shifting about and in fact that I have not been very tuff since I returned.. . . not very smart to day but . . . have been more like my self for the last week that I have before sence I was sick . . . it is now tremendous hot and takes the strength all away . . . I witnessed the big battle of Saturday and Sunday across the Chicka[hominy] River but we could not help them as there was abt ¾ Mile marshey land laid between us and them.

(ed: Brainerd resigned as Quartermaster in May after an extended illness but returned to the camp and battlefield as a civilian.)

(Vermont, pp. 82 – 83.)

- - - - -

June 14, 1862 – near Seven PInes battlefield
Lt. Charles Haydon, 2nd Michigan Infantry

It is now almost impossible to get a chance to wash your body or even to take off your shoes. Clean clothes are a rarity. This is partly owing to the water being so far from camp. I have sent my only shirt to be washed & have to wear my coat closely buttoned. Owing this we are all lousy [lice infested] & covered with sores & blotches. This no doubt partly owing to bad water.

(ed: In 1863 the 2nd Michigan will be transferred to the western theatre and Captain Charles Haydon will be badly wounded near Jackson, Mississippi. He mostly recovers from his wound and returns to duty. On a furlough home in February, 1864, he takes a turn for the worse enroute, checks himself into the Marine Hospital in Cincinnati, and on March 14, 1864, he dies from a form of pneumonia.)

(Haydon, by date & p. 362.)

- - - - -

Mid-June, 1862 – patrol in Charles City Cty.
Pvt. William C. Corson, Co. G – 3rd Virginia Cavalry

My Dear Jennie,
. . . I went on a reconnoitering expedition down into Charles City County where I regaled myself upon the luxuries of the season. We went nearly thirty miles below Richmond, and find no traces of the enemy, remained there several days feasting on vegetables, fried chicken and buttermilk. No soldiers had been there to annoy the citizens and they were quite kind to our . . . squadron.

(Corson, p. 84.)

- - - - -

June 17, 1862 – Poe's Farm-2 miles below Richmond
Pvt. James P. Williams, Richmond Howitzers

Dear Nannie,
. . . We are stationed at the same place we were, when Pa and Uncle John came down. . . . there has been no fight of importance since the battle of Seven Pines. . . . Our company arrived upon the field late Saturday evening and was subjected to a heavy infantry fire for 20 or 25 minutes, but finally succeeded in driving off the rascals with a few rounds of Canister and Shrapnel. . . . We remained that night in the enemy's old camp which was one solid mass almost of dead horses and men. It was the only time I have ever seen . . . fields covered with blood. . . . horses piled up on each other . . . They [Yankees] left splendid India rubber cloths and knapsacks and overcoats and blankets by the thousands. There were barrels of Sugar and Coffee . . . we have genuine coffee now twice a day. . . . I got me two good rubber cloths and a haversack and knapsack and a pair of Yankee spurs. The next day (Sunday) we remained . . . the sun was very hot . . . it was the most sickening offensive place . . . we helped bury a good many of our dead . . . I suppose Pa told you of my intention

to leave this company and join a maryland company . . . I have gotten the transfer signed . . . I shall join the other company which is now stationed on the river near Drury's Bluff . . . Tell Pa I got the shoes . . . and they are the very thing. Love to all

(Williams, by date.)

- - - - -

June 18, 1862 – Camp Jackson, Virginia
Pvt. Tally Simpson, 3rd S. Carolina Infantry

. . . I have sent three Richmond papers home here of late, two of which contain the account of Genl Stuart's brilliant exploit in rear of the enemy lines. . . . You will see by the daily papers that all things are quiet along the lines. I have no idea the cause of such a delay. McClellan was to have been in Richmond by this time, with our army prisoners together with Davis and Congress as a body. He has found to his cost that our capital is much harder to take than he supposed. He has become the greatest liar in America, and as the editor of one of the Richmond papers has said, he has undoubtedly mistaken his calling for he should be the editor of the N. Y. Herald.

(ed: On June 12, 1862, Confederate Brig. Genl. J. E. B. Stuart with some 1,200 cavalrymen and artillery starts out on a reconnaissance in force that develops into his famous 4-day ride around the entire Union army. This generated a great deal of the intelligence that completes General Lee's plan for the series of battles that will become known as The Seven Days.)

(Simpson, p. 128.)

- - - - -

June 19, 1862 – Poe's Farm, Virginia
Pvt. James P. Williams, Richmond Howitzers

Dear Mama,
. . . I expect to get the transfer to the "Chesapeake Artillery" to-

day and will probably join it tomorrow or next day.. . . . I will either get a Sergeantcy in the company or the position of gunner. In either case, instead of having two horses to drive and attend to, I will have one horse to ride and will be placed in the line of promotion. . . . The pair [of shoes] you sent will last me all the summer. I am in want of nothing now but one flannel undershirt which I expect however to get in Richmond and two more pair of socks. . . . I reckon you all are luxuriating in Cherries and Strawberries. I am quite surprised to hear I had another little cousin; you didn't tell me what her name was. . . . Hoping to hear from you again soon . . .

(ed: James originally joined the Second Company of the Richmond Howitzers. He is now transferring to the Chesapeake Artillery and will serve with them till just before Gettysburg when he will transfer to the First Company of the Richmond Howitzers and serve with them the balance of the war.)
(Williams, by date.)

- - - - -

June 20, 1862 – near Richmond, Virginia
Sgt. Benjamin Porter, Co. E – 11th Alabama Infantry

Mrs. & Mizs Porter

. . . I am in good health . . .I am very anceous to heare from you as I have not heard from in a long time. I have some Confederate notes I wish you had. . . . I have very little youse for money as every thing is very high & I neede but little. Two shirts, two par drawers & socks, one bottle ink, portfolio & paper in my knapsack. My olde blanket, haversack, canteen, gun & catridge box. All this I can through [throw] on my back double quick for several miles. . . .

Dear Sister, I want you to write to me of all the young ladys in the settlement. Tell them that I think of them all the time except a few settlement. Tell them that I think of them all the time except a few hours of the 31th of May and 1st of June. I was then thinking of something resembling a Yank. . . .

Prey for me as always is request,

B. F. Porter

(ed: The gear that Sgt. Porter describes is the basic marching gear of every Confederate soldier. They traveled light and lived lean. Most soldiers will also carry a tin cup which can also serve for cooking. You will notice that he does not mention a bayonet. Many rifles do not have attachments for bayonets and the soldiers learn, as the war progresses, that bayonets are primarily used for digging trenches and as a cooking utensil.)

(B. F. Porter, pp. 36-37)

- - - - -

June 21, 1862 – camp near Richmond
Pvt. William C. Corson, Co. G – 3rd Virginia Cavalry

. . . The Yankees are evidently strongly fortifying this side the Chicka-hominy. Their balloons are up twice a day watching us, in consequence of which we never move in force except at night. . . This regiment only has 250 men for duty [full strength would be about 750] so many are at home pretending to be sick. . . . I fear that our army will be much weakened by sickness this summer. Our soldiers are dying in the Richmond hospitals by hundreds.

(ed: A Confederate cavalry company at normal strength has 75 men and a regiment (10 Companies) has 750 men. With sickness, horse details home to re-horse, wounded, killed and men detailed for other assignments you seldom see companies near full strength and it gets worse as the war progresses. The swampy environment of the Peninsula from Williamsburg to the area around the Chickahominy took a serious toll on men and horses. Confederate cavalrymen own their own mounts so the army does not maintain a ready supply of re-

mounts. They must go home to rotate horses or buy a new horse in the local area.)

(Corson, p. 85.)

- - - - -

June 22, 1862 – camp near Richmond
Pvt. J. W. Reid, Mattison's S. C. Battalion

. . . Perhaps it would be interesting to know the current prices here for some articles in general use: Coffee is $2 per pound; sugar, 50 cents; Molases, per quart, $1: chickens (the size of robins), $1 apiece; eggs, per dozen, $1; butter, $1.25; a little fruit pie the size of my palm, 25 cents. I could at this moment eat $5 worth of them. . . . Yesterday I bought a loaf of bread for twenty-five cents, but it was hollow, though as big as my head, would not have weighed two ounces. I gave part of it to John McClinton and Warren McGee because they were sick . . .

(Reid, p. 96.)

- - - - -

June 28, 1862 (Saturday) – The Peninsula, Virginia
Maj. Gen. Lafayette McLaws, McLaws Division 8 ½ A.M.

my dear wife,
Yesterday our troops were engaged all day . . . the fighting has been carried out along opposite banks of the Chickahominy . . . we have been successful and the position of McClellans army is not an enviable one. . . . I have not written you my dear wife because my humor has not been for writing . . . Gen. Lee is rapidly regaining . . . the confidence of the army and the people as a skilled . . . and dashing officer. The criterion in military matters is success and up to this hour . . . General Lee [has] been of the most marked, decided & successful. You cannot imagine how gratifying is the feeling to soldiers, to know that their chief is competent to all positions. . . .

their chief is competent to all positions. . . . I received Willies letter and your short one and was much pleased . . . Tell Willie that I will try and write him before long . . . I hope Johnny will not only grow tall but grow smarter every day – although I know he is now a very smart fellow . . . I have my little daughter's daguerreotype before me, looking as sweet as possible. . . . I wonder how long it will be before I see her. . . .
Your devoted husband
L.McLaws

(ed: This letter is written after the battles of Mechanicsville (6-26) and Gaines Mill (6-27) which marked the end of the Peninsula Campaign and the beginning of the Seven Days Campaign. General Lee has been in command of the newly named Army of Northern Virginia for almost one month. He has gone from being called the "Ace of Spades" for the trench lines and fortifications he was working on around Richmond to a general of action. I included this letter for the warm, personal notes about family and the insight into the feelings toward the new general. I intentionally left out all of his detail regarding the two battles because this work ends in the aftermath of the battle of Seven Pines.)
(ed: A daguerreotype is a photograph where the image is made on a light sensitive silver-coated metallic plate. It was heavy and nonflexible. The image is accurate, sharp and detailed. It is named for the inventor, Mr. Louis J. M. Daguerre (1787-1851). The exposure took less than 60 seconds and the subject could not move or it would blur the image. All people have a serious expression because it is not possible to hold a smile for an extended period of time. If you have old family daguerreotypes it is important to avoid placing your fingers on the photo side of the surface because the oils in your skin will create harmful reactions to the surface.)
(McLaws, by date; AHD, p. 363.)

Postscript

War is not the same when you read the letters of the common soldiers and civilians. All of the pontificating of the generals and politicians goes out the window. Suddenly you are immersed in the harsh reality of life as a soldier or as a civilian whose farm, city and home are being directly impacted by the hostilities.

Very few of these soldiers saw more than two days of heavy fighting in the entire twelve months. A large number saw no direct action. However, they are all exposed to the harsh, unsanitary conditions of camp life, drilling, boredom, poor rations, unending rain, mud, pests and disease. The pests mentioned the most are mosquitoes, wood-ticks and lice. The diseases with the greatest impact are diarrhea and dysentery. In the swampy environs of the Virginia Peninsula, with poor camp sanitation, it was a prime environment for diarrhea, dysentery and other diseases. It is no wonder that more men died in the war from disease than from battle injuries. It is a fact that virtually every disease in the 1860s could be fatal. The smallpox vaccination and quinine were virtually the only items in the medicine chest to effectively counter specific diseases. Using some of the various treatments suggested in *Mackenzie's Five Thousand Receipts* might be even worse than the disease.

You will have noted that the Northern attitude toward the negro may have been different than what you supposed. There were never any Union recruiting posters with the slogan *"Join the Army and Free the Negro."* The Union recruiting posters focused on *"Restoring the Union."*

Freedom of the press may not have been what you expected.

I hope you felt as if you were on the *Monitor* and the Viginia as they fought in Hampton Roads. Their sailors left a remarkable array rof letters, diaries and articles regarding their ships and their activities. Very few people realize that the *Virginia* steamed around Hampton Roads for a month after the battle and the *Monitor* would not come out to offer battle. If the *Virginia* had not drawn so much water and had been equipped with a reliable engine and propulsion system, she could have created chaos and destruction in Hampton Roads and the lower Chesapeake Bay.

Soldiers in both armies longed for home and longed for letters from their loved ones. Soldiers in both armies needed key items from home. This is especially true of Southern soldiers with their need for socks, drawers, shoes and the occasional box with food.

Farms were ruined by the soldiers of both armies. You will note this in the journals from our two farmers and also from soldiers of both armies discussing the local farms where they are camped. It becomes easier to understand why families abandon their farms and become refugees.

I hope you found the magic in this collection of American voices, both Southern and Northern. If you were captivated by one or two voices, I encourage you to seek out the entire collection of that person's letters. In most cases the letters of my major voices have been published.

I leave these voices in your care.

Appendix One

The below information will provide a better understanding of muster reports, how many men are shown on a company roster, how many men in that same unit are available for battle, and a variety of other insights. Confederate units received reinforcements from the county where they were enlisted. Union units varied by state: Some received reinforcements like the Vermont regiment listed below and other states did not provide reinforcement but chose to create new regiments. Losses reduced those regiments not receiving reinforcements to battalions or in some cases, they were combined with other commands or ceased to exist.

3rd Vermont Infantry – Final Statement (capitulation of the numbers for the war)

Total Men - Volunteers, Drafted, Transfers:

Original Recruits for the Regiment: 881
Additional Replacements and Transfers in: 928

Total Men Into the Regiment during the war: 1809

Total Losses for the Regiment:

Killed in action: 131

Died of Wounds: 65

Died of Disease: 152

Died in Confederate Prisons: 11

Died in Accidents: 3

Total Action Losses: 362

Promoted to other regiments: 11
Discharged (mostly medical):   474
Dishonorable Discharge: 12
Deserted: 261
Unaccounted / Reason not available: 9

Transferred (medical corps, frontier corps, artillery, cavalry, couriers, teamsters, navy, etc):   101

Total Non Action Losses: **868 Total**

Total Wounded during War: **428 ***

Total Taken Prisoner: **78 #**

Wounded (*) is a very confusing number. Slight wounds never go to the hospital. Minor wounds go to the hospital and they return to duty in a week or two. Seriously wounded men spend weeks in the hospital and sometimes are sent home on medical furlough before coming back. Many men are wounded several times during the war and keep returning. In commands that are heavily engaged during the war you will see more men wounded than have served in the regiment. That is simply because many men are recorded multiple times as wounded over the 4 years. They are shown with the regiment on the regimental musters because they will be returning. If they get a medical discharge, like the 474 men listed in the report, they will drop from the regiment rolls. Those 474 were not all medical discharges for wounds, many of them were for incurable diseases and incapacity from those diseases. Reporting methods for wounded may vary and you always wonder what level of injury qualified to be reported. The report does show that 65 men died of their wounds.

Sick There is no number in this report recapping sick. In a normal unit that keeps good records you will note that more men have reported sick than are in the command. That is simply because many report multiple times during the war. Obviously with some of the men the sickness becomes chronic such as cases of diar-rhea or rheumatism and they are given medical discharges. We do not know how many of the 474 medical discharges were for disease and how many for wounds.

A regiment normally has 10 companies, plus the officers. In the-ory a normal company strength is 100 men. With 881 initial men the 3rd Vermont did not start out with full companies. If we as-sume that 70% of the wounded are on duty at any given time and 30% in the hospital, it becomes apparent that seldom do each of the companies have 70 men present for duty.

The number of men under arms constantly fluctuates and the muster reports may look like a company has 95 men until you start subtracting wounded, temporary duty, AWOL, on leave, prisoners, etc etc. The men present is the key number and re-searchers quite often use the other number.

As an example, below is a sampling of some Company I muster reports of the 61st Virginia Infantry:

Date 1864	Co	Present	Sick	W	Detail	POW	Leave	Arrest
June 2 Cold Harbor	43	28	3	3	7	2		
June 22 Wilcox Farm	41	21	7	5	7	2	1	
June 30 Crater	38	17	7	5	6	1		2

These are 1864 muster reports and you can see they show the company has about 40 men. In the span of one month they go from 28 rifles to 17 rifles. If the other 9 companies were in similar shape, and they were, the regiment had about 170 fighting men on June 30 instead of approximately 380 that is the reported full company strength. This is considerably fewer than their initial company strength of 100 at the start of their service. Men still have to be provided for various details: latrine construction, hospital workers, pioneer corps, etc. The Company, on June 22, had 7 men detailed, or 25% of their potential available rifles, if details were not required. A similar report is being maintained on the musters of the companies of the 3rd Vermont Infantry.

(Wikipedia – The Free Encyclopedia; The 3rd Vermont Infantry – Final Statement, Feb. 22, 2011, page 1074133531; No Soap, No Pay, Diarrhea, Dysentery & Desertion, Jeff Toalson, editor, Lincoln, 2006, p.203.)

Appendix Two

Understanding Post War Confederate Monuments:

There is tremendous misunderstanding today about the reasons for the Confederate and Union monuments that sit on courthouse lawns or on the village greens in thousands of towns both North and South. We are not discussing statues to generals, colonels and politicians. We are discussing the thousands of monuments erected between 1885 and 1920 to honor the soldiers and sailors from a given county. In a few cases, government workers, slaves and the local women were also recognized on these monuments.

These monuments honored the local citizens who served and answered the call of their state and their country. Many of them died and are buried in unmarked graves on battlefields and campgrounds far from home. Some died in prison camps and hospitals and word never reached home of their fate or where they might be buried. A monument, at the county courthouse or on the village green, became their grave marker and a place for their family to grieve.

The South was a third world country following the war. It was bankrupt; reconstruction hindered and virtually destroyed the ability to rebuild. The citizens who would be the leaders were prevented from holding elective office. The lack of monies for several years resulted in a barter economy. Stealing and pillaging of crops by vagrants was a problem, and designing methods for hiring farm workers, primarily former slaves, was a challenge. Many states passed laws regarding a minimum monthly pay, but did not get into specifics about housing, food, clothing, medical attention and all of the other items that had previously been provided. There were periodic bank failures and the Panic of 1893 brought bank failures to many of the Southern states and furthered the struggle of the South to regain a solid economic footing.

It was almost 1900 before the Southern economy had recovered enough that drives to raise money for local memorials could begin. Even then it was a stretch for some families to give a nickel or a dime. It was in the early 1900's that Southern drives, led by local chapters of the United Daughters of the Confederacy, finally began to achieve success. Hundreds of Union monuments had already been erected in counties in the northern states by 1900.

Here are excerpts from the diary of Rebecca Hunley Diggs of Mathews County, Virginia, and excerpts from research done by Mr. Starke Miller on the Confederate Monument in Oxford, Mississippi, which is on the campus of the University of Mississippi.

- - - - -

The Rebecca Diggs Diary:

"**1867, Virginia**: Scrounge for food, anything edible is now dinner. Females rule the farm as most men are now feared dead, because they never returned home. Been waiting for years and no husband and no word.

1868: start saving money for a grave marker to place on the farm to honor my husband and the father of my kids.

1875: Still trying to save money for a monument to my dearest love, Jonathan who gave his life in defense of Virginia.

1886: Daughters of the Confederacy informed me they would collect small donations for a collective account that would eventually buy a monument in town square, that we can mourn our lost ones at. Thank God we have an advocate in the United Daughters of the Confederacy. Reconstruction has been a total slap in all Southerners faces. It has been appalling at best, diminutively embarrassing at best. There is no extra money to even think of saving. I get older as the children grow and leave the farm. Oh, how I wish Johnathan survived that damned war.

Jetha and her husband Ephraim Diggs stopped by to help me get up the hay for winter feed. Jetha was a slave here before the emancipation. So was Ephraim. Thank you Jesus they stayed as freemen and women in Mathews County.

1889: word has come that a company in Ohio will make monuments, but we have saved no where near enough money to make a purchase.

We deeded land to our former slaves as they stayed back and helped us immensely thru these hardest of times, the Diggs have a nice farmstead and five growing children on the north end of our farm, which they now own and do well on. My son Johnny jr. runs a pound net off of Roys point and employs Ephraim and his young men bringing tons of fish to the docks at mobjack and ware River for cash money. God has blessed us with money to spare finally. We will have our monument in Mathews Courthouse to mourn my Johnathan and hundreds of other men both white and black who served and protected our beloved Virginia thru that ugly and horrible war.

1912: our monument was erected on the corner of Maple Ave and Court Street and beautiful it is. I have endured many years without my beloved husband yet today is bittersweet. I have a marker to grieve at, a place to cuss my husband for leaving me too soon.

He should have never left to fight that wretched war. But it was his duty to protect his homeland."

- - - - -

It should be noted that the entire inscription on this monument simply reads, "*In Memory of the Soldiers and Sailors of Mathews County.*"

(James City Cavalry Picket Lines, July, 2021, "Confederate Gravesites", Fred Boelt, p. 2. Fred is a native of Williamsburg and a historian specializing in local history. He is a co-author of two books on local cemeteries: James City County, Virginia, Cemeteries – Family, Historical, Indian, Military & Slave (2011) and James City County, Virginia, Church Graveyards (2013). Monument inscription text provided by Mrs. Marilyn Iglesias of Mathews County.)

- - - - -

Oxford's "Old Miss" Confederate Monument: Why Is It There?
Starke Miller

"The monument on the campus at Old Miss was erected in 1906 by the United Daughters of the Confederacy. It took 45 women 14 years to raise $2000 to erect it. . . . They raised money through a national depression (1893-1895) and a Yellow Fever epidemic (1898). They raised pennies, nickels, and dollars every way they could from cake sales, baby shows, speeches, baseball games, ice cream socials, fraternity and sorority lunches and more.

The monument is dedicated to the Lafayette County Civil War Confederate dead. It was and is not dedicated to the glory of the Confederacy. It was closure for many, many families and it was the only marker many of those dead ever received.

Twenty-five percent of the men who left Lafayette County to fight were dead in four years. 432 local men. Most of them did not get a decent burial." At Seven Pines, Sharpsburg, Gettysburg, the Wilderness, the Weldon Railroad and many other battlefields they were buried in mass graves. "Their families knew this. The women who raised the money had each lost one or more male relatives in the war. The percentage lost for the South was far greater than World War II. We modern Americans have no earthly idea what those families went through.

Imagine today, in 2020, if 25% of the 20,000 member student body plus 25% of the military aged men in Lafayette County died in a 4 year conflict. We would put up a monument! That is all those people did.

The monuments timing had nothing to do with Jim Crow laws. The nation went Civil War nostalgia crazy in the 1890s when the first "Big Five" Civil War National Battlefields were formed: Vicksburg, Shiloh, Chattanooga-Chickamauga, Sharpsburg and Gettysburg. Northerners had already placed hundreds of monuments on their courthouse lawns because they had money. Mississippi was in poverty and Southerners had no money until the 1890s."

Go on campus and go back to the Civil War cemetery where the statue now stands. Read the inscription on the monument. It is a memorial to the Lafayette County men who died in the war. It is their tombstone.

(Oxford's Confederate Monument – Why Is It There?, Starke Miller, The Local Voice, 6/25/2020 TLV News. Mr. Miller is a historian and Civil War tour guide who has been researching the local Lafayette County military units for more than 25 years. He is on the 11th Mississippi Memorial Committee. They have placed four monuments on three Civil War battlefields. A key focus of his research is the history of the University Greys, a company raised at the University of Mississippi. The University Greys (Co. A) and the Lamar Rifles (Co. G) were the Lafayette County companies in the 11th Mississippi Infantry Regiment. Other Lafayette County companies served in the western Confederate armies and their dead are buried in mass graves at Shiloh and other western battlefields. Starke also serves as a board member on the Mississippi Civil War Battlefield Commission.)

The above monument was supposed to be the Lafayette County Monument, but the committee, with some members out of town, placed the monument on campus. Therefore, a second fund was raised and in 1907 a monument to honor the men who died in the defense of "our Southland" was installed at the courthouse. The following dedication quotation from Commander J. L. Shinault, United Confederate Veterans, appeared in the *Oxford Eagle* on May 9, 1907.

"After efforts of several months we have succeeded in raising a monument to the memory of the young manhood of Lafayette County who you sent to the front from 1861 to 1865 to keep the enemy from our beautiful Southland. To this response our best manhood met the enemy four times their number upon many hard-fought battlefields; and in this conflict of might and strength, your husband, sons, and brothers, who fell on the numerous battlefields of our Civil War were buried in ditches and gullies hurriedly dug by their comrades, and often times by the enemy – and unknown there now rest. It is to the memory of those to who you said go and check the invading armies, and never returned, that the few survivors of that terrible struggle, in the evening tide of their lives, have erected on the courthouse Square in the city of Oxford, a shaft of beautiful design." (*Oxford Eagle*, Oxford, Mississippi, May 9, 1907.)

Lafayette County and Oxford are unique. They have two monuments, honoring the same soldiers, who gave their lives in defense of their homes. These men were buried in shallow graves dug by their comrades and also by the enemy. On major battlefields many of them lie in mass graves dug by the enemy. Some also died in hospitals and prison camps. The location of their burial locations is unrecorded in almost every instance. The monument, or in this case the monuments, became the gravestone for these 432 men and became the spot where their families could grieve and remember their loved ones.

Appendix Three

A History of Fort Magruder
Williamsburg, Virginia   1861 to Current

Presented on the occasion of the U.D.C. May 2, 2021,
Memorial Day Celebration

Jeff Toalson

On April 23, 1861, Benjamin Stoddert Ewell offered his services
to the Confederacy. He was appointed to the rank of Lt. Colonel and given two initial assignments: 1) raise and begin training
10 infantry companies in Williamsburg & 2) survey a line for defense across the peninsula at Williamsburg.

He initially recruited just over 30 men to form the Williamsburg
Junior Guard. More would follow. Also, additional companies
were raised on the lower peninsula and sent to Williamsburg to
train with the Junior Guard. Camp Page was set up in the area
of the current Capitol Landing Road and training began. These
local peninsula companies would become the 32nd Virginia Infantry. A1 see additional info in footnotes.

Ewell laid out a proposed line of fortifications stretching, across
the peninsula, from Tutter's Neck Pond to Queen's Creek. General Lee approved this concept and then sent Captain Alfred L.
Rives to review the plan. Rives specialized in defensive lines and
fortifications whereas Ewell had only had engineering classes
and theory at West Point and did not have practical experi-
ence. The key feature of the Rives changes involved moving Fort

Magruder (redoubt 6) forward much closer to the intersection of the Yorktown Road and the Lee's Mill – Hampton Road. (Redoubts 5 and 7 had their positions adjusted to provide a supporting field of artillery fire for Ft. Magruder.) Colonel Magruder and Gen. Lee both approved the final adjustments which included Fort Magruder and 13 other redoubts connected by rifle pits and crossing fields of artillery fire.

In late May, 1861, construction began. The men of the 32nd Virginia Infantry, conscripted slaves and men from many other CSA Infantry regiments would provide the manpower for construction. Camp Page grew larger. Regiments of Gen. Lafayette McLaws Division would spend many months here working on the defenses before being sent down the peninsula to serve with Gen. Magruder manning the Warwick Line. Of his 13 infantry regiments, the 2nd, 5th & 10th Louisiana, the 10th Georgia, and the 15th and 32nd Virginia would spend the most time in Williamsburg. The 32nd Virginia would stay in Williamsburg from recruitment in May of 1861 until the battle in May of 1862.

From June, 1861, through April, 1862, it was a constant struggle for manpower and supplies. Requests constantly went to Richmond, including to the Secretary of War, requesting up to 1500 slaves from the Richmond area in addition to horses, wagons, axes, spades etc. Manpower, other than soldiers, was not forthcoming.[1]

Disease ran rampant among the soldiers in Williamsburg. The mosquito ruled the land and typhoid fever, diphtheria, dysentery, mumps, measles, smallpox and all types of camp fever decimated the ranks. The Williamsburg hospitals were full of sick soldiers. On July 21st Gen. McLaws visited the General Hospital and wrote his wife that, *"there are about one hundred patients with measles, mumps, and all kinds of diseases as soldiers have. . . . it is a sickly country."*[2]

The majority of the sick were cared for in four area hospitals: 1) *The College Hospital,* which was located in the Wren building, 2) *The Female Academy Hospital,* which was located on the site of the former Colonial Capitol building, 3) *The Episcopal Hospital,* which was located at Bruton Parish, and *The African Church Hospital,* which was at the African Baptist Church across the street from the Lunatic Asylum. Dr. Galt's sister was the patron saint of the *African Church Hospital.* The vast majority of sick were cared for at the *College Hospital* and the *Female Academy Hospital.* When General McLaws wrote his wife about visiting his sick at the General Hospital he is no doubt referring to the *Female Academy Hospital.*[3]

Later in the summer, in another letter to his wife, he stated that he was supervising the construction of dams, obstructions and earthworks. He noted he was, *"off to put a work party to work cutting down fruit trees that obstructed the field of fire of a battery and entangling a ravine that led up in front of another battery."*

Regarding the work on Fort Magruder he mentioned, *"the main work here is fast approaching completion and on the right and left redoubts [#5 & #7) of formidable strength are already finished or will be within a week."*[4]

The men dying of disease at the area hospitals are recorded in the Bucktrout Order Book. Some were shipped home but most are buried in the Bucktrout plot at Cedar Grove Cemetery and they are laid out in rows by state. A large memorial erected by the U. D. C. marks the area. A significant number of these burials are from the various regiments commanded by Gen. McLaws.

Regiment	July – Dec., 1861	Jan. – Mar, 1862
2 Louisiana	22	2
5 Louisiana	7	2

10 Georgia	31	10
15 Virginia	3	3
32 Virginia **	2	

The 32nd Virginia was the 'local' regiment, spent the entire time here, but had built up immunity to local contagions. The 10th Georgia and the 2nd Louisiana, in particular, did not fare well. Many other regiments spent a limited time in Williamsburg and in particular the 14th Virginia (Armistead) with 15 dead, the 13th Alabama (Colquitt) with 11 dead, and the 5th North Carolina (Garland) with 5 dead fared poorly in the area.[5]

(Additionally, the 7, 8, 11 & 16 Georgia, Cobb's Legion, 17 Mississippi, & 15 North Carolina Infantry plus the Peninsula Artillery, Troup Artillery, Cabell's 1st Virginia Artillery, Magruder Lt. Artillery, 1st Co. Richmond Howitzers & 1st & 2nd Co. Washington Artillery were all in McLaws Division.) [6]

By late March of 1862, the 32nd Virginia Infantry was manning Fort Magruder and forwarding all troops from General Johnston's army down the peninsula to the Warwick line. General Joseph Johnston arrived on the peninsula the second week of April to take personal command. The CSA troops abandoned the Warwick line on May 3 and withdrew toward Richmond. McLaws division joined the 32nd Virginia in Fort Magruder and Redoubt 7 holding off Union troops arriving on the afternoon of May 4. As action heated up on May 5, several divisions under Longstreet were recalled to Williamsburg to stem the Union pursuit and the battle raged till nightfall. When Longstreet's troops arrived the men of McLaws division, including the 32nd Virginia, began their withdrawal toward Richmond.

At nightfall on the 5th the 11th Virginia Infantry was withdrawn from the 'Ravine' and sent to Fort Magruder. Here are the words of of Private Newton Camper of Company D – The Fincastle Rifles, "*In the night . . . Co. D was relieved and sent to Fort Magruda, a short distance in the rear. Here the men spent a miserable night. Having left their baggage in Williamsburg on the morning of the battle, the men were without blankets or protection of any kind from the weather. More than this, they had no fires, and were standing in mud and water, in many places over their shoetops . . ."* [7]

The correspondent of the *New York Daily Tribune* traveling with Mc-Clellan's army filed the following description from Williamsburg dated May the 7th, "*The second line of Rebel defenses above Yorktown consisted of 13 formidable earth forts, within sure artillery range of each other. One of them, Fort Magruder, was of great strength. Fort Magruder and most of the key forts were in front of General Heintzelman and on his left.*" This of course was the main area of battle including the 'Ravine' and the area from the 'Ravine' to the major road intersection in front of Fort Magruder.

Our un-named correspondent also noted the "*abandoned wounded in forts, in cornfields, in churches, in court houses, record offices, colleges, and hospitals. . . . What of the abandoned dead? They strewed the woods, they were in the fields, along the fence lines, on the edge of timbered portions and near the forts. Burial parties worked all day Tuesday (6th) and the labor begins again this morning.*" [8]

In a May 17 letter the sister of Sgt. Robert W. Johnson, Co. H – 8th New Jersey Infantry, asked him if bodies could be returned home for burial. He replied on May 21st, "It will be an utter impossibility to procu[re] those bodies I think for they are decayed a great deal by this time, and then they where not buried in cofins for we could not get them. Even the Officers where buried the same as the men no distinction in death." [9] They were buried by burial details in groups, wooden identification markers provided for many, simply wrapped in blankets in shallow graves. In 1864 and 1865 the Federal government began exhuming the bodies and relocating to the National Cemetery in Yorktown. Many of the markers did not survive and those soldiers became unknowns.[10]

Attached is artwork, from the Williamsburg Battlefield Association website, by Union soldier Robert Knox Sneden with his depiction of Fort Magruder following the battle. The Southwest Bastion of the fort is all that remains and it matches up very well with his drawing. Also shown, by Robert, is the location where 300 Union soldiers have been buried by the burial details. Some of his other artwork of the battlefield shows other burial locations.

(The Sneden artwork was printed on the program. You will need to consult his entire grouping of artwork shown in the two published works of his watercolors and diaries: Eye of the Storm: A Civil War Odyssey (2000) and Images from the Storm: 300 Civil War Images by the author of Eye of the Storm: (2001) both edited by Charles Bryan.)

Following the battle, Williamsburg became a Union occupied city and Fort Magruder became a Union fort and served as the headquarters for the area. There were a variety of raids on the town by Confederate forces in 1863 and 1864. This maintained a level of tension in the area. Union troops passing through and training in the area would camp near Fort Magruder. A few new redoubts were constructed facing up the peninsula. The following order was issued on June 14, 1864.

Headquarters U S Forces
Fort Magruder Va June 14th 1864

General Orders
No 11

The galloping or fast driving
of all public animals unless directed is
strictly prohibitde. Order to go beyond

By Command of Col W. H. P. Steere
E, V, Brown.
Capt & AAAG[11]

From January, 1864, through the end of May, 1864, there were United States Colored Troops in the area. The 4th, 5th, 6th and 10th USCTs are documented as being on the lower peninsula, camping or transiting through Williamsburg and making patrols and forays to New Kent and King & Queen County. These troops were all assigned to the Army of the James and most departed in May to join that army around Bermuda Hundred. These four regiments would all become part of the 3rd Division of the 25th Corp in December of 1864. [12]

USCTs who died on the lower peninsula were also buried in the National Cemetery in Yorktown.

There are no records regarding the Confederate battlefield dead. Most of them were buried on the battlefield by the Union burial details on May 6th and 7th. They logically were not marked with name or regiment. There are no records if they were ever disinterred and moved to a mass grave or individual graves. Many folks assumed the Bucktrout burials at Cedar Grove Cemetery were a post battle or a war mass gravem but that is not true. Carson Hudson and Michael Moore both suspect that a mass grave was dug somewhere in Cedar Grove, maybe near the Bucktrout burial area where the Monument stands in that cemetery. There is no entry in the Bucktrout Order Book in 1865 or 1866 with any type of confirmation. Fred Boelt believes that almost all of them remain where they were buried following the battle. The number of men involved is unknown. There is no documentation of reburial, and until some proof can be found we must assume Confederate bodies were not recovered. No doubt even a few

Union bodies remain on the battlefield. [13]

(see more detailed information in footnotes and also the 'addendum' that follows the footnotes.)

This remaining portion of Fort Magruder (the Southwest bastion), where we are standing today, was deeded from the Benel Corporation to the Williamsburg Chapter 673 of the U.D.C. on May 31, 1951. The ladies of the Williamsburg Chapter have maintained and protected this historic fortification for the past 70 years. They have preserved a history that belongs to Williamsburg, James City County, Confederate soldiers, Union Soldiers and in that last group, the often overlooked, U. S. Colored Troops. [14]

- - - - -

Footnotes:

A1) Jensen, Les; *The 32nd Virginia Infantry,* 1990, Lynchburg, p.3 & pp. 159-72. Seven companies would make up the 32nd Virginia. A normal regiment has ten companies and some 1,000 men. The 32nd Virginia would serve the entire war as an undersized regiment. Williamsburg provided Company C: *The Williamsburg Junior Guard*; Hampton provided Company A: *The Wythe Rifles* and Company E: *The Hampton Grays*; York County provided Company F: *The Nelson Guard* and Company I: *The York Rangers*; Warwick & Elizabeth City Counties provided Company H: *The Warwick Rangers* and Company K: *The Lee Guards*. Four artillery batteries were initially part of the 32nd but were soon transferred to artillery commands: Company G: *Lee Artillery/Garrett's Battery*; 1st Company H: James City Artillery/Hankin's Battery; 1st *Company I: Peninsula Artillery/Cosnahan's Battery;* 1st Company K: *Washington Artillery/Smith's Hampton Battery.* The additional 3 infantry companies were never added. When General Magruder and General Johnston withdrew from the Warwick and Williamsburg lines many of the lower peninsula volunteers (80+)

to protect their homes and families from invaders and were alienated by the withdrawal. This rendered a small regiment even smaller.

1) Chapman, Anne W., *Benjamin Stoddert Ewell: A Biography,* 1988, Dissertations, Theses & Masters Project Papers, 153962378. p. 125-164. Available on line under Benjamin S. Ewell and held by the SCRC, Swem Library at the College of William and Mary.

2) Moore, J. Michael & Quarstein, John, *Yorktown's Civil War Siege – drums Along the Warwick,* 2012, Charleston, pp. 53-57. The quotes are from *A Soldier's Journal: The Civil War Letters of Maj. General Lafayette McLaws.*

3) *Richard Manning Bucktrout Daybook & Ledger 1850-1866* (referred to as The Bucktrout Order Book) Mss.Acc 1997.15, by date, Special Collections Research Center, Swem Library, College of William and Mary *and correspondence with Mr. Carson Hudson.*

4) *Yorktown's Civil War Siege,* pp. 53-57.

5) Boelt, Higgs, Hull, Kaufmann & Myers, *James City County Cemeteries – Family, Historical, Indian, Military & Slave,* 2011, Yorktown, pp. 163-75.

6) *Yorktown's Civil War Siege,* pp. 158-59.

7) *A Short Sketch of the Fincastle Rifles,* Newton Camper, 1979, Fincastle, p. 6.

8) *New York Daily Tribune,* Saturday May 10, 1862, p.4 col. 1 & col. 2 "The Battle Near Williamsburg Revised."

9) Sgt. Robert W. Johnson Letter, 'Picket Lines' *– James City Cavalry Newsletter,* 11-2018, p. 4; SC01349 – Special Collections Research Center, Swem Library, College of William and Mary.

10) Correspondence and conversations with Historians Carson Hudson, J. Michael Moore, Drew Gruber & Fred Boelt.

11) General Orders #11, 'Picket Lines' – James City Cavalry Newsletter, 4-2018, p.4; SC00058 – Special Collections Research Center, Swem Library, College of William and Mary.

12) National Park Service Military Unit Website; Battle Unit Details - the site provides the organizational detail of the command

and a service history of the command as well as numbers of officers and men killed and wounded during the conflict.

13) Conversations and correspondence with Historians Fred Boelt, Carson Hudson, & J. Michael Moore; 1865 and 1866 entries in The Bucktrout Order Book; A possible source to be checked would be the *Virginia Gazette* for 1865 and 1866 for any articles on reburials of battlefield dead {see addendum below}.

14) Email from Mrs. Gerry Waring, President of the Williamsburg Chapter of the United Daughters of the Confederacy, February 20, 2021, detailing the transaction on May 31, 1951. Representing the U.D.C. on the deed, as parties of the second part, were Mrs. Ruby Saunders, Mrs. Hallie Wermuth and Mrs. Julia Armistead as Trustees for the Chapter. The original was mailed to Mrs. Saunders at 302 Harrison Avenue in Williamsburg.

ADDENDUM:

May 2 / 9:14 pm Note from Carson Hudson

The *Gazette [Eastern Virginia Gazette & Advertiser]* wasn't published after the early 1860s. The presses were confiscated **[probably following the battle in May, 1862]** and used to print a Union military paper – *The Cavalier* from 1862 to 1864 – first in Williamsburg and then in Yorktown. I believe the presses weren't returned until years later. I believe one of the Lively brothers had to appeal to the Federal Government and after much legal argument recovered the presses from Fort Monroe. The Gazette did not resume publishing, under a different name and publisher, till years later. There were 4 Richmond papers during the war that would occasionally mention events in Williamsburg, but I've never come across anything on reburials.

May 2 / 8:52 pm Note from Fred Boelt
I was thinking more about this on my drive home this afternoon – there were basically no Confederates on the peninsula after the bat-

tle of Williamsburg. Were the Union soldiers (in 1864-1865) going to disinter the Confederate dead and relocate? I think not. The few citizens left behind were the feeble and women and children.The vast majority of the enslaved moved on as well. I seriously believe that there would be some mention of it if there was an effort to move the bodies. No, they are still where they were placed on May 6 and 7.

May 3 / 6:57 am Note to Fred Boelt and Gerry Waring before I read Fred's note above.

My hope that maybe some 1864-1866 copies of the *Virginia Gazette* were in the Swem Archives, or somewhere, is dashed by Carson's note . . . It is not logical for the Union to waste any time with the Confederate battlefield dead [to disinter & rebury] when they are removing the Union dead for transfer to the National Cemetery in Yorktown. It is not logical for the Williamsburg citizens or the Williamsburg / J.C.C. governments to spend any of their miniscule treasury to recover the bodies for reburial in a mass grave.

Fred, your theory has all the logic. The Confederate dead are still buried on the battlefield.

Acknowledgments

My first thank you goes to the men and women who wrote the letters and maintained the diaries and journals that provide this history. Secondly, we must thank the people who saved those items and preserved them for posterity. Many have been transcribed and are available in print and many are in the archives of various historical institutions and libraries.

I would like to thank Curtis Watkins and Cathy Watkins Thomas for providing a scan of the 1864 wedding picture of Richard Curtis who served on the C.S. Ironclad *Virginia.* Curtis Watkins also, several years ago, gave me a copy of the pamphlet Richard Curtis printed recounting his service on the *Virginia.* Richard Dupuy Watkins (no relation to Curtis and Cathy) provided scans of the wedding picture of Richard and Mary Watkins of Prince Edward County, Virginia, and also the 1890 photograph of the couple.

Mr. Jay Gaidmore - Director of Special Collections, Swem Library at the College of William and Mary and Ms. Rosalyn Liljenquist – Publishing and Open Access Librarian, along with the archives staff, provided assistance on many fronts. They scanned the front and back of Pvt. Edgar Steele's carte-de-visite. It is a marvelous piece of history. They house a wonderful grouping of letters from the Peninsula Campaign written by soldiers from both armies and they hold the Nathaniel V. Watkins Papers which detail his service at Gloucester Point, the retreat to Richmond, and the battle of Seven Pines. Rosalyn was able to provide me with guidance on Fair Use doctrine and when photographs fall within Public Domain doctrine. Additionally, she provided a concise and informative evaluation tool that has been published by Purdue University, on these two topics. The staff at the Swem Archives have been integral to the research and production of all five books in my Butternut Series.

Sarah McLusky – Lead Archivist at the Bentley Historical Library of the University of Michigan provided me with a link to their image bank where they had a marvelous scan of a Lt. Charles B. Hayden photograph. Dr. Judith Silva – University Archivist and Jared Negley – Archives Technician at Slippery Rock University, Slippery Rock, Pennsylvania, provided access to the transcriptions of Private Luther Furst's diary and granted permission for their use. Andrea Laws – Permission Coordination at the University Press of Kansas in Lawrence, Kansas; Mr. Wert Smith of Dietz Press in Richmond, Virginia; and John Jackson – Special Collections at Virginia Tech in Blacksburg, Virginia; all answered questions and provided support for this project.

Two magnificent maps of the Yorktown – Warwick Line and the Seven Pines Battle are courtesy of Maps by Hal Jesperson at www.cwmaps.com.

A. R. Waud and William Waud drew hundreds of marvelous wartime sketches as they traveled with the Union army. These sketches were shipped back to New York where the engravers at *Harper's Weekly* quickly created the engravings that appeared in their newspapers. Turnaround time was amazing. The Nelson House Hospital appeared 3 weeks after A. R. sketched it. His Burning Horses at Seven Pines appeared in late June and the sketch was made in the first week of June. All of this artwork is part of the collection of the Library of Congress and is available with no restrictions.

Local historians Fred Boelt, J. Michael Moore and Carson Hudson have provided a wealth of information, documents, insights, and assistance during this project. I cannot thank them enough.

My team of proofreaders, many of whom have proofed on my earlier works, once again provided excellent service. Thank you to Jan Toalson, Paul and Joli Huelskamp, Fred Boelt, George and Martha Barnett, Ron Perry and William Molineux. It is impossible to catch all of the errors, but it would be great if we were successful. Those pesky errors that survived are mine.

Thanks also to the Pale Horse Books team of Sally Stiles and John Conlee. Their support has been key in publishing this very personal history of war in our backyard.

Sources

Manuscripts and Letters:

[   ], George [Private]   3rd Vermont Infantry

Vermont Brigade Dam #1 Letter of 5-17-1862, SC01698, Box 116, Folder 1, Special Collections Research Center, Swem Library, College of William and Mary, Williamsburg, Virginia.

Bumgarner, [S]. A. [Private]   CSA unknown

[Pvt] [S.] A. Bumgarner Letter, SC00720, Special Collections Research Center, Swem Library, College of William and Mary, Williamsburg, Virginia.

Furst, Luther Calvin (Private)   10th Pennsylvania Infantry

Civil War Diary of Luther Calvin Furst, 1-19-5-2, Slippery Rock University Archives, Slippery Rock University, Slippery Rock, Pennsylvania.

Head, Thomas J. (Private)   6th Georgia Infantry

Letter of Private Thomas J. Head, SCOO117, Special Collections Research Center, Swem Library, College of William and Mary, Williamsburg, Virginia.

Johnson, Robert W. (Sergeant)   Co H - 8th New Jersey Infantry

Letter of Sgt. R. W. Johnson, SC01349, Special Collections Research Center, Swem Library, College of William and Mary, Williamsburg, Virginia.

Martin, John T. (Farmer & Teacher) James City County, Virginia

1861 and 1862 quotes from his farm journal in the *James City Cavalry Picket Lines* issues of February and March, 2019, p. 3, Williamsburg. The Farm Journal of John T. Martin, 1848-1881; Library of Virginia, Richmond, Virginia. This journal was donated to the Library of Virginia in 2005.

Steele, Edgar (Private)   Co. B – 85th N. Y. Infantry

Private Edgar Steele Letter, SC01325, Special Collections Research Center, Swem Library, College of William and Mary, Williamsburg, Virginia.

Watkins, Nathaniel (Sergeant)   King & Queen Heavy Artillery

The Nathaniel V. Watkins Papers, 39.1 – W 32, Box 1, Folders 2 and 3, Special Collections Research Center, Swem Library, College of William and Mary, Williamsburg, Virginia

Williams, James P. (Private)   Richmond Howitzers

Papers of James P. Williams, 1854-1899; Accession 490, Alderman Library, University of Virginia, Charlottesville, Virginia.

Wynne, Thomas G. (Farmer)   James City County, Virginia

Excerpts of daily entries from the farm journal of Thomas G. Wynne in issues of the *James City Cavalry Picket Lines* appearing in April through December, 2009.

Newspapers:

New York Daily Tribune – May and June, 1862 selected issues. The issues I utilized are all in the Special Collections Research Center, Swem Archives, College of William and Mary, Williamsburg, Virginia.

Personal Reminiscences, Diaries and Journals:

Barrett, Milton (Private)   18th Georgia Infantry

Heller & Heller, editors; *The Confederacy is on Her Way Up the Spout,* Athens, 1982.

Branch, Hamilton (Sergeant)   8th Georgia Infantry

Joslyn, Mauriel P. – editor; Charlotte's Boys – *The Civil War Letters of the Branch Family of Savannah,* Berryville, 1996.

Buzhardt, Beaufort (Private)   3rd S. Carolina Infantry

See Simpson, Tally – portions of Private Buzhardt's diary are contained in that collection.

Camper, Newton (Private)   Co. D – 11th Virginia Infantry

Camper, Newton; *A Sketch of the Fincastle Rifles*, Fincastle, 1979.

Corson, William C. (Private)   Co. G – 3rd Virginia Cavalry

Corson, Blake – editor; *My Dear Jennie – Letters from a Confederate Soldier to his Fiancee* by William C. Corson, Richmond, 1992.

Curtis, Richard (Seaman / Bow Gunner) C.S. Ironclad *Virginia*

Curtis, Richard; *History of the Great Naval Engagement between the Iron-Clad Merrimac CSN and the Cumberland, Congress, & the Iron-Clad Monitor USN, March 8 & 9, 1862 as seen by a Man at the Gun,* Hampton, 1957 reprint of original.

Davis, W. W. H. (Colonel)   104th Pennsylvania Infantry

Eisenschiml & Newman, editors; *The Civil War – The American Iliad*, New York, 1956.

> **Dunbar, Henry E. (Corporal)**   Co. C - 3rd Vermont Infantry
>
> **Quinby, George (Captain)**   Co. D – 4th Vermont Infantry
>
> **Brainerd, Aldis (former Quartermaster)** 5th Vermont Infantry

Marshall, Jeffrey - editor; *A War of the People – Vermont Civil War Letters,* Hanover, 1999

Englis, George, M. (Private)   89th New York Infantry

Patch, Eileen M. Knapp, editor; *This From George – The Civil War Letters of Sergeant George Magusta Englis, 1861-1865 Co. K, 89th New York Infantry Regiment, Endicott, 2001.*

Fisk, Wilbur (Private)   2nd Vermont Infantry

Rosenblatt, Emil & Ruth, editors; *Hard Marching Every Day – The Civil War Letters of Private Wilbur Fisk*, Lawrence, 1983.

French, George (Corporal)
3rd Vermont Infantry

Vermont History – Vermont Historical Society; Fall 1981, Vol 49, #4.

Greene, Dana (Lieutenant and X. O.)
U.S. Ironclad *Monitor*

Greene, Dana ; *In The Monitor Turret* – an essay in B&L, Vol. 1 – p.719-729.

Haydon, Charles (Lieutenant)   Co. I – 2nd Michigan Infantry

Sears, Stephen – editor; *For Country Cause and Leader – The Journal of Charles B. Haydon*. New York, 1993.

Holland, William P. (Private)   Co. G – 11th Virginia Infantry

Holland, William P.; *Recollections of a Private*, Rocky Mount, 2009 re-print of 1936 edition.

Jones, John B. (Clerk)   CSA War Department

Jones, J. B., *A Rebel War Clerks Diary*, 2 vols., New York, 1935.

Johnson, Charles (Private)   Hawkins Zouaves (9th N. Y.)

Johnson, Charles F.; *The Long Roll – One of the Hawkins Zouaves – 1861-1863,* Sheperdstown, 1986.

Lyons, Patrick (Corporal)   2nd R. Island Infantry

"James City Cavalry Picket Lines" of March, 2020, Williamsburg, p.3 in an article on Olive Branch by Fred Boelt. Quoted from *A Soldier's Log* the diary of Patrick Lyons privately published in Providence in 1988.

McKinney, E. P. (Lieutenant)   Co. F – 6th N. Y. Cavalry

McKinney, E. P.; *Life in Tent and Field* , Boston, 1922.

McLaws, Lafayette (Lt. General)   McLaws Division

Oeffinger, John C., editor; *A Soldier's General – The Civil War Letters of Maj. General Lafayette McLaws,* Chapel Hill, 2014.

Porter, Benjamin (Sergeant)   Co. E – 11th Alabama Infantry

Williams, Ellen – editor; *Prey For Us All – The War Letters of Benjamin Franklin Porter – 11th Alabama,* Mobile, 2006.

Porter, John L. (Naval Constructor)   Gosport Naval Yard

Porter, John L.; *The Plan and Construction of the Merrimac II,* essay in B&L. Vol. 1, p.716-718.

Reid, J. W. (Private)   4th S. Carolina Infantry

Reid, J. W.; *History of the 4th Regiment of South Carolina Volunteers,* Dayton, 1975.

Rhodes, Elisha (Sergeant Major)   2nd Rhode Island Infantry

Robert H. Rhodes, editor: *All for the Union – History of the 2nd R. I. Volunteer Infantry by Elisha Hunt Rhodes,* New York, 1991.

Simpson, Tally (Private)   3rd S. Carolina Infantry

Everson & Simpson, editors; *Far, far from Home – The Wartime Letters of Dick and Tally Simpson of the 3rd South Carolina Infantry,* New York, 1994.

Twitchell, Marshall H. (Corporal)   Co. I – 4th Vermont Infantry

Tunnell, Ted – editor; *A Carpetbagger from Vermont – Autobiography of Marshall H. Twitchell,* Baton Rouge, 1989.

Watkins, Richard H. (Private & Lieutenant) Co. K – 3rd Virginia Cavalry

Flournoy, John J. (Private)   Co. K – 3rd Virginia Cavalry

Toalson, Jeff – editor; *Send Me a Pair of Old Boots & Kiss My Little Girls – The Civil War Letters of Richard & Mary Watkins, 1861-1865,* Bloomington, 2009.

White, E. V. (Lieutenant) Asst. Engineering Officer C.S. Ironclad *Virginia*

White, E. V.; *The First Ironclad Engagement in the World Between the Merrimac-Virginia CSN & the Ericsson-Monitor USN March 8 & 9, 1862,* New York, 1906.

Wood, George Randolph   student / river-boatman

Molineux, Will editor; *A Young Virginia Boatman Navigates the Civil War – The Journals of George R. Wood,* Charlottesville, 2010.

Wood, John Taylor (Lieutenant)   C.S. Ironclad *Virginia*

Wood, John T.; *The First Fight of the Ironclads,* essay in Battles &Leaders, Vol. 1, pp. 691-711.

Photographs, Maps, and Artwork:

(Note: Photographs prior to 1900 are now over 120 years old and with the exception of E. V. White the photographs used are over 155 years old. Placing them well in the 'Public Domain' 'PD' time frame and permission is not required. This is because, in the vast majority of cases, it would be impossible to find a person or entity with ownership to grant permission. There is also a 'Fair Use' 'FU' doctrine based on four categories and that would also grant allowance but is not necessary since they fall in 'Public Domain.' My source for obtaining all of the photographs and engravings is listed below.)

Battle Maps of the Warwick Line and Seven Pines: Courtesy of 'Maps by Hal Jespersen' at www.cwmaps.com/freemaps.html

William Corson & Jennie Caldwell: PD/FU – *My Dear Jennie – A Collection of Love Letters from a Confederate Soldier,* Blake W. Corson, editor, 1982, Richmond (Dietz Press).

Richard Curtis Photograph: Courtesy of Curtis Watkins, Cathy Watkins Thomas and Jim Brennan who are all descendants of Richard Curtis.

Wilbur Fisk Photograph: PD/FU - *Hard Marching Every Day: The Civil War Letter of Private Wilbur Fisk, 1861-1865* by Wilbur Fisk, edited by Emil and Ruth Rosenblatt copyright 1963, republished by the University of Kansas Press copyright 1992. www.kansaspress.ku.edu.

Dana Greene Engraving: PD/FU - Battles and Leaders / Century Magazine

Charles Haydon: The Charles B. Haydon Papers, 85446 Aaz Boxes 1 & 2, Image # HS17470, Bentley Historical Library, University of Michigan, Ann Arbor, Michigan.

Edgar Steele Photograph: SC01325, Special Collections Research Center, Swem Library, College of William and Mary, Williamsburg, Virginia.

Monitor & Virginia Engravings: PD/FU - Battles and Leaders / Century Magazine

Richard & Mary Watkins Photos: Courtesy of Richard Dupuy Watkins a great-grandson of Richard & Mary Watkins.

W. Waud and A. R. Waud Artwork: Library of Congress — Most appeared in *Harper's Weekly* and some appeared in Century Magazine & Battles and Leaders. No restrictions.

E. V. White: PD - *The First Ironclad Engagement in the World Between the Merrimac-Virginia CSN and the Ericsson-Monitor USN March 8 & 9, 1862 — New York, 1906.*

John Taylor Wood Engraving: PD/FU - Battles and Leaders / Century Magazine

Regimental and Unit Histories:

Bell, Robert T.; *The 11th Virginia Infantry,* Lynchburg, 1985.

Dickinson, John; *The 18th Virginia Infantry,* Lynchburg, 1984

Devine, John; *The 8th Virginia Infantry,* Lynchburg, 1984.

Fields, Frank; *The 28th Virginia Infantry,* Lynchburg, 1985.

Gunn, Ralph; *The 24th Virginia Infantry,* Lynchburg, 1987.

Jensen, Les; *The 32nd Virginia Infantry,* Lynchburg, 1990.

Jordon, E. L. & Thomas, H. A.; *The 19th Virginia Infantry,* Lynchburg, 1987.

Nanzig, Thomas P.; *The 3rd Virginia Cavalry,* Lynchburg, 1989.

Riggs, David; *The 7th Virginia Infantry,* Lynchburg, 1982.

Riggs, David; *The 17th Virginia Infantry,* Lynchburg, 1990

Wallace, Lee; *The 1st Virginia Infantry,* Lynchburg, 1984.

Wallace, Lee; *The Richmond Howitzers,* Lynchburg, 1993.

Other Primary Sources:

Cuhaj, George S. editor; *Confederate States Paper Money – Civil War Currency from the South,* Iola, 2012, Text by Arlie Slabaugh, Pricing by William Brandimore.

Denney, Robert E., *The Civil War Years – A Day-by-Day Chronicle,* New York, 1992.

Dubbs, Carol K.; *Defend This Old Town – Williamsburg During the Civil War,* Baton Rouge, 2002.

Foote, Shelby; *The Civil War – A Narrative,* 3 volumes, New York, 1963

Hughes, Dwight S., *Unlike Anything That Ever Floated – The Monitor & the Virginia and the Battle of Hampton Roads, March 8-9, 1862,* El Dorado Hills, 2021.

Johnson, Robert & Buel, Clarence, editors, *Battles and Leaders of the Civil War,* 4 volumes, New York, 1887 and I also used the 1956 edition.

Mackenzie, Dr., editor – *Mackenzie's Five Thousand Receipts in all the Useful and Domestic Arts: constituting a Complete Practical Library,* Pittsburg, 1853.

Newman, Ralph & Long E. B., editors, *The Civil War – Vol. II The Picture Chronicle,* New York, 1956.

Quarstein, John V. & Moore, Michael J.; *Yorktown's Civil War Siege – Drums Along the Warwick,* Charleston, 2012.

Sears, Stephen W.; *To The Gates of Richmond – The Peninsula Campaign,* New York, 1992.

Slabaugh, Arlie; *Confederate States Paper Money,* Iola, 2000.

Toalson, Jeff -editor; *No Soap, No Pay, Diarrhea, Dysentery & Desertion,* Lincoln, 2006.

Virginia Gazette – editor; *150 Civil War Sesquicentennial – Virtue, Valor & Sacrifice – Yorktown, Williamsburg, Jamestown and West Point,* Williamsburg, 2012.

Warner, Ezra, *Generals in Gray,* Baton Rouge, 1950.

Watkins, Sam, *Company Aytch – A Memoir of the Civil War,* Nashville, 2011.

INDEX

I have created a double index. One is **BIOGRAPHICAL** which records the name of the individual and the dates where his/her quote(s) appear. Name – 4-25 means the quote is on April 25, 1862. If it had been Name – **4-25** it would mean the quote was on April 25, 1861. If it is listed 4 / 5, 18, 22, 26 it means that there are quotes on four different dates in April, 1862. Should it list an 'I' before the 5, in this example, it means there is a quote in the chapter introduction. In the **SUBJECT** index under the topic of 'Diarrhea' you might find: 3/12 Johnson; 3/18 Smith; 4/6, 8 Rayburn; 4/18 Fox; 5-1 Watson, Johnson, Mitchell, & 5-11, 22 Washburn. On those 1862 dates you will find quotes by those individuals relating to diarrhea.

Biographical:

Corson, William (Pvt.)   **7/1, 2, 29; 8/10, 12, 18, 25, 26; 9/3, 28; 11/11;** 1862: 1/6, 12, 20; 2/8; 3/2, 5, 25; 4/1, 16; 5/1, 4, 27; 6/4, 9, 14, 21.

Curtis, Richard (Seaman)   3/8, 8, 8, 8, 9, 9, 9

Curtis, Frederick (Gun Capt.)   3/8

Davis, W. W. (Capt.)   5/31

Dickey, Lyman (Pvt.)   5/11

Dunbar, Henry (Cpl.)   4/16

Eggleston, John (Lt.)   3/8

Englis, George (Pvt.)   2/23

Fisk, Wilbur (Pvt.)   3/25, 27; 4/4, 6, 16, 24; 5/9, 10, 18, 19; 6/7, 7.

Flournoy, John (Pvt.)   2/24

French, George (Cpl.)   4/17

Furst, Luther (Cpl.)   3/20; 4/4, 7, 15, 16, 20; 5/4, 5, 6, 10, 11, 15, 17, 20, 21, 27, 30, 31; 6/2, 11.

Galt, John M. (Dr.)   5/6

Galt, Sally (Miss.)   3/10

Greene, Dana (Lt.)   3/7, 8, 9, 9, 9, 9, 9, 9; 5/15

Haydon, Charles (Lt.)   3/18, 20, 21, 28; 4/6, 8, 13, 16, 20; 5/1, 3, 4, 5, 6, 8, 10, 14, 15, 16, 21, 25, 31, 31; 6/2, 5, 6, 14.

Head, Thomas J. (Pvt.)   **6/15**

Holland, William (Pvt.)   5/6, 12, 31, 31

Jack, E. A. (Asst. Eng.)   5/11

Johnson, Charles (Pvt.)   **4/11; 6/22, 26; 7/17, 26.**

Johnson, Robert (Sgt.)   5/21

Jones, Catesby (Lt.)   2/18; 3/9

Jones, John B. (Mr.)   5/10, 14, 15, 16, 23, 31; 6/1, 3.

Landers, Eli (Pvt.)   4/16

Laughton, Joseph (Cpl.)   5/5

Lyons, Patrick (Cpl.)   5/7

Martin, John T. (Mr.)   **11/11;** 1862: 1/17; 2/24, 28; 3/8; 5/5, 6, 8, 15.

McDonald, Joseph (Fireman)   3/8

McKinney, E. P. (Lt.)   4/30; 5/3 & 4, 21; 6/11

McLaws, Lafayette (Maj. Gen.)   **7/2, 18, 24, 25, 30; 8/18, 26; 9/29; 10/3, 10, 23; 11/29; 12/20, 30;** 1862: 1/4, 14; 2/7, 19; 3/31; 4/23, 25; 5/1, 13, 20; 6/10, 28.

Norris, William (Capt.)   3/8, 9

Pendergast, Austin (Lt.)   3/8

Petty, James (Pvt.)   5/31

Phillips, Dinwiddie (Surgeon)   3/8, 8, 9

Porter, Benjamin (Sgt.)   5/29, 6/2, 20

Porter, John L. (Mr.)   2/18; 3/10

Quinby, George (Capt.)   4/25

Ramsay, H. A. (Chief Engineer)   3/8, 9; 5/11

Reid, J. W. (Pvt.)   4/18, 24, 30; 5/4, 5, 5, 5, 5, 14; 6/2, 7, 22.

Rhodes, Elisha (Sgt. Major)   3/9, 10, 26, 27, 28, 31; 4/12, 14, 25, 30; 5/7, 11, 12, 16, 20, 24, 26; 6/4.

Shotwell, Randolph (Pvt.) 5/5

Simpson, Tally (Pvt.)   4/7, 13, 18, 20, 24, 30; 5/4, 14, 21, 23; 6/18, 19.

Smith, William R. (Sgt.)   5/31

Steele, Edgar (Pvt.)   4/13

Stimers, Alban (Chief Engineer)   3/7, 10

Twitchell, Marshall (Cpl.)   4/16; 5/6, 23; 6/5

Watkins, Sam (Pvt) [an *editorial comment* under Twitchell on 5/23].

Watkins, Nathaniel (Pvt.)   3/28; 4/2, 4, 7, 9, 12, 15, 18, 22, 24, 27; 5/3, 8, 13, 26, 27; 6/1, 7, 11.

Watkins, Richard H. (Pvt./Lt.)   **8/23; 9/12, 17, 24; 10/2, 15, 18, 26,; 11/10, 13, 17, 23, 27; 12/7, 19;** 1862: 1/6, 14; 2/9, 20; 3/16, 27; 4/1, 18, 22, 24, 25, 27; 5/1, 4-6, 11, 11, 20, 30; 6/1, 3, 5.

White, E. V. (Lt.)   **4/21, 6/15;** 1862: 1/16; 3/8, 8, 8, 8, 9, 9; 5/11.

Williams, James P. (Pvt.)   **5/8;   6/24;   7/31;   8/29;   10/14;   11/4; 12/27;** 1862: 1/20; 3/13; 4/27; 6/17.

Wood, John T. (Lt.)   3/8, 8, 8, 9, 9, 9, 29; 4/11; 5/8.

Wood, George R. (Mr.)   **4/20, 23; 9/15; 12/25;** 1862: 5/4, 11, 13, 14.

Worden, John (Capt.)   3/9

Wynne,Thomas G. (Mr.)   **4/22, 26;   5/11, 16, 23;   6/10, 12, 18, 28; 7/11, 19, 22, 24;   8/8, 21, 31;   9/2, 7, 18, 25, 30; 11/1, 9, 23; 12/ 10, 14, 15, 21.**

SUBJECT

Battles:

Battle of Hampton Roads March 8 & 9: Half of the March chapter involves the destruction of the Union fleet and the battle of the *Monitor & Virginia.* Many Union and Confederate voices provide multiple comments. See in great detail in 'Naval' section of index.

Big Bethel: **6/11** Wynne, Johnson, **6/15** Head

Dam #1: 4/15 Bumgarner, 4/16 Furst, Twitchell, Landers, Fisk, Corson, 4/17 French, 4/18 R. Watkins, 4/19 Branch

Eltham's Landing: 5/7 Barrett

Fort Donelson: 2/19 McLaws, 2/20 R. Watkins, 3/27 R. Watkins

Donelson surrender dooms Nashville: 2/19 McLaws; 2/22 R. Watkins

Manassas: **7/19** Wynne, **7/26** Johnson

Mobile: 5/28 Porter

New Orleans: 4/30 Rhodes, 5/1 McLaws, 5/28 Porter

Savannah & Fort Pulaski: 4/26 Branch

Winchester: 3/27 R. Watkins

Camp Life:

General:

Balloon: 4/6 Haydon, 6/21 Corson

Bands: 1/4 McLaws

Bathing: **6/24** Williams, **7/3** Corson, **8/12** Corson, **12/7** R. Watkins, 4/24 Fisk, 5/13 N. Watkins, 5/28 Corson, 6/14 Haydon

Boxes from home: **7/31** Williams, 5/17 George

Burial Details and Recovering Wounded: 5/4 Haydon, 5/6 Twitchell,

Camp Site Conditions: **8/12** Corson, **10/26** R. Watkins, 1/14 R. Watkins, 1/29 Corson, 4/6 Haydon, 4/8 Haydon, 4/15 Furst, 4/22 R. Watkins, 4/25 Quinby, 5/3 Haydon, 5/5 Camper, 5/6 Furst, 5/10 Haydon, 5/19 Fisk, 5/20 R. Watkins, Rhodes, 5/21 Furst, 5/25 Haydon, 5/26 N. Watkins, 5/31 Holland

Camping w/ tents or Winter Quarters: **10/14** Williams, **11/17** R. Watkins, **11/29** McLaws, **12/7, 12** R. Watkins **12/27** Williams, 3/31 Rhodes,

Camping without tents or shelter: **10/14** Williams, 3/25 Fisk, 4/20 Simpson, 5/5 Camper, 6/4 Rhodes, 6/5 R. Watkins.

Changing Underclothes: **12/7** R. Watkins

Church Service & Religion: 4/14 Haydon

Conscription & Conscription Bill: See under 'Re-Enlistment'

Court Martial: 3/31 Haydon

Deaths / Burials: **7/26** Johnson, 4/24 Reid, 4/25 McLaws, 5/4 Haydon, 5/5 Laughton, Camper, 5/6 Furst, Haydon, 5/7 Rhodes, 5/9 Fisk, 5/21 Johnson, 6/2 Porter, 6/5, 6 Haydon, 6/7 Reid, 6/17 Williams.

Desertion / Prisoners – Confederate: 5/3 McKinney, 4/12 Rhodes, 6/3 NYDailyTrib

Desertion / Prisoners – Union: **10/18** R. Watkins, 5/3 N. Watkins, 5/30 R. Watkins

Details (army wide) to gather vegetables to fight scurvy: 5/23 Simpson

Digging Trenches, Rifle Pits, Fortifications: 4/12 N. Watkins, 4/24 Fisk, 4/25 Williams

Dreams: 1/6 Corson

Drilling, Parade & Inspection: **6/15** Head, **7/31** Williams; 3/27 R. Watkins, 3/28 Haydon, 4/20 Simpson, 4/25 McLaws, 4/30 McKinney, 4/30 Reid

Election of Company Officers: See under 'Re-Organization of Armies'

Excess Clothing & Baggage Disposal: 5/1 Corson

Field Correspondent for Newspaper 3/25 Fisk

Fishing: **8/12** Corson, 4/30 Reid, 5/11 Furst

Flag of Truce: 5/21 Johnson

Foraging Details: **11/10, 13, 23** R. Watkins, 6/17 Corson

Furloughs: **11/23, 27** R. Watkins, 2/9 R. Watkins, 6/5 R. Watkins

Haircut: 5/28 Corson

Head cut with axe: **8/18** Corson

Headquarters Tent Hub-bub: **12/30** McLaws

Horse Health: **8/12** Corson, **12/12** Watkins, 6/9 Corson

Houses of Prostitution: 3/20 Furst

Marching: 3/10 Rhodes, 3/28 Rhodes, 4/18 Reid, 4/20 Simpson, 5/6 Camper, 5/8 N. Watkins, 5/20 Rhodes, 5/22 Twitchell

Parent visit Camp: 1/20 Williams

Peach Brandy: **12/25** Wood

Petition to go home for winter / return in spring: **10/2** R. Watkins, **12/12** R. Watkins

Picket/Vidette/Guard Duty/Scout/Skirmishing: **5/26** Corson, **9/3** Corson, **10/18, 26** R. Watkins, **11/17** R. Watkins, 1/12 R. Watkins, 2/9 R. Watkins; 3/13 Williams, 3/27 Fisk, 4/1 Corson, 4/7 Furst, 4/24 Fisk, 4/30 Rhodes, 5/1 Haydon, 5/3 McKinney, 5/4 Reid, 5/7 Lyons, 5/8 Haydon, 5/11 R. Watkins, Furst, 5/20 Furst, R. Watikns, 5/22 McKinney, 5/24 Rhodes, 5/27 Corson, 5/30 R. Watkins, J. Jones, 5/31 Holland, 6/17 Corson

Pictures / Daguerreotypes − 1/14 McLaws, 3/5 Corson, 4/1 Corson; 4/13 Steele, 5/17 George, 528 Corson, 6/28 McLaws

Playing the Violin: **6/15** Head, **7/31** Williams

Promotion: 3/9 Rhodes, 4/22 R. Watkins, 4/27 R. Watkins, 5/20 McLaws

Rain & Mud: **10/10, 22** McLaws, **11/10** R. Watkins, **11/11** Corson, 1/10 McLaws, 1/12 Corson, 1/14 R. Watkins, 1/29 Corson, 2/19 McLaws, 2/20 R. Watkins, 2/23 Englis, 3/5 Corson, 3/20 Furst, 3/25 Corson, 4/7 Buzhardt, 4/8 Haydon, 4/20 Furst, 4/22 R. Watkins, 4/24 Furst, 4/25 Quinby, 4/27 Williams, 5/1 Haydon, 5/3 Haydon, 5/4 Reid, 5/5 Furst, Camper, Reid, Martin, 5/6 Camper, 5/7 Rhodes, 5/9 Fisk, 5/12 Holland, 5/15 Furst, 5/24 Rhodes, 5/27 Furst, 5/30 Furst, 5/31 Davis, 6/2 Porter, Furst, Reid, 6/4 Rhodes, 6/5 Haydon.

Re-enlistment: 2/9 R. Watkins, 3/2 Corson, 3/13 Williams, 3/16 R. Watkins, 4/18 R. Watkins, 4/25 R. Watkins,

Conscription Bill: 4/18 Simpson, 4/25 Reid, R. Watkins, 4/30 Simpson

Substitutes: 5/20 R. Watkins, 5/26 N. Watkins, 6/1 R. Watkins

Re-organization of Army: 4/25 R. Watkins

Election of New Officers: 2/24 Flournoy

Sanitation: 3/25 Corson

Sewing Pants: 4/22 N. Watkins

Shotguns Issued: **9/28** Corson

Sick Call: See 'Sick Call – Reported Sick' under 'Disease' in Medical section

Sick Horses: **12/12** R. Watkins, 1/14 R. Watkins, 6/9 Corson.

Signal Corps: 5/27 Furst, all entries under Furst relate to the Signal Corps, see also 'Norris' who served in the Confederate signal corps.

Size/Regiments in Command: 5/20 McLaws

Sleeping on the beach: 3/25 Fisk

Squirrel Hunting: **9/28** Corson

Stealing Negro Oyster Boats: 3/20 Haydon

Substitutes: See Re-Enlistment sub topic

Torpedoes/Land Mines: 5/4 Haydon, 5/21 Johnson

Train Transportation: 3/28 N. Watkins

Viewing a comet: **7/17** Johnson

Water: **9/17** R. Watkins, 5/4 Corson

Clothing & Uniforms:

Boots 1/4 McLaws

Blanket: 5/30 Watkins

Burnt by order at Yorktown (excess): 5/28 Corson

Flannel Shirts: **10/10** McLaws, 6/19 Williams

Hat: 6/2 Reid

Lost Clothing: 2/8 Corson

Marching Uniform of C.S. soldier: 6/20 Porter

Pants: 4/22 N. Watkins

Shirts: 1/4 McLaws

Shoes: 4/22 N. Watkins, 6/17 Williams, 6/19 Williams

Socks: **7/31** Williams, **10/10** McLaws, **12/7** R. Watkins, 1/4 McLaws, 1/6 R. Watkins, 5/20 McLaws, 6/19 Williams.

Underclothing: **10/10** McLaws, 1/4 McLaws,

Uniform: **10/10** McLaws

Letters/Writing:

"Bring me food": 4/14 Bumgarner

Christmas thoughts away from home: **12/27** Williams

Direct Mail to: 1/6 R. Watkins, 4/9 N. Watkins

Envelopes & Paper Borrowed: 4/1 R. Watkins, 4/22 R. Watkins

"How happy letters make me": **10/15** R. Watkins

Letter Transit Time in Virginia: 3/27 R. Watkins

Letters receiving: **6/15** Head, **7/17, 31** Johnson, **9/3** Corson, 4/12 Rhodes, 4/27 Williams, 5/20 McLaws, 5/26 N. Watkins, 6/5 R. Watkins, 6/28 McLaws.

Letters sending: 3/16 R. Watkins, 6/1 R. Watkins

Letters sending home (carried) with soldiers & civilians: **11/27** R. Watkins, 6/1. 5 R. Watkins.

Letters from children: **8/18** McLaws; 4/23 McLaws

Love and Kisses: 3/31 McLaws, 4/1 R. Watkins, 4/23 McLaws, 4/25, 27 R. Watkins, 5/1 McLaws, 5/30 R. Watkins

"May God keep you and children safe" – 4/24 R. Watkins

Mail departing / too late / no time to write: 4/18 Reid, 4/18 R. Watkins, 4/24 Reid, 4/27 R. Watkins, 4/30 Reid

Missing loved ones: **6/15** Head, **7/29** Corson, **8/25** Corson, **10/2** R. Watkins,

Names for a baby: **12/30** McLaws

Newspaper Subcription: **7/18** McLaws

"No letters from you" – 4/7 N. Watkins, 4/9 N. Watkins, 5/1 McLaws, 5/20 R. Watkins.

"Sent Candy for Emmie & Minnie" – 6/5 R. Watkins

Stamps: 5/21 Johnson

"With you in my dreams" – 5/3 N Watkins

Questions/Requests about items at home:

    Bill to Exempt Overseers from military: 3/16 R. Watkins

        Cattle: **10/2** R. Watkins

        Cutting the tobacco: R. Watkins

        Guano Purchase: 1/6 R. Watkins

        Hogs: **10/2** R. Watkins, 1/6 R, Watkins

        Horses: **10/2** R. Watkins

        Orchard: 1/6 R. Watkins

Overseer not to neglect Mother's farm: 3/27 R. Watkins

Pork in Smokehouse: 2/23 Martin

Potato Crop: **11/4** Williams, 4/1 R. Watkins

Sheep: **10/2** R. Watkins

Where is my brother?: 3/27 R. Waktins

Winter Clothes – Making: **11/4** Williams

Saved letters: **11/17** R. Watkins

Want to see you: **11/23** R. Watkins, 1/6 R. Watkins, 2/9 R. Watkins.

Write about young ladies at home: 6/20 Porter

Write Often: **11/23** R. Watkins, **11/29** McLaws, 6/20 Porter.

Rations:

Bacon: **6/24** Williams, **9/24** R. Watkins, 3/31 Rhodes, 4/15 Branch

Beef: 3/5 Corson, 3/31 Rhodes

Biscuits: **6/24** Williams, **7/20** McLaws, **9/24** R. Watkins, 4/18 N. Watkins, 5/8, 27 N. Watkins

Box from home: **7/31** Williams

Bread / No Bread: **6/15** Wynne, 4/6 Haydon

Butter: 4/15 Bumgarner, 4/18 N. Watkins, 5/21 Haydon, 5/23 Simpson

Buttermilk: **6/18** Wynne, **7/30** McLaws, **12/10** Wynne

Cabbage: **12/10** Wynne

Cakes: 2/7 McLaws;

Cattle: 4/6 Haydon

Chicken: **9/24** R. Watkins, 5/15 Furst

Clams: **7/29** Corson

Coffee: **9/17 R.** Watkins, **10/10** McLaws, 3/28 Haydon, 4/18 N. Watkins, 6/7 N. Watkins.

Coffee Substitute: 3/25 Corson

Corn: **8/12** Corson, 4/6 Haydon, 5/13 Simpson, 5/28 Porter

Crackers (Hardtack): 3/28 Haydon, 4/8 Haydon, 4/24 Fisk

Crabs: **7/3** Corson

Crout (like Saurkraut): 4/15 Bumgarner

Dried Fruit: 4/15 Bumgarner

Eggs: **12/10** Wynne, 4/18 N. Watkins,

Fish: **7/29** Corson, **8/12** Corson, **9/24** R. Watkins, 4/18 N. Watkins, 4/24 Simpson, 4/30 Reid,

Fried Meat: 4/18 N. Watkins

Guinea Hen (Tough): 5/22 McKinney

Ham: **9/17** R. Watkins, **10/10** McLaws, **11/9** Wynne, 3/31 Rhodes

Hoe Cakes: **9/17** R. Watkins

Honey: 4/15 Bumgarner, 5/21 Furst

Lard: **6/24** Williams

Mutton: 5/23 Simpson

Nuts: 2/7 McLaws

Onions: 4/15 Bumgarner, 5/23 Simpson

Oranges: 1/4 McLaws

Oysters: **7/3** Corson, **9/24** R. Watkins, **10/10** McLaws, 4/18 N. Watkins,

Peas: **9/24** R. Watkins, 5/24 Rhodes

Poor Food / Scanty Rations: **7/29** Corson, 3/31 Rhodes, 4/18 R. Watkins, 4/20 Simpson, 4/24 Fisk, 5/6 Camper, 5/10 Fisk, 5/11 Rhodes, 5/13 Simpson, 5/22 McKinney, 5/28 Porter

Potatoes: **9/24** R. Watkins

Prices in Richmond excessively high: **8/21** Wynne

Salt: 4/8 Haydon, 5/11 Rhodes

Sausages: 1/4 McLaws

Strawberries: 5/21 Haydon, 5/24 Rhodes

Sweet Potatoes: **9/24** Watkins, 3/31 Rhodes,

Sugar: 4/8 Haydon

Sugar Plums: 2/7 McLaws

Tallow mistaken for Lard: **6/24** Williams

Tomatoes: **7/30** McLaws, **9/24** R. Watkins

Watermelons: **7/29** Corson, **8/12** Corson

Purchased from farmers: **6/18 & 7/22** Wynne

Supplied meals and foodstuffs to troops: **6/28, 7/24, 10/9, 12/10 & 14** Wynne

Cities / Geographic Locations / Key Sites:
Gloucester Point:

Arrival: 4/2 N. Watkins

Climate – Summer Conditions: **6/24** Williams

Columbiads – Awaiting Shipment from West Point: **5/8** Williams

Description of the Point & Work: **5/8** Williams

Food in Camp: **5/8** Williams, 4/18 N. Watkins

Forests are pine woods: 4/24 N. Watkins

Fortifications – Construction: **5/8** Williams, **5/11** Wynne, 4/14 N. Watkins

"Gloucester Point is one huge bank of sand.": 4/24 N. Watkins

Guard Duty at the Fort: 4/4 N. Watkins

Officers of K&Q Artillery all Baptist – No Drinking: 4/2 N. Watkins

Preparing to Evacuate the Fort: 5/3 N. Watkins

Shots exchanged with Yankee ships: 4/15 N. Watkins, 4/24 N. Watkins

Transfer to K&Q Artillery possible for Bro. Dick Watkins: 4/12 N. Watkins

York River Width: **5/8** Williams

Peninsula Locations:

Lower:

Adams Ranch: **8/25, 26** Corson, **9/3** Corson, **9/17** R. Watkins

Back River – Messox Point: **10/18** R. Watkins

Bartlett's Farm: **8/12** Corson, **11/17** R. Watkins

Bethel (Big & Little): **6/11** Johnson, Wynne, **6/15** Head, **6/29** Corson, **8/9** Williams, **9/17** R. Watkins, **11/14** Williams, **11/17** R. Watkins; 3/27 Fisk, 3/31 Haydon, McLaws, 4/9 Furst

Broken Bridge: **12/27** R. Watkins

Camp Cockle / Cockletown: **8/10** Corson, **12/10** Wynne

Camp Butler: **6/18** Johnson

Camp Phillips: **9/24** R. Watkins, **9/28** Corson

Camp Shields: 1/14 R. Watkins, 2/9, 20 R. Watkins

College Creek – Williamsburg: **4/21** Wood, **9/15** Wood

Custis Farm (lower peninsula): 4/18, 20, 24, 30 Simpson

Fort Crafford: **4/21** Wood, **8/21, 31, 9/2** Wynne

Fortress Monroe: **8/9** Williams, **8/23** R. Watkins, **9/12** R. Watkins, **10/14** Williams, 2/23 Englis, 3/18 Haydon, 3/25 Fisk, 3/28 Rhodes, 6/4, 10 New York Daily Tribune

Half-Way House: **9/24** R. Watkins **10/2, 15, 26** R. Watkins, **11/23, 27** Watkins

Hampton: **4/21** Wood, **7/29** Corson, **8/9** Williams, **8/10** Corson, 3/20 Haydon, 3/21, Haydon, 3/25 Fisk, 3/28 Rhodes, 4/7 Furst, 4/13 Steel, 4/30 McKinney

Harrod's Mill: **12/27** R. Watkins, 1/20 Williams

James City County: See all entries by John T. Martin and Thomas Wynne

Jamestown Island: **4/21** Wood, **8/18** McLaws

Jones Farm: 1/29 Corson, 2/8 Corson

Kings Mill & Kings Mill Landing: **4/21** Wood, 4/15 Branch,

Lebanon Church: **11/23; 12/15, 21** Wynne, 1/12 Corson, 4/1 R. Watkins, 4/15 Branch, 4/18, 22, 24, 25, 27 R. Watkins

Lee's Mill / Farm: 4/13 Simpson, 4/24 Fisk

Mulberry Island: **4/21** Wood, 1/12 Corson,

Newport News: **6/26** Johnson, **7/29** Corson, **10/14** Williams, 3/27 Fisk, 3/31 Rhodes, 4/4 Fisk, 4/12 Steel,

'Poquosin' River: **8/12** Corson, **9/24** Watkins

Sawyer Swamp: **11/17** R. Watkins

Warwick Cty. & Warwick CoHo: **9/7** Wynne, 4/6 Fisk, 4/12 Rhodes, 4/14 Rhodes, 4/20 Furst, 4/13 Steel

Wynne's Mill: 4/27 Williams

Yorktown Line: **9/7, 18** Wynne, 3/13 Williams, 4/24 Reid

Young's Mill: **8/9** Williams, **9/29** McLaws, **10/3, 10** McLaws, **10/14** Williams, **11/23, 29** McLaws, **12/15** Wynne, **12/20** McLaws, 1/4 McLaws, 1/12 Corson, 2/7, 19 McLaws, 3/2 Corson, 3/16, 27 R. Watkins, 4/1 R. Watkins, Corson, 4/30 Rhodes

Upper:

Bottom's Bridge: 5/20 Watkins, 5/25 Haydon, 5/27 Corson

Camp Jackson – Richmond: 6/18 Simpson

Charles City County: 6/17 Corson

Chickahominy River / Swamp: 5/11 R. Watkins, 5/12 Simpson, 5/14 Reid, 5/20 Furst, 5/22 McKinney, Twitchell, 5/24 Rhodes, 5/25 Haydon, 5/30 Furst, 5/31 Haydon, 6/7 Fisk, 6/10 McLaws, 6/11 Furst.

Cold Harbor Crossroads: 5/21 Furst

Golding's Farm: 6/5 Twitchell

'Glenwood' – Home of a Mr. Stubbs: 5/20 McLaws

Hanover CoHo: 5/27 Furst

Jamestown Island: 5/2 Branch, 5/5 Wood

King's Mill Wharf/Landing: 5/1 R. Watkins, 5/2 Branch, 5/4 Corson, 5/5 Wood

Lee's Mill: 5/1 Corson

New Kent CoHo and County: 5/10 Furst, 5/13 McLaws, 5/13 N. Watkins

Macon Farm (Dr. Macon): 5/15 Furst, 5/16 Rhodes, 5/20 Rhodes

Mechanicsville: 5/24 Rhodes

Olive Branch: 5/9 Lyons

Poe's Farm: 6/17, 19 Williams

West Point: 5/22 N. York Daily Tribune

White House (Custis Farm & Lee Farm): 5/11 Furst, 5/12 Rhodes, 5/18 Fisk

Pamunkey: 5/21 Johnson

Pamunkey/Cumberland Landing: 5/15, 16 Haydon

Pamunkey/Mt. Airy: 5/17 Furst

Williamsburg:

Aid at African Baptist Hospital: 3/10 Galt

Construction of Fortifications: **7/2** McLaws

Description of the Town: 5/21 Johnson

Drilling Artillerymen: **7/31** Williams

Fort Magruder (Redoubt 6): **7/2, 30** McLaws

News of CSS *Virginia* crushing the Union fleet: 3/9 Coleman

Rain Damage to Fortifications: **7/24** McLaws

Redoubts 5 & 7 Construction: **7/30** McLaws

Fifth Louisiana Infantry: **11/1** Wynne

Tenth Louisiana Infantry – Arrival & time on Jamestown Island: **8/18** McLaws

Work Parties – Clearing Fields of Fire: **7/25** McLaws

Work Parties – Marking Torpedoes, Exploding: 5/21 Johnson

Work Parties – Putting Tree Brush into Ravines: **7/25** McLaws

Work Party – Negro – Earth moving at Redoubt #1: **7/25** McLaws

Yorktown:

Arrive by boat from West Point: 4/7 Simpson

Bombardment of the Yorktown forts: 5/1 McLaws

Climate – Summer Conditions: **6/24** Williams

Construction of Fortifications: **6/15** Head, **6/24** Williams

Cornwallis Cave: **6/15** Head

Cornwallis Surrender Site: **7/1** Corson

Description: **6/15** Head, **9/12** R. Watkins, 4/30 Reid

Evacuate the Yorktown- Warwick Line: 5/1 Corson, 5/3 Barrett

Formidable CSA Works: 5/4 Haydon

House where Cornwallis surrendered": 4/24 Reid

Phosphorescent Lights of Sea Water in river: 1/12 Watkins

Steamer *Logan* regular West Point to Yorktown runs: 1/26 Williams

Scouting Party: 1/6 Corson

Troops Arriving: **11/1** Wynne

Yankee Ships on York River & Chesapeake Bay: **9/3** Corson, 1/12 R. Watkins,

Cost of Goods:

Bacon: **11/11** Martin, 6/11 Furst

Boots: 5/23 J. Jones

Bread: 6/11 Furst, 6/22 Reid

Butter: 5/21 Haydon, 5/23 Simpson, 5/23 J. Jones, 6/22 Reid

Chickens: 4/15 Bumgarner, 6/22 Reid

Cheese: 5/21 Haydon, 6/7 Fisk

Coffee: **11/11** Martin, 6/22 Reid

Eggs: 4/15 Bumgarner, 6/22 Reid

Horse: **10/10** McLaws

House Rent: 5/23 J. Jones

Meat: 5/23 J. Jones

Milk: 6/11 Furst

Molasses: **11/11** Martin, 3/5 Corson,

Mutton: 5/23 Simpson, 6/10 McLaws

Onions: 6/11 Furst

Pants: 4/22 N. Watkins

Pies: 4/14 Bumgarner, 6/7 Fisk, 6/22 Reid

Salt: **11/11** Martin; 1/6 R. Watkins, 1/17 Martin, 4/30 Reid

Shoes: 4/22 N. Watkins, 5/23 J. Jones

Shirts: 5/23 J. Jones

Strawberries: 5/21 Haydon, 6/9 Corson

Sugar: **11/11** Martin, 6/10 McLaws, 6/22 Reid.

Tea: 5/23 J. Jones

Destruction of Property:

Burning of Hampton: **8/8** Wynne, **8/9** Williams, 3/21 Haydon, 3/25 Fisk, 3/28 Rhodes; 4/13 Steel

Camped on farm in fields CSA: 4/22 R. Watkins, 5/5, 6 Martin

Camped in apple orchard CSA: **9/7** Wynne

Camped on farm in fields USA: 5/8 Martin

Carpenter Shop in Hampton: **6/26** Johnson

Destruction – The Grim Visage of War: 4/27 Williams

Farms Abandoned: 5/20 Rhodes

Farms Abandoned, become refugees: **12/21** Wynne

Farms Fences: 4/22 R. Watkins

Farm Fields and Crops: 4/22 R. Watkins

Stealing/Killing Livestock: **8/26** McLaws, 5/6 Martin, 5/7 Lyons, 5/10 Furst, Fisk, 5/11 Rhodes, 5/12 Rhodes, 5/15 Furst

Stealing, Foraging, Confiscating Crops: 5/10 Furst, 5/17 Furst, 5/21 McKinney

Stealing Negro Oyster Boats and Oysters: 3/20 Haydon

Stealing Negroes: **7/2** McLaws, **7/24** Wynne, **8/26** McLaws

Yankee Destruction of Hampton Homes: **8/9** Williams

Letters (See 'Camp Life')

Military Operations: Ironclads, Peninsula, Williamsburg & Seven Pines:

Virginia against the Union Wooden Fleet (3-8) and the *Monitor* (3-9)

A massive section on the naval activities in Hampton Roads and on the James River is contained in the 'Naval' section.

Peninsula – The Yorktown/Warwick Line:

Unfavorable for military operations: 3/31 McLaws

Warwick River Defensive Line: 3/31 McLaws, 4/15 Branch, 4/22 R. Watkins, 4/27 N. Watkins

West Point capture would leave Union 40 miles from Richmond: 3/31 McLaws

- - - - -

Inspecting Fortifications: **5/11, 16** Wynne

Louisiana Troops are merest rowdies: **7/24** Wynne

Louisiana Zouaves to Yorktown: **6/12** Wynne

Amphibious transportation for Union army: 3/ introduction

Yanks Advancing, driving in pickets, skirmishing: 4/1 R. Watkins, Corson, 4/4 Fisk

Deployment of Skirmishers – Method: 4/4 Fisk

Balloon Operations: 4/6, 16 Haydon (see all entries by Furst for Signal Corps operations)

Close to the Rebel Works: 4/6 Fisk, 4/7 Furst

Marched to Lee's Farm: 4/7 Simpson

Sharpshooters/Snipers: 4/7 Furst

Prisoners Taken near Warwick CoHo: 4/12 Rhodes

Wynne's Mill Union Attack: 4/12 N. Watkins

"Hemmed in on 3 sides by water, Rebels on 4[th"]: 4/13 Steel

Estimates of Troop Strength: 4/13 Steel

Lee's Mill Pond Separates our pickets: 4/13 Simpson

3000 Negro Men working on breast works: 4/13 Simpson

Yanks moving siege guns in by rail: 4/13 Simpson

"To Williamsburg by boat, march to Yorktown line near Young's Mill": 4/14, 15 Branch

Examined old CSA line at Young's Mill: 4/14 Rhodes

Dam #1 Battle: 4/15 Bumgarner, 4/16 Dunbar, Furst, Twitchell, Landers, Fisk, Corson, 4/17 French, 4/18 R. Watkins, 4/19 Branch

Heavy artillery fire at Yorktown: 4/15 N. Watkins

Dead Recovered under flag of truce (Dam #1): 4/16 Fisk

"Genl. McClellan will have to do some pretty fighting": 4/18 R. Watkins

Lee's Mill & House, HQ, Center of the line: 4/22 R. Watkins

Digging Trenches, cutting timber: 4/22 Simpson

Tour of Young's Farm on the Warwick River: 4/25 Rhodes

Comparing Gen. Magruder & Gen. Johnston's styles: 4/27 Williams

Wynne's Mill trench – Union cannon fire: 4/27 Williams

Teaser shells 2nd R. Island at Young's Farm on the Warwick River: 4/30 Rhodes

Seven Pines – Crossing the Chickahominy until late June operations:

"It will take weeks for McClellan to make preparations": 5/22 Simpson

"I scarcely think our general will wait (Johnston) . . . he will give battle": 5/22 Simpson

Set fire to a railroad bridge at Hanover CoHo: 5/27 Furst

3 days rations – in line of battle: 5/27 N. Watkins

Attacked train south of Hanover with 4 cars of munitions for Richmond: 5/28 Rhodes

Heavy rain, lightning strikes pine 20 yds. of tent: 5/30 Furst

"On picket, sitting in a swamp": 5/30 R. Watkins

Great rain, Chickahominy swollen, opportune for C.S. attack: 5/30 J. Jones

Ordered to march to the front: 5/31 Holland

Rain in torrents, lightning and enemy attack: 5/31 Davis

In 3 hours lost 1/3 of our men – no reinforcements: 5/31 Davis

Kemper's brigade drives enemy from trenches: 5/31 Camper

Camped in captured trenches then moved at 9 p.m.: 5/31 Camper

Shot in thumb, went to field hospital: 5/31 Holland

2nd Michigan over-run with lice and woodticks: 5/31 Haydon

Formed line to stop Union stragglers – arrested 1000 men in one hour: 5/31 Haydon

Lights flickering over field as men search the dead for booty: 5/31 Smith

Catching Confederate stragglers: 6/1 R. Watkins

General Johnston wounded: 6/1 R. Watkins, 6/2 Reid

Our Company had half killed & wounded: 6/1 N. Watkins

Ambulances bringing wounded into Richmond: 6/1 J. Jones

"We drove them from their own redoubts: - 6/2 Porter

Mass of dead horses and men: 6/5, 6 Haydon, 6/17 Williams

"They left their tents, knapsacks, provisions & everything" – 6/2 Porter, Reid, 6/4 Corson, 6/7 N. Watkins, 6/17 Williams.

Losses by the 2nd Michigan: 6/2 Haydon

Casey's Division met with disaster: 6/2 New York Daily Tribune (NYDT)

Our Company gathered arms on the battlefield: 6/3 R. Watkins, 6/4 Corson

Excuses for straggling: 6/3 R. Watkins

General Lee assumes command: 6/3 J. Jones

540 C.S. prisoners shipped to Governor's Island, NY: 6/3 NYDT

Richmond to fall in days or hours: 6/3 NYDT

Removing dead & wounded from battlefield: 6/4 Corson

"We have withdrawn to old lines" – 6/7 N Watkins

Sutlers & extravagant prices: 6/7 Fisk

4000 Union wounded shipped from W. Point: 6/10 NYDT

New Hospitals at Fort Monroe: 6/10 NYDT

Gen. McClellan continues to entrench: 6/10 McLaws

Transferred from Chickahominy swamp to Drury's Bluff: 6/11 N. Watkins

Battle was across flooded Chickahominy: 6/13 Brainerd

Clean clothes & a bath are a rarity: 6/14 Haydon

Stuart's 'Ride Around McClellan' – 6/18 Simpson

Williamsburg – A Rear Guard Action Covering the Withdrawal:

Evacuation of wounded & supplies at Kings Mill: 5/1 R. Watkins, 5/2 Branch, 5/4 Corson, Watkins, 5/5 Wood

Evacuation of the Yorktown trenches: 5/4 Barrett, Simpson

Stench of dead animals & human waste at Yorktown: 5/3 Haydon

Marched into Yorktown: 5/3 McKinney, 5/4 Furst

Reached Williamsburg the night of the 4th: 5/4 Simpson

Yanks on river heading to W. Point & Eltham: 5/4 Barrett

Picket Lines in the rain: 5/4 Reid

Abandoned tents, stores and stench of death: 5/4 Haydon

Rebs drove Hooker about half a miles: 5/5 Furst

Attacks at and near Ft. Magruder: 5/5 Reid

Kearny counter-attack: 5/5 Haydon

Move to Redoubt #9 & attack redoubt to our left: 5/5 Reid

Redoubt #11 – 5th N. C. driven back with heavy loss: 5/5 Reid

More ammo delivered at 2 a.m. near Redoubt #9: 5/5 Reid

Entered empty Fort Magruder at daybreak: 5/6 Rhodes

Battlefield strewn with dead and wounded: 5/6 Haydon, 5/7 Rhodes

Comparison of the image of CSA and USA troops: 5/6 Coleman

Withdraw at 0800 toward Richmond: 5/5 Reid

3 day mud march in the rain: 5/6 Camper

Passing the Lunatic Asylum: 5/6 Holland, 5/6 Galt

Yankee protection of Southern property: 5/6 Cary

Hood blunts Union move at Eltham Landing: 5/7 Barrett

Battlefield burials: 5/7 N. York Daily Tribune, 5/21 Johnson, 5/7 Sneden footnote

Mass grave of 96 men of the 5th N. Carolina: 5/7 N. York Daily Tribune

Large number of wounded in Williamsburg; 5/8 Haydon

Quantities of dead on the battlefield: 5/9 Fisk

2nd Michigan losses at Williamsburg: 5/10 Haydon

"One rifle ball put through my clothes" 5/11 Dickey

Two week withdrawal from Wmsbg. to Chickahominy: 5/11 R. Watkins

Hancock praised in 'False' newspaper reports: 5/15 Haydon

Hancock gets praise for capturing an empty fort: 5/21 Johnson

Hooker & Kearny's men deserve all the praise: 5/21 Johnson

 Query about recovering bodies of the buried to return home: 5/21 Johnson

Cavalry retreats 2 miles a day & Bro Nat on foot does 20 miles a day: 5/30 R. Watkins

Medical:

Disease & Sickness:

Bilious Fever Cause/Remedy: **6/18** Johnson

Chills & Fever: **6/22** Johnson, **7/1** Corson

Cold: 3/25 Corson

Cholera Morbus: **11/23** R. Watkins

Cholera Morbus Symptoms/Remedy: **11/23** R. Watkins

Deaths: **8/12** Corson, **11/11** Corson

Diarrhea: 3/31 Haydon, 4/17 French, 5/2 Branch, 6/5 Twitchell

Diarrhea Symptoms/Remedies: 3/31 Haydon, 4/17 French

Dysentery/Dysentery Symptoms/Remedy: 4/17 French

Fever: **6/15** Head, **6/18** Johnson, 2/24 Flournoy

Indigestion: 2/7 McLaws

Kidney Stones: 6/1 N. Watkins

Kidney Stone Symptoms/Remedy: 6/1 N. Watkins

Measles: **7/18, 21** McLaws, **11/11** Corson

Measles Symptoms/Remedy: **11/11** Corson

Mumps: **7/18, 21** McLaws

Pain in the side: **12/7** R. Watkins

Rheumatism: **7/2** Corson, **11/10** R. Watkins

Rheumatism Symptoms/Remedy: **11/10** R. Watkins

Scurvy: 5/23 Simpson

Scurvy Symptoms/Treatment: 5/23 Simpson

Sick Call – Reported Sick: 3/25 Corson, 3/31 Haydon, 4/1 Corson, 4/18 R. Watkins, 4/25 McLaws, 5/2 Branch, 5/20 R. Watkins, 5/21 Johnson, 5/29 Porter, 6/1 N. Watkins, 6/4 Rhodes, 6/5 Twitchell, 6/7 Reid, 6/9, 21 Corson.

Sickly country: **7/18** McLaws; 4/24 Reid; 5/3 Haydon, 6/21 Corson.

Tumor on head: **11/27** R. Watkins

Typhus Fever: 3/25 Corson

Typhus Symptoms and Remedy: 3/25 Corson

Vomiting: 3/31 Haydon

"Great deal of sickness, soldiers dying daily" – 6/7 Reid, 6/9, 21 Corson

"Men dying like flies" – 6/13 McKinney

Hospitals:

African Baptist Church Hospital – Williamsburg: **7/30** McLaws; 3/10 Galt

Bartlett Farmhouse Hospital – Yorktown: **11/17** R. Watkins

Chimborazo Hospital – Richmond: 5/28 Porter, 6/1 N. Watkins

College Hospital 'Wren Building' – Williamsburg: **7/30** McLaws, 5/5 Shotwell, 5/6 Furst

Episcopal Church 'Bruton Parish' Hospital – Williamsburg: **7/30** Mclaws

Female Academy 'General' Hospital – Williamsburg: **7/21, 24** McLaws

Fort Monroe Hospitals:

    Chesapeake Hospital: 5/26 N. York Daily Tribune

    Hygea Hospital: 5/26 N. York Daily Tribune

    U. S. Hospital: 5/26 N. York Daily Tribune

Ladies Aid: **7/31** McLaws

'Ladies Hospital' probably Robertson Hospital in Richmond: 5/31 Holland

Neglect by CSA Supply Department: **7/21** McLaws

Seven Pine C.S. Field Hospital: 5/31 Holland

State Insane Asylum in Williamsburg: 5/6 Galt, Holland, 5/8 Haydon

Yorktown 'Nelson House' Hospital – Yorktown: **11/4** Williams, **11/11** Corson

Treatment of Wounded in Hospitals: 5/10 N. York Daily Tribune, 5/5 Shotwell, 5/6 Furst, Haydon, 5/7 Rhodes, 5/8 Haydon, 5/31 Holland

Treatment of wounded at Seven Pines: 5/31 Davis

Evacuation of CSA sick at Kings Mill Wharf: 5/1 R. Watkins, 5/2 Branch

Evacuation of USA sick/wounded: 5/22, 26 New York Daily Tribune

Medicines & Treatments:

Boiling Water: 6/5 Haydon

Calomel: **6/18** Johnson

Castor Oil: 6/1 N. Watkins

Clysters: **6/18** Johnson, **11/23** R. Watkins

Ipecac: 4/18 R. Watkins

Laudanum: **11/23** R. Watkins

Mustard Poultices & Blisters: **11/11** Corson, 6/1 N. Watkins

Opium: 4/18 R. Watkins, 6/1 N. Watkins

Turpentine: 6/1 N. Watkins

Whiskey: **8/18** Corson

Pests:

Gnats: 5/14 Haydon

Lice: 5/22 Twitchell, 5/22 S. Waktins (note with Twitchell letter), 5/31 Haydon

Maggots: 6/5 Haydon

Mosquitoes: **7/30** McLaws, **8/26** Corson, **9/3** Corson, 5/14 Haydon

Tar Repellant for Mosquitoes: **7/30 McLaws**

Woodticks: 5/14, 21 Haydon

Money, Pay, & Confederate Currency:
Confederate Currency:

First Issue: **April, May, June Introduction**

Second Issue: **July, August, September Introduction**

Third Issue: **July, August, September Introduction**

Fourth Issue: April, 1862, Introduction

Money at Home & in Camp:

Buy a horse: **10/10** McLaws

Money available with Broker/Crop Agent: **9/17** R. Watkins, 6/5 R. Watkins

Money to children: 4/25 McLaws

"notes I wish you had" – 6/20 Porter

Sending money home: **10/10** McLaws, 6/10 McLaws

Sight Draft to draw monies: **9/17** R. Watkins, 2/9 R. Watkins

Pay:

"Have no Money": 3/28 Haydon

Not Paid: **8/26** McLaws, 5/17 George

Partial Pay: 1/29 Corson

Promise to Pay: 3/28 Haydon

Paymaster Problems: **8/26** McLaws

Naval Activity, Battles, Navy Yards, & Transportation of Men & Material:

Amphibious Transportation:

Arrivals at Fortress Monroe: **4/21** Wood, 2/23 Englis, 3/18 Haydon, 3/26, 27, 28 Rhodes

Baltimore & Washington to Fortress Monroe: 2/23 Englis, 3/Introduction, 3/18 Haydon, 3/26, 27, 28 Rhodes, 4/16 Furst, 4/13 Steel, 4/30 McKinney

Cumberland Landing on the Pamunkey: 5/15 Haydon

Richmond to Kings Mill Wharf: 4/14 Branch

West Point to Gloucester: **5/8** Williams

West Point to Yorktown: **9/12** R. Watkins, 1/20 Williams, 2/8 Corson, 4/7 Buzhardt

Ironclads:

Monitor:

Enroute New York to Hampton Roads: 3/7 Greene

Leaks, Taking on Water: 3/7 Greene, Stimers

Loss of Engines: 3/7 Greene

Evacuation of Engine Rooms: 3/7 Greene, Stimers

Not Very Sea Worthy: 3/7 Greene

Almost Lost Twice Enroute: 3/9 Greene

Arrive at Mouth of Chesapeake Bay: 3/7 Greene, 3/8 Greene

Arrive at Fortress Monroe 3/8 Greene

Secured for Night at 1:00 a.m beside *Minnesota* on 3/9: 3/9 Greene

Physical Condition of Crew: 3/9 Greene

Condition & Morale of U. S. Fleet: 3/9 Greene

Seaworthiness Opinion: "equal to any weather I saw at sea": 3/10 Stimers

Experimental Ships, Untried, No Training, Baptism by Battle: 3/9 Wood

Virginia (formerly *Merrimac*):

Armament of the *Virginia:* **6/14** White

Appointment as Junior Engineering Officer: 1/16 White

Construction of the *Virginia:* **6/14** White

Coordinate Army action with '*Merrimac*': 2/7 McLaws

Description of *Virginia*: 3/8 Phillips

Launching of *Virginia:* 2/17 Cline, Porter

No Armor Plate at Waterline: 2/7 C. Jones

   Post battle add armor: 3/29 J. Wood

Poor Steering – Forever to Turn: 3/8 Norris, J. Wood

Raising and Converting the *Merrimac:* **12/30** McLaws

Speed of *Virginia:* 3/8 Norris, J. Wood

Wretched Engines: 3/8 Norris

Battle with the Wooden Fleet on March 8:

Dragon on picket sees *Virginia* coming: 3/8 McDonald

Sortie from Norfolk to attack the fleet: 3/8 Phillips, Curtis, White

Opening Bow Gun Shot Hits *Cumberland*: 3/8 Curtis

Ramming the *Cumberland*: 3/8 Curtis, White, Curtis, J. Wood

Rapidly Sinking: 3/8 Curtis

Upriver to Turn to attack *Congress*: 3/8 J. Wood

Attack and Damage to *Congress:* 3/8 Curtis, White, Curtis, White, J. Wood

Hoisting the White Flag / Surrender: 3/8 White, Pendergast

Arrangement for Surrender: 3/8 White, F. Curtis, Colston, Curtis

Union Firing on their White Flag: 3/8 White, Curtis

Hot Shot Orders: 3/8 White, J. Wood, Curtis, Eggleston, Ramsay

Abandon Ship: 3/8 F. Curtis

Night anchorage at Sewell's Point watching *Congress* burning: 3/8 Curtis, White

Brief Attack on *Minnesota* before darkness: 3/8 White

Roanoke, Mystic & St. Lawrence retreat to Fort Monroe: 3/8 F. Curtis

Killed and Wounded from 3/8 fighting: 3/8 White, Curtis, White, Buchanan, 3/9 Phillips

Damage to *Virginia*: 3/8 White, Curtis, Buchanan

Battle Between the *Virginia* and the *Monitor* on March 9:

New Captain of *Virginia* to replace wounded Buchanan: 3/9 Curtis

Virginia sorties toward *Minnesota:* 3/9 Curtis

First shot from bow gun hits *Minnesota* and starts fires: 3/9 Curtis

Fireman McDonald pulled off *Dragon* through gun-port of *Minnesota:* 3/9 Norris

Sighting of the *Monitor:* 3/9 Curtis

The Ironclads engage: 3/9 Worden

Turret Firing & Loading Shortcomings: 3/9 Greene, J. Wood

Speaking Tube broken on *Monitor:* 3/9 Greene

Firing and Maneuvering of *Virginia* difficult: 3/9 C. Jones

Monitor very maneuverable and nimble: 3/9 C. Jones, White, J. Wood

Virginia runs aground: 3/9 White

Constant fighting from 0845 till evening: 3/9 Greene

Trying to ram the *Monitor:* 3/9 Greene

Half loads of powder: 3/9 Greene

Monitor well handled: 3/9 J. Wood

Virginia had no 'solid shot' on board: 3/9 J. Wood

No serious damage to either vessel: 3/9 Wood

Evening return by *Virginia* to anchorage at Craney Island: 3/9 Ramsay

Damage from fight with *Monitor:* 3/9 Norris, 3/10 Porter

Survey of 97 dents, 20 from 10" shells: 3/10 Porter

6 top steel plates broken, 0 lower plates: 3/10 Porter

Smokestack riddled: 3/10 Porter

Civilian and Military Observations:

Word of a great naval victory over wooden fleet: 3/9 Coleman, 3/13 Williams

Monitor is a ridiculous looking craft: 3/18 Haydon

Monitor is a 120' long pumpkin seed with a cheese box on top: 3/18 Haydon

Soldiers are frightened by *Virginia*: 3/21 Haydon

Saw *Monortor* and Rebel *Merimac:* 4/13 Steel

James River Fleet:

Beaufort: 3/8 McDonald, J Wood, 5/11 Wood

Jamestown: 3/8 White, J. Wood,

Patrick Henry: 5/11 Wood

Raleigh: 3/8 McDonald, J. Wood, 5/11 Wood

Teaser: 3/8 White, J. Wood, 5/11 Wood

Thomas Jefferson: 5/11 Wood

Yorktown: 3/8 J. Wood

With Virginia after sinking Cumberland, attack and sink Whilden & a schooner: 3/8 White

Capture of Reindeer by Jamestown & Teaser: 3/8 White, J. Wood

Joining battle with Virginia against Congress: 3/8 J. Wood, Colston

April & May Sorties against Union forces in Hampton Roads:

Sailed into the Roads - Virginia & 6 gunboats / Monitor absent: 4/11 J. Wood

Traded shots with batteries at the Rip-Rap: 4/11 J. Wood

Commodore ordered Jamestown to capture 3 merchant vessels at Hampton: 4/11 J. Wood

Towed away the prizes: 4/11 J. Wood

Returned a few days later – no Monitor: 4/11 J. Wood

CSA plan was to attack & board from 4 sides: 4/11 Wood

Teaser goes up Warwick River and shells 2nd Rhode Island at Young's Farm: 4/30 Rhodes

Monitor, Galena, Naugatuck, near Sewell's Pt., retreat at our approach: 5/8 J. Wood

5/11 Virginia blown up on Craney Island: 5/11 J. Wood, Ramsay, White, Jack

Union salvage contract on Virginia for mementoes: 5/27 N. York Daily Tribune

Defense of Drewry's Bluff:

James River Fleet sent to Drewry's Bluff: 5/11 J. Wood

5/13 Union fleet approaching City Point: 5/13 Wood, 5/14 J. Jones

5/14 Union fleet at Aiken: 5/14 Wood,

5/15 Union fleet defeated at Drewry's Bluff: 5/15 Wood, J. Jones

President Davis watches battle: 5/15 Wood

Serious damage to *Galena:* 5/15 Wood

Disagreeable life 'inside' *Monitor* in the summer heat: 5/15 Greene

Navy Yard – Portsmouth (Gosport):

Set on fire: **4/20** Wood, **4/21** White

Ships Burned: **4/20** Wood, **4/21** White

Post Battle Repair of *Virginia*; Add Armor, Increase Draft, Reduce Speed:
3/29 J. Wood

Pilots:

Evacuation: **4/21** Wood

Status: **4/21** Wood

Request for City Point / James River Pilots: 5/14 Wood

Negroes:

Contraband Population at Fortress Monroe: 2/23 Englis

Custis Plantation at White House: 5/11 Furst

Dozen Contraband Servants if you wished: 2/23 Englis

"Dirty and Ignorant": 5/18 Fisk

Hunting Terrapins: 1/12 R. Watkins

If Purpose of War was to Free Negro – Union soldiers would quit: 5/18
Fisk

Measurements for Negro Shoes on the farm: **9/17** R. Watkins

Negro understands commotions has a connection to him: 5/18 Fisk

Negroes are queer people but seem to understand the war: 5/254
Rhodes

Negroes leave for Fort Monroe as soon as in our rear: 5/24 Rhodes

Pay for Negroes used in construction: **9/18, 25, 30** Wynne

Prisoners of war arriving in New York: 6/3 NYDT

Servants in camp with some of 3rd Virginia Cavalry: **9/17** R. Watkins

Six Negroes Shot in Norfolk: 5/30 New York Daily Tribune

Stealing Negroes by Yankees: **7/2** McLaws, **8/26** McLaws

Strong Negroe prejudice in Yankee army: 5/18 Fisk

Theft of Oysters & Oyster Boats from 'Darkies": 3/20 Haydon

Want to be free – Do they have to work?: 5/11 Furst

Winter Clothing for farm workers: **10/2** R. Watkins

Work Party at Redoubt in Williamsburg: **7/25** McLaws

Work on fortifications at Grove Wharf: **7/11** Wynne

Work on fortifications at Mulberry Point – Fort Crafford: **8/21, 31; 9/2** Wynne

Political Thought:

Blockade of Southern Ports: **11/11** Martin, 1/6 R. Watkins

Confidence in 'Our Cause and Jeff Davis": 3/27 R. Watkins

Desire to have our own government: **12/12** R. Watkins

Draft Ages in Confederacy: 2/9 R. Watkins

Draft / Conscription Legislation by C.S. Congress: 4/18 Simpson, Reid

Draft Proclamation from Gov. Letcher of Virginia: 4/18 R. Watkins

Emancipation Act – Military Governors: 6/7 Fisk

England may support the Confederacy: **12/12** R. Watkins, **12/20** McLaws

"Floyd is unfit to be Secretary of War": 3/27 R. Watkins

Freedom of the Press ?: 3/27 R. Watkins

"Large army about Yorktown": 3/8 Martin

Lee gaining the confidence of the army: 6/28 McLaws

"Justice and Right Must Prevail": 2/20 R. Watkins

"McClellan is not a great general": 5/20 R. Watkins, 6/13 McKinney

"McClellan is greatest liar in America": 6/18 Simpson

Peace propositions: **8/18** Corson

Political Generals: **9/29** McLaws

Population Fleeing: **7/2** McLaws

Presidential Proclamation: Day of Fasting: 2/28 Martin

Property Degradation: **7/2** McLaws

Richmond Examiner is now anti-administration: 3/27 R. Watkins

    Anti-administration newspapers: 3/27 R. Watkins

    Fate of Anti-Lincoln newspapers in North: 3/27 R. Watkins

Secession – Ordance of: **4/26** Wynne

Secession- Ratification of Ordance: **5/23** Wynne

Southern Defense in the face of Yankee Crimes: **6/20** Johnson

"They are right to drive us from their soil": **6/20** Johnson

Thoughts of a comet: **7/17** Johnson

Trent Affair: **12/12** Watkins

Union Restored & Peace Again (I want to see): 6/4 Rhodes

Rations and Food: (See ' Camp Life')

Printed in the USA
CPSIA information can be obtained
at www.ICGtesting.com
LVHW040324030324
773357LV00001BA/47